TWENTY-FIRST CENTURY
BIBLICAL COMMENTARY SERIES®

THE GOSPEL OF

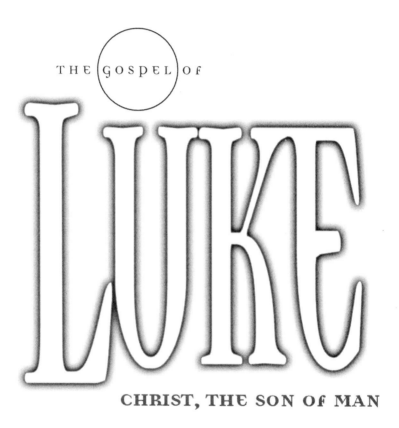

CHRIST, THE SON OF MAN

Advancing the Ministries of the Gospel

AMG Publishers

God's Word to you is our highest calling.

TWENTY-FIRST CENTURY
BIBLICAL COMMENTARY SERIES®

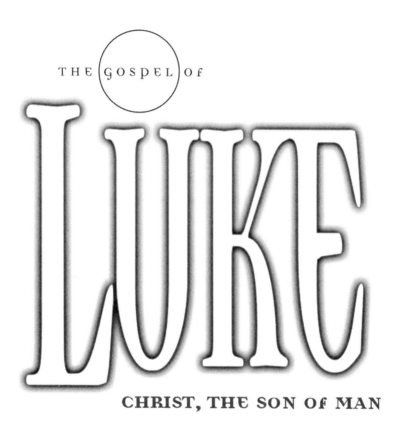

THE GOSPEL OF

LUKE

CHRIST, THE SON OF MAN

MAL
COUCH
GENERAL EDITOR

ED HINDSON

The Gospel of Luke: Christ, The Son of Man
Twenty-First Century Biblical Commentary Series®
Copyright © 2006 by Tyndale Theological Seminary

Published by AMG Publishers
6815 Shallowford Road
Chattanooga, TN 37421

Unless otherwise noted, Scripture quotes are taken from the NEW AMERICAN STANDARD BIBLE, Copyright © 1960, 1962, 1963, 1968, 1971, 1972, 1973, 1975, 1977, by the Lockman Foundation. Used by permission. (www.Lockman.org)
Scriptures marked KJV are from the King James Version of the Bible.
Scriptures marked NIV are from the HOLY BIBLE NEW INTERNATIONAL VERSION®. NIV®. Copyright © 1973, 1978, 1984 by International Bible Society. Used by permission of Zondervan.

TWENTY-FIRST CENTURY BIBLICAL COMMENTARY SERIES is a registered trademark of CLW Communications Group, Inc.

ISBN–13: 978–0–89957–822–4
ISBN–10: 0–89957–822–5

First Published: December 2006

Cover Design by ImageWright, Inc.
Editing and Text Design by Warren Baker
Editorial assistance provided by Weller Editorial Services, Chippewa Lake, MI
Typesetting by Jennifer Ross

Printed in the United States of America
11 10 09 08 07 06 –R– 7 6 5 4 3 2 1

Twenty-First Century Biblical Commentary Series®

Mal Couch, Th.D., and Ed Hindson, D.Phil.

The New Testament has guided the Christian Church for over two thousand years. This one testament is made up of twenty-seven books, penned by godly men through the inspiration of the Holy Spirit. It tells us of the life of Jesus Christ, His atoning death for our sins, His miraculous resurrection, His ascension back to heaven, and the promise of His second coming. It also tells the story of the birth and growth of the Church and the people and principles that shaped it in its earliest days. The New Testament concludes with the book of Revelation pointing ahead to the glorious return of Jesus Christ.

Without the New Testament, the message of the Bible would be incomplete. The Old Testament emphasizes the promise of a coming Messiah. It constantly points us ahead to the One who is coming to be the King of Israel and the Savior of the world. But the Old Testament ends with this event still unfulfilled. All of its ceremonies, pictures, types, and prophecies are left awaiting the arrival of the "Lamb of God who takes away the sin of the world!" (John 1:29).

The message of the New Testament represents the timeless truth of God. As each generation seeks to apply that truth to its specific context, an up-to-date commentary needs to be created just for them. The editors and authors of the Twenty-First Century Biblical Commentary Series have endeavored to do just that. This team of scholars represents conservative, evangelical, and dispensational scholarship at its best. The individual authors may differ on minor points of interpretation, but all are convinced that the Old and New Testaments teach a dispensational framework for biblical history. They also hold to a pretribulational and premillennial understanding of biblical prophecy.

The French scholar René Pache reminded each succeeding generation, "If the power of the Holy Spirit is to be made manifest anew among us, it is of primary importance that His message should regain its due place. Then we shall be able to put the enemy to flight by the sword of the Spirit which is the Word of God."

The Gospel of Luke has long been recognized for its eloquent style, historical accuracy, and profound portrait of the Son of Man—Jesus Christ. Australian scholar Leon Morris has emphasized that Luke's purpose is not only to introduce Jesus as the Messiah, but as the Savior of the world. He points out that Luke is the only one of the four evangelists to write an immediate sequel to his Gospel as he takes his reader, Theophilus, from the gospel account on into the book of Acts.

William Hendriksen observes: "Luke must have regarded Theophilus as a representative of that large company of contemporaries who either had already become committed to Christ or were seriously considering doing so. Both earnest enquirers and beginning believers were included in his purview." Darrell Bock of Dallas Theological Seminary reminds us that Luke's gospel is a theological narrative about Jesus Christ. He says, "It often makes its points through dialogue, speeches, characterization, plot and narrative comment. Such teaching often emerges implicitly, within the story and through the interaction of its characters." Thus, the gospel accounts tell a story that teaches us the truth about God's purpose for our lives.

Leon Morris adds: "The great thought that Luke is expressing is surely that God is working out His purpose. This purpose is seen clearly in the life and work of Jesus, but it did not finish with the earthly ministry of Jesus. It carried right on into the life and ministry of the church." Thus, Luke's gospel not only sets the stage of the book of Acts but for the whole of Church history. God is still at work in His Church today, and He will continue that work until the Church is raptured home to heaven.

Contents

Background of Luke

While the book of Luke has many things similar to the synoptic Gospels of Matthew and Mark, the narration of the life and times of the Son of Man seems to have more details and particulars. The book is rich with many accounts of the healings of Jesus, which were always questioned by the skeptical Jewish leadership. The book describes this constant encounter between Jesus and his skeptics, but also gives an exciting account of much that the Lord said and did as He walked among both the common people and those who were in places of religious authority.

What is fascinating about the book of Luke is that it is the first of two volumes of the ministry of Christ. The book of Acts follows and describes how the church went forth in both triumph and persecution as it witnessed to both the people of Israel and the Gentile world. With both books together, the apostle Luke is the largest contributor to the New Testament in terms of the volume of words and chapters. Looking at the close of Luke's gospel and the beginning of Acts, one can see how the author has fitted the two books together to carry the reader along in a thrilling spiritual adventure.

> Comparison with the practice of Josephus, the first-century Jewish historian, makes it reasonably certain that Luke conceived of his two books as parts of a single whole. At the beginning of Book II of his work *Against Apion*, Josephus refers to Book I as the former book or first volume of his work. Luke was aware of the habit of historians of the Hellenistic period and adapted his writing to this model.[1]

As with the other Gospels, Luke presents the Lord Jesus as the promised Son of Man, the Messiah, the one so vividly described in Daniel 7:8–28. The Son of Man would someday come to earth and rule over the nation of Israel and bring blessings to the entire world during His millennial reign. He was presented as such in Luke, but He would first be rejected and slain by His own people. Luke closes with the return of Christ to His Father following His resurrection, and Acts picks up the story of the coming of the Holy Spirit and the beginning of the church.

Who Was Luke?

Luke was a missionary, historian, and physician. He was a Greek whose name was *Loukas* with a Latin equivalent of *Lucanus*. From the book of Colossians (4:14) we find that he is a physician, but there is uncertainty as to when he began his profession. Comparing the Gospel of Luke with the book of Acts, it is clear that the author, Luke, was educated and able to interview witnesses, write, research, and carry out remarkable observations. He had a commanding knowledge of Greek literature and language. Some argue that almost all physicians had been slaves, but this may not have been true in Luke's case.

Luke says that he was not an eyewitness about the things he reports nor a minister or disciple from the beginning (Luke 1:2). He comes into view in Acts 16:10-11 where he joined Paul at Troas and sailed with him as his companion to Macedonia. In this chapter the narration picks up with the personal note of "we" and "us." Clearly, he was becoming involved in many of the initial dramas of the establishment of the early church. He apparently did not share Paul's persecution (16:25—17:1), nor did he leave Philippi when Paul was expelled from the city, because the narration turns to "they" and does not include his eyewitness accounts. Luke reappears with Paul on his third missionary journey (20:6), where the first person plural "we" picks up through the end of Acts.[2]

Why did Luke escape the persecution that came upon Paul and Silas? Some speculate that he was a Gentile with an honorable profession and therefore escaped the anger of the crowds and the officials at Philippi. Luke was without doubt a faithful follower of Paul until the end (2 Tim. 4:11). The final New Testament references describe him as "the beloved physician" (Col. 4:14) and "fellow worker" (Philem. 1:24).

Theodore the Lector (early sixth century) gives the tradition that Luke was a painter, though this cannot be proven. Some say he was a Syrian from Antioch and that he was converted under Paul. A quote from the third century says Luke had neither wife nor children and that he died in Bithynia at the age of seventy-four. But this is not certain. Gregory of Nazianzus (A.D. 330–389) tells us that Luke became a martyr under Emperor Domitian, but again this cannot be verified. Tradition also adds that his bones were carried from Achaia to Constantinople and buried there in the twentieth year of Constantius.[3]

Marvin Vincent writes:

> It has been assumed that [Luke] was a freedman, from the large number of physicians who belonged to that class, the Greeks and Romans being accustomed to educate some of their domestics in the science of medicine, and to grant them freedom in requital of services. Physicians often held no higher rank than slaves, and it has been noticed that contractions in *as*, like *Lucas* for *Lucanus*, were peculiarly common in the names of slaves.[4]

The Gospel of Luke and the Book of Acts

Most Bible teachers have observed that the books of Luke and Acts appear to be two large sections of one volume. After Luke had penned the life and teachings of the Lord Jesus in his gospel, he continued on in the account of the early church in the volume most well known as "The *Acts* of the Apostles." Both works begin with almost the same introductory material and the same wording.

The opening salutations of Luke and Acts are strong and straightforward. They point out that what Luke is writing has to do with what was handed down by the apostles, eyewitnesses, and servants of the Word (Luke 1:1). Luke is compiling a vast amount of material that comes with "convincing proofs" (Acts 1:1–3) and was "carefully investigated" from the beginning and recorded by him.

Reading Luke and Acts back to back, one can feel the excitement generated by the author as the story continues from Christ, to the apostles, to the Jews, and finally to the Gentiles. The two books end up firmly establishing the documented truth about the Lord Jesus and about the spread of the gospel throughout the Mediterranean region.

To Whom Was the Book Addressed?

Both Luke and Acts were addressed to a Greek named Theophilus (Luke 1:1–4; Acts 1:1–2). Theophilus means "loved of God." While little is known about him, some facts seem obvious; for example, he was educated and a professional. Many believe Luke could have sent Theophilus the Gospel of Mark but that this account of the life of Jesus was too short. Thus, he assembled a more detailed record. Both the gospel and the Acts of the Apostles were written in a refined *Koine* (popular) or even near-Classical Greek. By the many Old

Testament quotes in the Septuagint (the Greek translation of the Old Testament) by Luke, Theophilus could appreciate the narration better.

Some have surmised the name Theophilus was not an individual's name but referred to any "friend of God." Yet the majority of scholars still regard it as referring to a specific individual who was more than likely a wealthy, well-educated aristocrat. By calling him "most excellent" or "most noble" (Greek, *kratistos*), Luke seems to bestow an honorary rank or high social status upon him. The word is used in Acts 23:26; 24:3; and 26:25 to address the procurator of Judea. The noun *kratos* means "power, rule, sovereignty." Clearly, Theophilus was a man of rank and possibly possessed great authority. Because Luke does not use this designation in Acts 1:1, some believe Theophilus had by then become a follower of Jesus, since believers in the early church did not use *kratistos* in addressing other Christians.[5]

If the dating of the book of Acts is around A.D. 63, then more than likely Luke was compiled a few months or years before, especially if it is true that the apostle simply continued to research and then went on to write his narration and history found in Acts.

The *Monarchian Prologue of Luke* says that he wrote this gospel in the region of Achaia, but this cannot be proven. Nothing is affirmed about the place.

The Muratorian Canon

The Muratorian Canon was compiled around A.D. 170 and gives one of the first references to the Lukan authorship and tradition of the Gospel of Luke. The Canon reads:

> The third book of the Gospel: According to Luke. This Luke was a physician. After the accension of Christ, when Paul had taken him along with him as one devoted to w he wrote it under his own name from hearsay. For he himself has not seen the Lord in person, but, insofar as he was able to allow [it all], he thus began his account with the birth of John.[6]

Throughout the early Church period, into the third century, there was little doubt about the Lukan authorship of the gospel. Form criticism began its destructive work of tearing down the fact that Luke wrote the book. The great Oxford scholar Sir William Ramsay opposed with factual accuracy the damage done by the German Tubingen school of criticism. Ramsay summarized the trustworthiness of Luke as attested by so many of the earliest writers of early Christianity. He also confirmed the historical and geographical information that proves beyond a doubt the factual nature of this gospel.

What Are the Themes Found in Luke?

The work of the Holy Spirit has an important role in the book of Luke. The Spirit is said to indwell John the Baptist (1:15), is active at the conception of Jesus (v. 35), comes upon Jesus when He is baptized (3:22), fills Him for the work He will do (4:1), and imparts strength in the temptation (vv. 1–2).

The temple plays a special role, beginning in the birth narratives (1:9, 21–22; 2:27, 37), including Christ's visit there as a boy (vv. 41–51). Toward the end of the book, the disciples are seen at the temple (24:53). Luke seems to emphasize the work of redemption and substitution of the Lord by specifically referring to Isaiah 53 in 22:37. Isaiah 40–66 is also alluded to in 24:27, 44, 46. Luke focuses often on the popular response to the ministry of Christ. He often speaks about how Jesus was surrounded by large crowds that were shocked by His works (5:26; 7:16–17; 11:14; 13:17).

While all of the gospel accounts give a marvelous picture of the life and ministry of Jesus, there is something rich and special about Luke's narration. R. C. H. Lenski writes:

> Luke made an accurate examination of all the gospel facts before he wrote. It was natural that he should want to know all the gospel facts at firsthand. As an educated man he would embrace the golden opportunities that came his way. There was added to his own spiritual interest the urge of his gospel work under Paul's direction; for this he needed to know all he possibly could concerning the life of Jesus. Finally there came his contact with Theophilus and the latter's need. This induced Luke to write. If this is the human side of it, we know another—the divine. The Holy Spirit selected Luke for the great task in the interest of the church of all ages and enabled him with divine help to write the two books that constitute such a fountain of saving truth for us today.[7]

Many commentators hold that the overall theme of Luke is the salvation of mankind. "Succinctly stated, the purpose of the third gospel, along with the Acts of the Apostles, is to demonstrate that the twofold promise of salvation of the Jews and the Gentiles predicted in the Old Testament is in the process of being fulfilled in Jesus Christ."[8] These two themes, the salvation of Jew and Gentile, come together and are prominent in Luke's portrait of Christ. The overall subject is clear: Christ came to save the whole of humanity.

Dispensational Issues

The ministry of the Lord Jesus takes place under the dispensation of the Mosaic Law. Christ was faithful to the Law and even says that He came to fulfill or complete it (Matt. 5:17). He did this by living a perfect life. He never violated the injunctions or even the intent of the Law.

Jesus said He would **fulfill the Law** by obeying it perfectly and would fulfill the prophets' predictions of the Messiah and His kingdom. But the responsibility of the people was made clear. The **righteousness** they were currently seeking—**that of the Pharisees and the teachers of the Law**— was insufficient for entrance into **the kingdom** Jesus was offering. The righteousness He demanded was not merely external; it was a true inner righteousness based on faith in God's Word (Rom. 3:21–22).[9]

Jesus presents Himself as the prophesied king of Israel. He also presents the kingdom to the nation of Israel, but the people as a whole reject Him and His message. Repentance by the people would have brought about the kingdom. However, in God's absolute foreknowledge, He knew the nation would reject the Lord. While the offer of the kingdom was valid, it was also true that "the Son of Man must suffer many things, and be rejected by the elders and chief priests and scribes, and be killed, and be raised up on the third day" (Luke 9:22). And before He reigns, "first He must suffer many things and be rejected by this generation" (17:25; 22:15; 24:26; Acts 3:18).

At the Jerusalem Council the issue of postponement of the kingdom was discussed. When Peter finished telling how God was saving Gentiles, the apostle James stood up and said, "Simon [Peter] has related [exegeted, *exageomai*] how God first concerned Himself about taking from among the Gentiles a people for His name" (Acts 15:14). The word "first" is picked up by James in the verses that follow. And with this the words of the Prophets agree, just as it is written,

> After these things I will return,
> And I will rebuild the tabernacle of David which has fallen,
> And I will rebuild its ruins,
> And I will restore it,
> In order that the rest of mankind may seek the Lord,
> And all the Gentiles who are called by My name
> Says the Lord, who makes these things known from of old.
> (vv. 15–18)

James is specifically referring to Amos 9:11. He expands upon and explains further the context of this verse. James begins by saying, "After these things," which is not in Amos. This must refer to "God . . . taking from among the Gentiles a people for His name" (Acts 15:14), meaning the Church. Thus, God will work with the Gentiles before He restores the kingdom to Israel. Luke records some of the final words of Christ to His disciples that seem to have this in view. Jesus said that after His resurrection (Luke 24:46) "repentance for forgiveness of sins should be proclaimed in His name to all the nations, beginning from Jerusalem" (v. 47). Opportunity for the national repentance of Israel would end, but it would go to the Gentiles by means of this "new thing," the dispensation of the Church age. The early Church would have many Jews who trust Jesus as Savior, but as the apostle Paul predicted, salvation would pass mainly from the Jews (though not totally) to the nations. Paul told the Jews of Rome, "Let it be known to you therefore, that this salvation of God has been sent to the Gentiles; they will also listen" (Acts 28:28).

Along with the other Gospels and the book of Acts, Luke tells the story of that great rejection of Christ by the Jewish people living during His lifetime in the Holy Land.

SECTION I

Purpose for Writing

Luke 1:1–4

The first four verses of Luke set the stage for why this document was written. The verses describe the intensity and attention to detail that the apostle Luke must have used as he penned his work. Frederic Godet writes:

> How different Luke's prologue, and in what an entirely different atmosphere it places us from the first! . . . The author does not seek to put himself in the rank of the Christian authorities; he places himself modestly among men of the second order. . . . He does not permit himself to undertake the work of writing a Gospel history until he has furnished himself with all the aids fitted to enable him to attain the lofty aim he sets before him. There is a striking contrast between his frank and modest attitude and that of a forger.[1]

CHAPTER 1

Greetings to Theophilus
Luke 1:1-4

Preview:

Luke tells how he set out to assemble the facts about the life and ministry of the Lord Jesus. He spoke with the earliest apostles of the Lord who were eyewitnesses and who followed Him as His servants. Luke was meticulous in his research and desired to give Theophilus an authentic and reliable chronology. The purpose was to confirm what Theophilus had heard and had been taught.

"*Inasmuch as many have undertaken to compile an account of the things accomplished among us*" *(1:1).* This verse and the three verses that follow are packed with indicators as to how Luke went about his research. Such meticulous details would be expected of a physician who was trained in the rudimentary science of medicine. Luke was clearly a thinker and one who wanted to be sure of his evidence. This is not to say that he himself had doubts about the life of Christ, but he desired to confirm the facts to those who were responding to the gospel.

What is important here is that Luke provided corresponding evidence as to what the apostles reported. In other words, this was another voice that confirmed the accounts of the ministry of Jesus. Luke then was a corroborator of what was spreading far and wide about the Lord. In verse 1 Luke calls his report a *diēgēsis*, a "narrative, report," an "explanation, digest" about Christ. This word as a noun is used only here in the New Testament, and it carries the idea "to always give the meaning, the explanation" about something. Luke then is not only giving information about the life of the Lord, but he is explaining what Jesus was all about.

In verse 2 Luke uses the word *autoptēs*, which literally means "to see with one's own eye." Luke interviewed firsthand witnesses and is not simply reporting hearsay or secondary sources. Luke's credibility is on the line in the document he presents to Theophilus. He notes that he "investigated everything carefully," adding "from the beginning" (v. 3). This would mean that he had to interview many witnesses and had to compare their stories. If there had been inaccuracies in Luke's writing, someone could have objected and called the account untrue. Thus, there are many checks and balances in what Luke is setting forth for examination.

Luke says that he "wrote it out" (v. 3) in "consecutive [chronological] order" so that Theophilus would "know" the "exact truth" about "the things [he had] been taught." Being an aristocrat, Theophilus would consider it important that he know what was true and false. Some go further and speculate that Theophilus may have assisted in the publication of Luke's work. Thus, only the truth would be adequate! In all of this, there is a wide circle of people who knew people, and so on. To falsify information about Jesus the Messiah would be virtually impossible.[1]

Because the apostle Luke was a close follower of Paul, Irenaeus believes that when Paul said "my gospel" in Romans 2:16, he had in mind Luke's gospel record. This idea was widely held by many of the church fathers, though more than likely Paul was simply referring to the doctrine of the gospel as it was given to him, including the way he presented it. But the fact that Irenaeus reported this shows how respected the Gospel of Luke actually was by the early Christians. Both Origen and Jerome believed Paul's statement about a certain brother "whose fame in the things of the gospel has spread through all the churches" (2 Cor. 8:18) was offering praise to Luke's account.

When Luke writes in verse 4, "so that you might know," he uses the intense word *epiginōskō*, which can be translated "to fully and completely know." Luke is going to great lengths to explain correctly all about the life and ministry of Christ. He adds, "as you have been taught," using the Greek word *katechō*, which means "to hold firm." The English word *catechism* derives from *katechō*. The word here is used in the technical sense, "to formally and systematically give instruction," in the general sense of "having been informed." The subjects of instruction of Christians in these early years following Christ's ascension were the teaching, acts, and experiences of Jesus.

> This preface gives a lively picture of the intense, universal interest felt by the early Church in the story of the Lord Jesus: Apostles constantly telling what they had seen and heard; many of their hearers taking notes of what they said for the benefit of themselves and others, ... creating a thirst for more and yet more; imposing on such a man as Luke the task of prepar-

ing a Gospel as *full, correct,* and *well arranged* as possible through the use of all available means ... oral testimon[ies] of surviving eyewitnesses.[2]

The question is often raised, did Luke dedicate his Gospel to the man named Theophilus? Many of the old German scholars often claim that the book is indeed a dedication, but are there problems with this view?

Generally most scholars argue that Luke set out to win this noble individual to Christ by his observations and by his objective arguments. He certainly does more than simply make a dedication, if that is what he was doing. In most secular writings such a dedication would be put forth in plain language, but Luke omits any statements of this kind. He gives no hint that this is his purpose. Luke does not want to allow such a dedication to interfere with his attempt to touch the heart of Theophilus.

Some argue further that if Theophilus thought such a literary dedication was intended by Luke, this would have been an affront to him and he would have refrained from reading the book for himself. However, there is no indication that Luke desired to have this work published for anyone other than Theophilus. Luke wrote with great sincerity, and he wrote for Theophilus alone! When Theophilus became a Christian, which many believe he did, he showed his great treasure to others, with the result that the book's publication took care of itself.

Study Questions

1. Could Luke be inclusive of the entire Christian community when he says he wanted to give an account of what was "accomplished among us" and handed down "to us"?

2. When Luke says he searched out the truth from those who were there from the beginning, could this have included accounts by Mary, Elizabeth, and Zacharias?

3. What impression do you have of Luke as an investigator?

4. From verse 4, what is most important about Luke's research?

5. What do we know historically about Theophilus?

SECTION II

Revelation of the Son of Man

Luke 1:5—4:13

Luke goes into great detail about the birth of John the Baptist, who is the forerunner of Christ. He also shares specific information about how the angel Gabriel presented to Mary the news of her pregnancy and the birth of Jesus the Messiah. Luke gives readers a glimpse of the hearts of those involved in this drama. He shares the emotional response of Mary, and of Zacharias, when they realized the roles they were to play in the fulfillment of so many Old Testament prophecies about the coming of the Messiah. Luke rushes forward to tell about how John the Baptist began his ministry, but then he backs up and confirms the genealogy of the Son of Man in 3:23–38. A concern for detail is the hallmark of Luke's digest of the coming of both John, the forerunner of the Lord, and of the Lord Jesus Himself.

CHAPTER 2

Announcement of the Coming of John the Baptist
Luke 1:5-25

Preview:

Luke identifies the period of the births of John the Baptist and Christ as the days of Herod the king. A detailed account follows of how the angel Gabriel came to a righteous priest, Zacharias, and told him he would be the father of the forerunner of the Messiah. He did not believe the angel and was struck mute. His wife Elizabeth realized that God was working a strange miracle with her. She was thankful that her days of being barren were over.

With great language ability, Luke makes an accurate account of the historical facts and events of his day. There is no doubt that Luke was a man of high education and polished writing skills. His Greek grammar is sophisticated and borders on classical Greek. The first two chapters read like one of the Old Testament prophets who lived about the time of Saul or David. Many think Luke was faithful to the original sources he worked from with spiritual keenness and masterful observations. Some believe he worked originally with Aramaic sources that gave him the information he edited and recorded for the first two chapters. Without question Luke knew Aramaic and possibly shows that knowledge in his transfer of this material into Greek. Working from this source information led him to mold the Greek to a high degree to give a grand vision of the early events of Christ's life.

Because Luke's research is so thorough, many specific details add to the authenticity of the gospel events. These details had to have come from those who were close to the characters mentioned in this drama. Because John the Baptist's role as herald of the Lord's arrival is so important, Luke takes us to the very beginning of his ministry.

Birth of John the Baptist Predicted (1:5–22)

"In the days of Herod, king of Judea" (1:5). The story begins under the reign of Herod the Great (v. 5), the despotic and cruel ruler who reigned over Judah. Herod's father, Antipater, had been governor of Judea. In 48 B.C., when Julius Caesar defeated Pompey, he had chosen Antipater's sons, Phasael and Herod, to inherit the throne. Yet before things could fall into place, Phasael committed suicide. Because of much intrigue within the Roman government, it was not until 40 B.C. that Mark Anthony finally persuaded the Roman senate to confirm Herod as king of Judea.

> Herod ruled for 33 years, an ally and friend of the Romans but loathed and feared by his Jewish subjects. He was a cruel and evil despot who stopped at nothing to fulfill his insane desire for power and prestige. Herod murdered three of his sons and many others, including his wife Mariamne, when he felt even remotely threatened. The Emperor Augustus commented, "It were better to be such a man's swine than his son." Evidence of Herod's megalomania can be seen today in the ruins of his huge building programs. This included the new seaport of Caesarea, a chain of fortresses (e.g., Masada), the most magnificent palace in the Middle East, and even embellishments to the Temple in Jerusalem (the Western Wall he had constructed still stands).[1]

Herod died about one year after the birth of Jesus, in 4 B.C., in misery and great suffering. He had hardening of the arteries or cancer or was afflicted with some loathsome sexual disease. When some fanatics found out he was dying, they attempted to remove the golden eagle, symbol of paganism, from the gable of the great Jerusalem temple that he had built. He had them burned alive. Nearing the end, he had all the leaders of Jerusalem assembled in a hippodrome so that upon his death they would be killed and the nation would have to mourn them instead of rejoicing at his death. With great suffering, and five days after he had his son Antipater put to death, Herod was gone. His son Archelaus took the throne and ruled until A.D. 6.

During these terrible times, Zacharias had gone to Jerusalem to serve out his priestly duties. His wife Elizabeth traced her lineage to Aaron (v. 5b), and Zacharias was a descendant of the prestigious priestly clan of Abijah, the first order and division of priests (1 Chron. 24:10). They both were "righteous in the sight of God, walking blamelessly in all the commandments and requirements of the Lord" (Luke 1:6). Since children were a sign of blessing from God, their neighbors may have questioned their piety, for they "had no child, because Elizabeth was barren, and they were both advanced in years" (v. 7). However, Zacharias longed for a child and probably petitioned the Lord frequently for offspring (v. 13).

Zacharias's time had come for his period of service at the temple (v. 8). He was chosen by lot to have the blessed privilege to burn incense before the Lord (v. 9). While Zacharias was standing at the altar of incense, the angel Gabriel suddenly appeared (v. 11). As most mortals would react when confronted by a heavenly personality, Zacharias was troubled and seized with fear (v. 12). The angel, however, gave him comfort, urged him not to be fearful, and revealed the good news that his wife, Elizabeth, would give him a son who was to be named John, which means "God is gracious" (v. 13).

Was it simply by chance that Zacharias was ministering at the altar of incense? No, it was in the providence of God. This altar, with its sweet smell ascending up to the Lord, owed its standing to the fact that a sacrifice had been made, the blood of atonement had been offered (Ex. 30:10). Holy fire on the altar caused the sweet perfume to ascend. The Lord was pleased to accept the blood sacrifice in the form of a pleasing fragrance.[2] John was privileged to minister in a place that called forth the graciousness and kindness of the heavenly Father. This may be why Zacharias would "have joy and gladness" and "many [would] rejoice at [John's] birth" (Luke 1:14).

The joy the angel speaks about would be a part of the day of salvation. It would begin with John's parents and then come upon "many," first the Jews and then the Gentiles. "Joy and gladness" stand in opposition to the great fright that had come over Zacharias in verse 12.

The Old Testament prophets were repeatedly concerned with turning the wayward Jews back to God and bringing about repentance (v. 16). No one stands out more than Elijah, who defied Israel's false God on Mount Carmel (1 Kings 18:20–40) and called for the people's repentance. Luke does not call John the reincarnated Elijah, yet he qualifies his comment with the words "in the spirit and power of Elijah" (v. 17). Luke uses the very words of Malachi 4:5–6 (see also Mal. 3:1) to compare the work of John with that of Elijah.

John will "turn the hearts of the fathers back to the children" must be interpreted with reference to Malachi 4:6 and the next phrase in this context (v. 17). If these words are parallel to "wisdom of the righteous," then the disobedient fathers may be turning to follow the example of their children who are now listening to John's words. The grammar may indicate that when the disobedient turn to listen to the words of wisdom, their Jewish ancestors of long ago would be thankful. In the context of the older testament, the words "turn the hearts" had to do with forestalling the wrath of God, a concept that was part of the work of John the Baptist.

"People" (Greek, *laos*) is an important word in Luke's gospel. *Laos* is used nineteen times in the other three Gospels, but in Luke alone it is used some thirty-six times. In contrast to *ochlos* ("crowd"), *laos* generally has a reference to Israel as the chosen people who forever hold and retain a special place in the Lord's heart and mind. By using this word, Luke is trying to make sure his audience understands the Jewishness of the Messiah. This would then mean that Luke wants to make sure his readers understand the Jewish nature and origins of Christianity.

The angel gave Zacharias a list of things that would mark John's ministry (vv. 15–17). (1) He would be great in the sight of the Lord, (2) he would not drink wine or liquor, (3) he would be filled with the Holy Spirit from his mother's womb, (4) he would turn many in Israel back to the Lord, (5) he would serve as a forerunner of the Lord in the spirit and power of Elijah, (6) he would turn the hearts of the fathers back to the children, (7) he would cause the disobedient to have an attitude of the righteous, and (8) he would make ready a people prepared for the Lord. In other words, he would prepare the nation of Israel for receiving the prophesied Messiah. God had made it clear that someday His Anointed (Messiah) would come (Ps. 2:2), who would be designated the King (v. 6) and would in the future reign from Mount Zion (v. 6b). He would be called God's Son, and He would inherit the nations (v. 8).

The prophecy about John the Baptist is given to us in Isaiah 40:3:

A voice is calling,
"Clear the way for the LORD in the wilderness;
Make smooth in the desert a highway for our God."

The child born to Zacharias would be this voice!

The Lord reveals in Malachi 4:5–6 that the prophet Elijah would be sent from God "before the coming of the great and terrible day of the LORD" (v. 5), referring to the coming judgment of the Messiah before He establishes His earthly rule. The Lord continues by saying that Elijah "will restore the hearts of the fathers to their children, and the hearts of the children to their fathers, lest I come and smite the land with a curse" (v. 6). While John was certainly not Elijah, the angel added these words from the book of Malachi to show that in this role of acting as heralds, John and Elijah would have a similar work. The restoration of the relation of parents to children must give some indication of the sad spiritual and domestic condition the nation was in. It would be the same when Elijah came. Barnes says that when the Messiah came, He "would restore peace to the families, and reconcile those parents and children who had chosen different sects. ... The effect of true religion on a family will always be to produce harmony."[3]

Zacharias seemed to doubt what he was hearing and asked for a sign. "How shall I know this for certain? For I am an old man, and my wife is advanced in years" (v. 18). His lack of faith carried a penalty in that he would be unable to speak because he did not believe the angel's words" (v. 20). Zacharias came out of the temple as a mute, and could only make signs to the people who were waiting for him. Detecting that something was wrong, "they realized that he had seen a vision in the temple" (v. 22).

Zacharias Returns Home (1:23–25)

"And it came about, when the days of his priestly service were ended" (1:23). A division of priests served only for a limited time. Zacharias returned to his hometown in the hill country of Judea. This was not far from Jerusalem and was possibly the city of Hebron. As prophesied, Elizabeth became pregnant, and "she kept herself in seclusion for five months, saying, 'This is the way the Lord has dealt with me in the days when He looked with favor upon me, to take away my disgrace among men'" (vv. 24–25). Elizabeth realized that God had been good to her in causing her to be pregnant, and she understood that her reproach and disgrace would be removed by having a child. Yet her words seem to hold some resignation. Why did she stay in seclusion for five months? Some commentators believe this was done out of custom, or from a certain belief that the woman might lose the child if she was too active, especially at Elizabeth's age. (This view is negated by the fact that it was divinely certain the child would be born!) *The Preacher's Homiletic Commentary* notes that Elizabeth may have remained secluded until it became clear that she was pregnant and then evident that God had indeed taken away her reproach of childlessness. Her womanly pride and humble gratitude to God are very natural character traits. No one could then claim that she or Zacharias had perpetrated a false rumor.[4]

Study Questions

1. How many men named Herod ruled over Israel?

2. When verse 8 speaks of Zacharias doing his priestly service in "the appointed order of his division," to what is this referring?

3. Was John's being "filled with the Holy Spirit while yet in his mother's womb" akin to believers being filled with the Holy Spirit?

4. Why does Gabriel relate "drinking no wine or liquor" to being "filled with the Holy Spirit"?

5. What is meant by John acting in "the spirit and power of Elijah"?

6. What is the source of the Old Testament quote in verse 17, and what is its relevance?

7. What is the importance of the people wondering at the delay of Zacharias in the temple?

CHAPTER 3

Announcement of the Birth of the Son of Man
Luke 1:26–56

Preview:

The angel Gabriel came to Mary with the startling announcement of the birth of the promised Messiah. Mary was apparently frightened at first but was comforted by the words of the angel. Her Son was conceived by the Holy Spirit. She would remain a virgin until after she had brought forth the one called the "Son of God." When Mary shared her good news with her relative Elizabeth, the baby in her womb leaped for joy! Mary created an inspiring poem, a song of her gladness that she had been chosen to bring forth the King of Israel!

Apparently six months after Elizabeth became pregnant, the angel Gabriel came to make the announcement to Mary of her own impending pregnancy. It is surmised that Mary was about sixteen years of age, which was the normal age that girls were married in Israel.

The Angel Appears to Mary (1:26–38)

"Gabriel was sent from God to a city in Galilee" (1:26). The mission of the angel Gabriel was a divine one, in that he came directly from God to deliver one of the most important messages of history. Mary and Joseph lived at this time in Nazareth, located but a few miles west of the sea of Galilee. The fact that they were residing in this city has prophetic significance. Isaiah 11:1–2 says "a shoot will spring from the stem of Jesse, and a branch from his roots

will bear fruit. And the Spirit of the LORD will rest on Him." The word "branch" is the Hebrew *nēṣer* from which later the name Nazareth would come. During the time of Isaiah there was no city of Nazareth. Obviously, the Lord in His providence was bringing about a divine connection between the word "branch" and the later city of Nazareth! Unger writes about Isaiah 11:1:

> But, **a Branch** (*nēṣer*, "a shoot, a scion"), a sign of vital life, **shall grow out of his roots,** that is, from the lowly "stump of Jesse." But "the Branch" is nevertheless also the "root" (v. 10; Rev. 5:5; 22:16), and as the "root and offspring of David" comprehends the Lord's "servant, the BRANCH" (Zech. 3:8) and "the man whose name is the BRANCH," who will "build the [millennial] temple of the Lord" (6:12; cf. Isa. 4:2; Jer. 23:5; 33:15).[1]

The word *nēṣer* is also mentioned in Matthew 2:23, where it is said that the prophets spoke of the Messiah as "the Nazarene."

The Angel Gabriel	
Appears to Daniel in a vision	*Dan. 8:15*
Instructed by a "man" to give a message to Daniel. The "man" could be the preincarnate Lord Jesus Christ	*Dan. 8:16*
Gives Daniel an understanding of "the time of the end"	*Dan. 8:17*
Sent to Daniel because the prophet was "highly esteemed"	*Dan. 9:23*
Possibly was the angel who appeared to Zacharias and revealed the future birth of John the Baptist	*Luke 1:11*
Reveals the mind of God: that the Lord had heard the petition of Zacharias for a son	*Luke 1:13*
Stands in the presence of God	*Luke 1:19*
Brings to Mary "good news"	*Luke 1:19*
Was sent to Mary "from God"	*Luke 1:26*
Mary could communicate with him	*Luke 1:34, 38*

Mary is called a "virgin" (Greek, *parthenos*) (v. 27), the most accurate word for an unwed and chaste girl. The word is a direct allusion to and quote of Isaiah 7, where in verse 13 a miraculous prophecy is said to be given to the royal house of David. "Therefore the Lord Himself will give you a sign: Behold, a virgin will be with child and bear a son, and she will call His name Immanuel" (v. 14). The Hebrew word for describing a very young girl, who would be without a doubt a virgin, is *b^ethûwlâh*. However, the word here is *'almâh*, which means "a veiled one." This word carries a lot of implication, as it was used by the Jewish people to describe virginity. It implied that indeed this young woman was technically a virgin and was also about sixteen, being of marriageable age. Being "veiled" was the sign showing these facts. Mary, then, was a young woman of marriageable age who was a virgin. Both Luke and Matthew use the most obvious word to describe this condition about Mary and call her a *parthenos*.

In the Greek text, the word for "engagement" is *mnēsteuomai*. The Greek perfect tense may imply that Mary and Joseph had been engaged for some time and that relationship had brought them up to this moment. In Israel an engagement was a serious affair, tantamount to marriage but without the physical consummation. Even in this engagement stage, an adulteress could have been stoned, though such punishment was being carried out less often. Matthew tells us that, when Joseph, who was a righteous man, heard that Mary was pregnant, he considered the issue and decided to put her away secretly, "not wanting to disgrace her" (Matt. 1:19). However, the angel of the Lord intervened and told him in a night dream that what was conceived was "of the Holy Spirit" (v. 20). Joseph then arose from sleep and took her as his wife that night (v. 24).

As was typical, Joseph was more than likely an older man. Some even surmise that he may have been about forty. Both Mary and Joseph were descendants ("of the house") of King David. Mary would be the chosen maiden who would bring forth the promised King and Savior of the world! She would have the greatest privilege any pious young Jewish woman could imagine. A future great king was promised through the line of David's son, Solomon, who would bring unlimited blessings to Israel and to the world. Through the prophet Nathan, the Lord made a promise to David: "And your house and your kingdom shall endure before Me forever; your throne shall be established forever" (2 Sam. 7:16).

This great King would be given one long name that would reflect the fact that He was God! Isaiah puts Hebrew nouns together to create one long descriptive name (Isa. 9:6). He would be called "Wonderful Counselor, Mighty God, Eternal Father, Prince of Peace" and He would reign "on the throne of David and over his kingdom, to establish it and to uphold it with justice and righteousness" (vv. 6b–7b). This King would be born ultimately through the seed of Jesse, David's father (Isa. 11:1). His reign at the end of history would be a rule of righteousness and peace for the nations. Isaiah the prophet adds, "Then it will come about in that day that the nations will resort to the root of Jesse, who will stand as a signal [banner, flag] for the peoples [nations]; and His resting place will be glorious" (11:10).

Messianic Promises

The prophesied Seed of the woman who would crush the head of the serpent (Satan) (Gen. 3:15)

The Peacemaker (Shiloh) from the tribe of Judah who would bear the scepter (Gen. 49:10)

The "I AM" who appeared to Moses from the burning bush (Ex. 3:14; John 8:58)

The Prophet Moses predicted who would someday come (Deut. 18:15)

The descendant of David through Solomon who would someday establish the earthly, Davidic kingdom (2 Sam. 7:13–17; Luke 1:32–33)

To be virgin born (Isa. 7:14; Luke 1:27)

The Anointed One (Messiah) (Ps. 2:2)

The King who will someday rule from Zion (Ps. 2:6)

The Son of God (Ps. 2:7)

The One whose hands and feet would be pierced (Ps. 22:16)

The One who would come forth from the grave (Ps. 16:10)

The Child born and the Son given who would someday rule Israel (Isa. 9:6–7)

The "branch" of Jesse (David's father) (Isa. 11:1)

The One upon whom the Spirit of God would someday rest (Isa. 11:2–5)

The One for whom the Jews would someday mourn and weep (Zech. 12:10)

The One whose existence has been from long ago (Mic. 5:2)

The young virgin Mary stands out in contrast to the elder priest Zacharias, who was far beyond the age for conceiving children. The word "virgin" was used to address one who had not had sexual relations. Mary's questioning in Luke 1:34 and the further mention (v. 27) of her being "engaged to a man" make this fact certain. Because an engagement (or betrothal) often took place soon after puberty, this young woman may have just begun her years as a teen. Such an engagement was just as legally binding as marriage, but intercourse would not take place until after the wedding. Only divorce or death could break an engagement. In the latter event, the young woman, though still not married, would yet be seen as a widow.

In verse 27 Luke describes Joseph as a descendant of the great King David. While the genealogy record found in 3:23–38 is generally seen as showing Mary's lineage, this is never specifically stated. And nowhere in the New Testament do any of the writers mention that Mary was from the royal line of King David. Joseph is mentioned here but also in 3:23 and is definitely tied to the royal linage. Therefore, we should probably assume that Luke saw Jesus as the rightful descendant of the royal line by what is now classified as the right of adoption. This has a powerful and important bearing on the promise in verse 32b.

In verse 28 Luke ties together another contrast with the narrative that went before by relating Gabriel's greeting (vv. 30–32) to the virgin. Zacharias did not receive such a greeting.

"Favored one" comes from *kecharitōmenē* and has the root meaning of the word for "greetings" (*chairō*), and "favor" as from the word *charis*, v. 30. Mary is the "favored one" because she is the one who was so blessed by God's grace. It has been suggested that the apostle makes the point that a certain grace has marked Mary's character. Though this may be true, the parallel in Ephesians, the only other time the verb is used the New Testament, shows that the grace mentioned here in Luke is that which is given all believers apart from any personal merit. Mary "found favor with God" (v. 30) and as well was the recipient of His grace (v. 28). Mary's only answer therefore was to utter, "My spirit has rejoiced in God my Savior" (v. 47), and "The Mighty One has done great things for me" (v. 49).

In a direct manner, the angel Gabriel greeted Mary, whose name comes from *Mariam*, the name of Moses' sister (Ex. 15:20). While the word *mary* itself implies bitterness, it does not reflect the nature or attitude of this young woman. Mary was by the time of Christ a common name. The angel said to her, "Hail," which is a vocative in grammar meaning, "Be glad, be rejoicing." He adds that she had been favored (Greek, *kecharitōmenē*, perfect passive participle) of the Lord, with the idea that "God has been progressively working a *work* of grace upon you. He is now about to fulfill that work!" It was natural that such a message and vision would be overwhelming to a young girl. Mary "was greatly troubled," or "completely shaken, thrown into confusion, terrified" (Greek, *diatarassō*, v. 29). In fact, she kept pondering (reasoning) in her mind what this message from the angel meant (v. 29b). To comfort her, Gabriel added, "Do not be afraid, Mary; for you have found favor with God" (v. 30). He then gave her more details about the impending pregnancy, birth, and career of her child: she would conceive in her womb, bear a son, and call Him Jesus (meaning "Jehovah saves"). He would be great, would be called the Son of the Most High, and would be given by the Lord the throne of His Father David. He would reign over the house of Jacob (the Jewish nation) forever, and His kingdom would have no end (vv. 31–33).

Much of what Gabriel said is from the Old Testament. Mary's child is called God's Son and the Son of the Most High (Ps. 2:7; Dan. 7:13–27). He will possess the throne of His father David (2 Sam. 7:16) and will reign over Jacob, the restored Jewish people (Zech. 12:1–10), and His kingdom will be eternal (Isa. 9:7). Some argue that this reign of the Messiah is not really over Israel, but over the church that has replaced the Jewish people in the plan of God. In other words, these promises are *spiritualized* or *allegorized*. The question is, How did Mary receive these promises? If verse 31 is referring to the Messiah's literal and actual birth, then His reign, as promised in a literal sense in the Old Testament, must also come to pass in a literal and historic way (vv. 32–33). One cannot change an interpretive horse in the middle of a stream! Both His first coming (His birth up to His ascension), and His second coming to reign later, must be seen in the same light: literal history! It is interesting to note that from verse 32, the early Church understood that Mary was also from the line of David. The last of the verse reads, "The Lord God will give Him the throne of His father David." Since Mary would be the sole human parent of Jesus, it is implied that she is related to David. (More on Mary's lineage on 3:23.)

Many Bible teachers think that it is significant that whereas in verse 15 Gabriel had qualified his prophecy about the greatness of John's prophetic ministry ("He will be great"), here in verses 32–33 his declaration of the greatness of Mary's Son is not specifically qualified at all. The important phrase "Son of the Most High" (vv. 32, 35, 76) leads to a bold and glorious messianic declaration about the "throne of his father David." The deity of Jesus as the divine Son is without a doubt linked to his messiahship in fulfillment of 2 Samuel 7:12–14 and Psalm 2:7–9 (see also Ps. 89:26–29). The messianic destiny of the Lord Jesus Christ follows the statement of His Sonship, and that Sonship is related to verse 35 and His divine origin. Without question Luke is given by the Holy Spirit a revelation of the messianic ministry as a divine mission of God's Son, rather than understanding Sonship as only an aspect of His being the Messiah!

The Old Testament ideas about the throne (v. 32), Davidic line (v. 32), reign (v. 33), and kingdom (v. 33) are described with a sense of eternity—that is, all of these things will have no end. While this overall concept is prophesied in Micah 4:7, it is not common in Jewish thinking today.

Mary did not ask for a confirming sign as Zacharias did but only for insight as to how the Lord would accomplish this wonder. As Luke records, the question she raised did not relate directly to the child she was about to bear. Instead, her inquiry had to do with her virginity. She responded with "How can this be, since I am a virgin?" (v. 34). Technically this expression is "I do not know a man." This statement is actually in the present tense and implies that she was not currently and never had been having sexual relations with any man. Virginity had been her pious way of life.

Since Mary was betrothed or engaged, it is clearly assumed that she thought she was to have normal marital relations at some time in the future. It is difficult, therefore, to know why she saw a problem in what the angel Gabriel had said. The biblical text of Luke does not show that Mary had Isaiah 7:14 in mind and wondered how she, still a virgin, could bring forth a child. Possibly Luke's compressed record is meant to suggest that Mary assumed an immediate fulfillment before marriage, or that the reader of his gospel might understand the issue as so clearly prophesied in Isaiah 7:14. This is hinted at in verse 31 when the apostle writes, "You will conceive in your womb, and bear a son, and you shall name Him Jesus."

Mary must have been puzzled when she asked, "How can this be, since I am a virgin?" (v. 34). "I am a virgin" actually reads in the Greek text, "For a man I know not!" She had never had sexual relations. The angel answered and then explained that what was about to happen was a miracle of God. His Holy Spirit would come upon her, and the power (*dunamis*) of the Most High would "overshadow" her (v. 35). She would soon give birth to a "holy offspring" who would be called "the Son of God" (v. 35b). The angel added that even Elizabeth, Mary's elder relative, was going to conceive miraculously (v. 36), because "nothing will be impossible with God" (v. 37). Being a godly young woman who wished to please the Lord, she answered, "Behold, the bondslave (*doulē*) of the Lord; be it done to me according to your word" (v. 38). "Nothing is said about the relation of Mary's submission to her consciousness of the shame a premarital pregnancy could bring her. Her servanthood is not a cringing slavery but a submission to God that in OT times characterized genuine believers and that should characterize believers today (see also v. 48)."[2] The work of revealing one of the greatest events of history was completed. The angel departed (v. 38b).

Mary and Elizabeth Meet (1:39–45)

"Mary arose and went with haste to the hill country, to a city of Judah" (1:39). Now Luke shifts his narration and combines the two strands about Elizabeth and Mary. Up to this point the narrative has not stressed Jesus' superiority to John. But now the attention will center on Christ and His mother (v. 43). Even so, the pattern will switch back and forth, giving John his own divine calling and important place as the prophet who goes before the Lord.

Mary must have started on her journey as soon as possible (v. 39). Luke does not make a definite statement about the town she went to, but we are able to surmise that it was fifty to seventy miles from Nazareth to Zacharias's home (v. 40). Many believe, as mentioned, the city was Hebron. This would be a major trip for Mary in her condition.

Spending time guessing how Mary's salutation caused the child in Elizabeth's womb to jump (v. 41) would be to miss the larger story of God's providence and sovereignty in this narrative in which the stirring of the unborn child becomes a wonderful prelude to Elizabeth's being filled with the Holy Spirit. Elizabeth's words were used to enlighten Mary about the identity of the child Mary was about to bring forth into the world (v. 42).

It must be noted at this point that nowhere in the New Testament is Mary ever called "Mother of God." Deity is not confined only to the person of Jesus, the Son of God and second person of the Trinity. It may be said that *Jesus is God*, but it cannot be said that *God is simply Jesus*. Yet it can be said that Mary was, however, the mother of Jesus the Messiah and Lord. It may also be said that He is *very God and very man*.

"Blessed" (v. 45) describes the happy situation of those God favors. Elizabeth gave the blessing Zacharias's muteness prevented him from giving. The blessing he later gave the infant Jesus is narrated in verses 68–79. Luke uses the blessing Elizabeth gave Mary to call attention to Mary's faith.

Coming back to the specifics of the narration story and reviewing: Mary took a quick journey to the city in the hill country of Judea where Zacharias and Elizabeth lived (v. 39), possibly when Mary explained what happened to her, the baby John leaped in Elizabeth's womb (v. 41). This was seen as a miraculous sign that two great events were coming together: the birth of the forerunner of the Messiah and the birth of the Messiah Himself! Elizabeth would be given new insights by the work of the Holy Spirit. She would be "filled" (*plēroō*) or "controlled" by this divine influence. The Spirit gave Elizabeth a marvelous revelation about Mary: "Blessed among women are you, and blessed is the fruit of your womb!" (v. 42). Elizabeth could not help but ponder why she was so fortunate (v. 43).

Mary's Song of Praise to God (1:46–56)

"My soul exalts the Lord" *(1:46).* In the shared excitement of the two women over what was about to happen, Mary created a song, a poem of thanksgiving to the Lord. Traditionally, this has been called by the Latin word *Magnificat,* meaning that Mary *magnifies* the works of God.

The Magnificat is saturated with Old Testament concepts and phrases, revealing Mary's deep piety and knowledge of Scripture. It would not be unusual for a pious young Jewish girl to know the ancient manuscripts and love Scripture. Mary's song reveals a God who vindicates and defends the downtrodden and ministers to the hungry (cf. 1 Sam. 2:1–10). It is similar to Hannah's great hymn. If Hannah spoke of the poor being raised to sit with nobles (1 Sam. 2:8), Mary sees the nobles falling from their high pinnacles of power (Luke 1:52). Yet Hannah's song is not without its elements of God's judgment in which God deals with the evil and arrogant who oppose Him (1 Sam 2:3, 4, 10; cf. Luke 1:51, 53). But because of the messianic element, Mary's Magnificat markedly goes beyond Hannah's poetic expression and implies Mary's consciousness of her exalted role in the coming birth of Israel's Messiah (v. 48). The song also should be taken as prophetic in the broad biblical sense, in which case the Holy Spirit who instructed Elizabeth may well have led both Mary and Luke in the composition and transmission of the song.

Mary begins her song by saying, "My soul exalts the Lord, and my spirit has rejoiced in God my Savior" (vv. 46–47). Her soul *is* "making great" (Greek, *megaluō*) the Lord. On soul (Greek, *pseuchē*) Vincent notes:

> The *soul* is the principle of individuality, the seat of personal impressions, having a side in contact with the material element of humanity, as well as with spiritual element. It is thus the mediating organ between the spirit and the body, receiving impressions from without and from within, and transmitting them by word or sign. *Spirit* is the highest, deepest, noblest part of our humanity, the point of contact between God and man.[3]

Using a present tense with the verb "has rejoiced," Mary implies that God is growing ever more wonderful for what He is doing with her. In certain theological traditions, some have considered Mary as sinless, but it is interesting to note that she implies her own need for redemption when she calls God "my Savior" (v. 47b). Mary continues by lavishing praises on God for all that He is doing through her. She says, "He has had regard for the humble state of His bondslave," meaning herself, and "all generations will count me blessed" (v. 48). Before turning to speak of how the Lord has blessed the world, she adds, "For the Mighty One has done great things for me; and holy is His name" (v. 49).

In verses 50–53, Mary goes beyond herself and speaks of God's judgments but also of His continual care for others. He has scattered the proud of heart (v. 51), brought down rulers and exalted the humble (v. 52), cared for the hungry and sent away empty the proud rich (v. 53).

Verses 54–55 are most insightful because they bring to mind that God is keeping His promises with Israel despite their suffering persecution under the cruel Roman puppet king, Herod the Great. Mary recalls God's mercy: "He has given help to Israel His servant," and "He spoke to our fathers, to Abraham and his offspring forever." She sees the coming birth of the promised Messiah as part of a larger prophetic unfolding of the Abrahamic covenant. The angel of the Lord had told Abraham how great and influential his descendants would be. "I will greatly bless you, and I will greatly multiply your seed as the stars of the heavens, and as the sand which is on the seashore; . . . And in your seed all the nations of the earth shall be blessed" (Gen. 22:17–18). Many rightly suggest that the word "seed" here should be taken in the singular and refer to Jesus. Unger writes about verse 18, "This expanded blessing [is] centered in Christ, the coming seed (see Gal. 3:16; cf. John 8:56), and could only be realized in Him."[4] There is no doubt that "Mary was aware that the birth of her Child was a fulfillment of the covenant promises to Abraham and his people."[5]

Study Questions

1. What does Matthew 1:18–25 add to the story of the birth of Christ?

2. Considering all of the gospel accounts, what do we know about Joseph?

3. What indicators in Luke 1:29–30 point out Mary's fear as to what was happening?

4. From verses 27–33, would a normal reading make one believe that the kingdom here meant the Church?

5. From the description of Mary as a pious and righteous young woman found in Matthew and Luke, does this convey that she was absolutely perfect and holy, as some churches try to say?

6. What is the significance of Elizabeth being filled with the Holy Spirit?

7. In verse 47, who is Mary referring to when she says, "God my Savior" ?

CHAPTER 4

Birth of John the Baptist
Luke 1:57–80

Preview:

Elizabeth and Zacharias were apparently greatly admired and seen as a righteous couple. Their neighbors and relatives rejoiced with them following the birth of their son, for Elizabeth had suffered for many years because of her barrenness. After the naming of the child John, Zacharias gave forth a profound prophecy about the ministry of his son and of the Messiah who was also soon to be born. In a good sense, John grew up to be a spiritual rebel whom God could use mightily in reaching the Jewish people.

Delivery of Elizabeth and Naming of John (1:57–66)

"Now the time had come for Elizabeth to give birth" *(1:57)*. Zacharias and Elizabeth's son, John, was born six months before Jesus. Their friends and family greatly rejoiced because John was born to this couple in their old age (v. 58). Luke says God *"displayed* His great mercy toward" Elizabeth (v. 58, italics mine). This is the same word (Greek, *megaluō*) as found in verse 46, where Mary says, "My soul exalts the Lord." Here in verse 58 it is an imperfect or past tense. Luke is saying that, with the beginning of Elizabeth's pregnancy until her delivery, God was "making large," that is, displaying His mercy toward her.

With the birth of John we come to the fulfillment of the promises of God which have occupied the first half of the birth narrative. The parallelism between the promises of the births of John and Jesus is continued in the accounts of their actual births and the acclamations that followed them.

33

The narrative emphasizes the way in which God fulfills his promises and brings joy to his people. . . . designates John as the prophet who will go before the coming of the Lord, and speaks of the redemption and salvation which God is preparing for his people in the house of David.[1]

As with Jewish custom and the Law, John was circumcised on the eighth day (Lev. 12:3). Modern medicine now knows that on the eighth day, vitamin K is at its highest level in an infant, and this vitamin helps with clotting and prevents massive bleeding. Jewish custom would have the child named for the father on that day (v. 59), but Elizabeth overruled and said, "No indeed; but he shall be called John" (v. 60). Dissension broke out among friends and family who said, "There is no one among your relatives who is called by that name" (v. 61). The dissenters made motions to Zacharias as to what he wanted to call his son (v. 62), and Zacharias acquiesced and wrote on a tablet, "His name is John" (v. 63). John would always bear this name and be designated as "God is gracious." In a sense, Zacharias had redeemed himself before the public and especially before the Lord. He had months to ponder the blessings of God and the miracle that was about to happen through him and Elizabeth. When he agreed with the name, his mouth opened and "he began to speak in praise of God" (v. 64). The word of all that had happened swept like a firestorm throughout all of the hill country of Judea (v. 65), with people continually saying, "'What then will this child turn out to be?' For the hand of the Lord was certainly with him" (v. 66).

Prophecy of Zacharias (1:67–80)

"Zacharias was filled with the Holy Spirit, and prophesied" (1:67). As with Elizabeth, Zacharias was "controlled" by the Holy Spirit and began to speak a prophetic message (v. 67). He first blessed the Lord God of Israel and said He had now accomplished redemption for His people (v. 68). By the revelation of the Spirit of God, Zacharias understood that the coming birth of Jesus would be like "a horn of salvation for us in the house of David His servant— as He spoke by the mouth of His holy prophets of old—Salvation from our enemies, and from the hand of all who hate us" (vv. 69–71). The promised Messiah was about to be born! What is so interesting is that Zacharias is quoting Psalm 106:10, which is part of a historical summary of God's redemption of the Jewish people from Egypt. Zacharias saw a parallel and applied in illustration form this psalm to what was about to take place through the birth of Christ. Through the Spirit, Zacharias was also shown that the birth of Jesus would be a part of the fulfillment of the Abrahamic covenant. He said that this salvation was coming

To show mercy toward our fathers,
And to remember His holy covenant,
The oath which He swore to Abraham our father,
To grant us that we, being delivered from the hands of our enemies,
Might serve Him without fear,
In holiness and righteousness before Him all our days. (vv. 72–75)

Comparing Elijah to John the Baptist	
Elijah was a prophet of the Old Testament (1 Kgs. 17—21).	John was a prophet of the New Testament (early chapters of the Gospels).
Elijah means "My God is Yahweh."	John means "Yahweh is merciful."
Elijah judged Israel when the nation was in idolatry—he told the people to choose either Baal or the Lord God (1 Kgs. 18:25).	John judged Israel and called the nation to repentance—he called for the people to confess their sins (Matt. 3:6).
Elijah performed miracles such as raising of the dead (1 Kgs. 17:17–24).	It is not recorded that John performed miracles.
Elijah went up to heaven in a whirlwind and a chariot (2 Kgs. 2:11).	John was murdered by Herod (Matt. 14:8).
Elijah was not a reincarnated John the Baptist (John 1:21, 25).	John came in the spirit and power of Elijah (Luke 1:17).
Elijah appeared, along with Moses, at the Transfiguration of the Lord (Matt. 17:3).	John heard from heaven the voice of God say, "This is My beloved Son" (Matt. 3:16–17).
Elijah came to herald the second coming of Christ (Mal. 4:5–6).	John came to herald the first coming of Christ (John 1:29).
Elijah would come to turn the hearts of the fathers back to the children (Mal. 4:5–6).	John came to do the same thing (Luke 1:17).

Zacharias rightly understood that the birth of Christ was a prelude to the establishment of the millennial reign of the Son of David. The literal and historic earthly kingdom was imminent. However, as the gospel accounts unfold, a problem becomes evident that will change things: the Jewish people must first repent for the forgiveness of their sins (3:3). This would be John's message more than thirty years later as he heralded the revealing of Jesus as the King. Without repentance, the promised messianic reign could not begin. The offer of the kingdom at that time was a legitimate offer. However, in God's divine foreknowledge, He knew the nation of Israel would reject His Son at His first coming. Many verses of Scripture confirm this (Matt. 16:21; Mark 8:31–32; 9:12, 31; Luke 17:25; 24:26, 46; Acts 3:18; 17:3; 26:23). The Lord's mysterious providence concerning the death of His Son was working in human affairs! Zacharias also mentions this work of personal salvation in his prophecy. He states, by quoting Isaiah 40:3, which predicts the arrival of John as the Messiah's herald, that this one would "go before the Lord to prepare His ways" (v. 76), "to give to His people the knowledge of salvation by the forgiveness of their sins, because of the tender mercy of our God" (vv. 77–78a). Though the order is reversed, Christ's first coming as a Savior is alluded to in verse 77, and His second coming to rid Israel of national oppression would come later (v. 71). The timing and chronology were not completely spelled out at this stage, even to Zacharias. Yet he describes this salvation and forgiveness of sins by quoting Isaiah 9:1–2 as a light shining on those who sit in darkness under the "shadow of death." Their feet will be finally guided into the way of peace (Luke 1:79; cf. Isa. 57:19–21).

This section closes with a footnote about how John grew up and what he did as a young man. He "continued to grow, and to become strong in spirit and he lived in the deserts until the day of his public appearance to Israel" (v. 80). "Strong in spirit" does not mean self-willed in a negative sense, but in the sense that he was independent of will. Being of the priestly family, he could have capitulated to the politics of the priestly hierarchy, but in fact, he resisted the traditional legalism, formality, and status quo of that institution. "Deserts" is plural, so John must have wandered from place to place, thinking, studying, and praying in a solitary manner. This isolation allowed the Spirit of God to work, creating a tenacity and determination that would make John bold and outspoken. In his solitude he was able to grow spiritually without adverse outside influences.

Study Questions

1. Give your thoughts as to how the people reacted to the coming birth of John.

2. What previous verses do you think caused Elizabeth to name John "God is gracious"?

3. Why was John to be circumcised on the eighth day?

4. From verse 64, why did Zacharias give God praise?

5. Why did the neighbors of Zacharias begin to fear after John was born and Zacharias began to speak again?

6. In the prophecy of Zacharias, how many verses does he give to the coming ministry of his son?

7. Where were the deserts, mentioned in verse 80 where John the Baptist lived?

CHAPTER 5

Birth of the Son of Man
Luke 2:1–20

Preview:

In this passage the political setting is established for the birth of Christ. His birth took place in the days of Caesar Augustus. Because of a national census in Judea, Joseph and Mary would have to travel to their city of origin, Nazareth.
Angels attended the birth of Jesus with heavenly praise: "Glory to God in the highest." Lowly shepherds were the first to visit the newborn, and they too glorified and praised the Lord.

Political Setting (2:1–3)

"A decree went out from Caesar Augustus, that a census be taken" (2:1). Caesar Augustus reigned in Rome from 27 B.C. to A.D. 14. He continued the policy of Roman emperors of making sure Judea was secure by strong leadership and tyrannical governors. Herod the Great was the overall titular king over the Jewish people, but a Roman authority was always present to make certain the full interests of the government were not neglected.

Caesar Augustus (Octavian). Rome had been in political and military turmoil with many factions and generals at war with each other. In time, Cassius and Brutus were defeated by Mark Antony and Octavian. Octavian would over a period of years be given control over Asia and finally would be made head over all of Rome and its possessions. Octavian was a grandnephew of Julius Caesar, meaning that his mother Atia was the daughter of Julia, the sister of

Julius Caesar. His granduncle, showered many honors upon him. When his uncle was murdered (44 B.C.), he was declared the son of Caesar and heir. In 27 B.C. the Roman senate gave him the title Augustus, meaning the supreme, highly esteemed one. From then on he would be known as Caesar Augustus. He ruled as emperor from 27 B.C. to A.D. 14. It is difficult to get a fix on his character. Early on he was ruthless but then seemed to mellow out and become a wise ruler. He allowed some home rule for conquered territory if the subjects submitted to Roman authority. He strengthened the family and passed laws against adultery, He stimulated art, created great buildings, and gave the world a lengthy period of peace. He was known as a kindly ruler and "the father of his country."

Quirinius. Under the rule of Augustus a census was to be taken of "all the inhabited earth" (v. 1), here meaning the vast regions of Roman rule. This is called the "first census" taken while Quirinius was governor of Syria (v. 2), the region north of Palestine. Liberal scholars take exception to Luke's account and argue that there is no evidence that a general census was taken during the reign of Augustus. This flies in the face of Luke's accuracy of accounting and the preservation of the biblical records by the work of the Holy Spirit. Furthermore, Luke's work was certainly read and studied by his contemporaries, including the apostles, and probably even by Mary, the mother of Jesus. Such a factual error, even from the human standpoint, is impossible.

The taking of a census was quite common in the Roman Empire. Augustus took one in 28 B.C. They were taken in Gaul in 27 and 12 B.C., in Cyrene in 7 B.C., and in Egypt starting in 9 B.C. To argue that we know of all the periods of census taking is historical foolishness. Hoehner well argues that

> Augustus [was] the first one in history to order a census or tax assessment of the whole provincial empire. This is further substantiated by the fact that Luke uses the present tense indicating that Augustus ordered censuses to be taken regularly rather than only one time. Thus, it is reasonable to believe that there was an order of a general census in the time of Augustus.[1]

Greek scholar Hoehner also notes that in verse 2 the word "first" (Greek, *protos*) may be used adverbially as the Greek word *pro*. In this case, the verse should read, "This census took place *before* Quirinius was governor of Syria."

> Luke . . . is merely stating that the census at the time of the nativity took place some time before Quirinius held office. This gives good sense to the passage at hand. . . . Quirinius was governor of Syria in A.D. 6–7 and possibly also, . . . in 3–2 B.C. If [Luke 2:2] has reference to his governorship in A.D. 6–7, then this census is before the governorship when he had conducted the well-known census mentioned in Josephus and Luke. On the other

hand, this also fits nicely if he were governor in 3–2 B.C.; for Luke is then stating that just before Quirinius was governor in Syria in 3–2 B.C. there was a census in Herod's domain.[2]

Herod the Great. It is in the book of Matthew that we learn the most about the role of Herod the Great in the birth story (2:1–22). But he certainly is the backdrop for the events as they are brought forth in Luke.

By God's providence and sovereignty, Herod was in the right place at the right time. Herod's father, Antipater, had been governor of Judea. In 48 B.C., when Julius Caesar had defeated Pompey, he chose Antipater's two sons, Phasael and Herod, to inherit the throne of Judea. But when Phasael committed suicide, Mark Antony in 40 B.C. urged the Roman senate to confirm Herod as king of Judea. This appalled the Jews because Herod's father was a half-breed, being part Jewish and part Idumean. Herod was not of the kingly Davidic lineage.

Herod would become an evil taskmaster. He would be cruel and ambitious, bringing on himself the hatred of the Jews. His genius would foster great building programs, including the construction and expansion of the great temple in Jerusalem. The project would continue well after his death. In the middle of his reign (25–13 B.C.), he could do anything he wished. He built amphitheaters, hippodromes, temples to Augustus, and water channels. By conservative calculations, he died about one year after the birth of Christ in misery and suffering. Matthew records that he was adamant to find the Christ child when Jesus was born (2:3–8). History shows why. He feared that the Jews would either kill him or depose him and put on the throne one from the house of David, specifically, the Messiah! His son Archelaus followed in his father's footsteps and was equally fearsome. This is why, when coming out of Egypt, Joseph took Mary and Jesus by an alternate route back to the Galilee region and the city of Nazareth (v. 22). (For more on Herod see commentary on 1:5–22).

Picking up the narration in Luke 2, before the birth of Christ, and under the governorship of Quirinius, everyone had to be registered for the census in his city of origin (v. 3). This is why Joseph and Mary, who was pregnant, would have to travel south to the place of family beginnings, Bethlehem.

Birth Account (2:4–14)

"Joseph also went up from Galilee … to Judea, to the city of David" (2:4). Probably traveling with other family members from Nazareth, Joseph took Mary to "the city of David, which is called Bethlehem ("house of bread"), "because he was of the house and family of David" (v. 4). The couple was already expecting the

soon birth of the Christ; Mary was heavy with child (v. 5). When the time of her delivery had arrived (v. 6), Mary and Joseph must have been camping out of doors with many people, because Luke tells us "there was no room for them in the inn" (v. 7). Many views are given as to what the word "inn" (Greek, *kataluma*) implies, for the word simply means "lodging, shelter." There also has been much speculation about the inn. Some think it may have been simply a walled enclosure outside someone's dwelling in which families could stay or an actual courtyard surrounding a house. In any case, they could not get shelter.

Many scholars believe that when Mary's birth pangs began, the family moved into the protection of a cave, since Jesus was laid down (Greek, *anaklinō*) in a manger. A manger (Greek, *phatnē*) is a feeding trough carved out in the wall of a cave. Around Bethlehem, the hillsides are dotted with caves, many of which still have mangers.[3] "Manger" became a word that encompassed both the feeding trough and the cave itself. Luke in 13:15 quotes Christ as speaking of leading the "ox or . . . donkey" away from the "stall" (*phatnē*, manger). Verse 7 also tells us that Mary gave birth to her first-born (Greek, *prototokos*) son. The Greek text clearly implies that other sons would be born later to Joseph and Mary. In fact, following the birth of Jesus, Matthew writes that Joseph "kept her a virgin until she gave birth to a Son" (Matt. 1:25). The word "until" (Greek, *eos*) implies that later they had marital relations and other children were born to them. That the Lord Jesus had half brothers and sisters, those born to Joseph and Mary, seems clear from Matthew 13:55–56a: "Is not this the carpenter's son? Is not His mother called Mary, and His brothers, James and Joseph and Simon and Judas? And His sisters, are they not all with us?"

Verse 7 also makes the point that baby Jesus was "wrapped" (Greek, *sparganoō*) in cloths. In the writings of Euripides, Aristotle, and Hippocrates, the word is used to describe medical bandages, and wrappings used to bind up the dead.[4] This is probably old clothes torn up and used for swaddling to keep the infant warm. Christ's first coming was to die for the sins of the world. Such wrappings of this Child told His ultimate destiny—to be slain for sinful humanity and have his body wrapped and placed in a tomb.

Nearby in the same region or *district* (Greek, *chora*), shepherds were in the fields caring for their sheep, watching them during the night (v. 8). In an instant an angel of the Lord (probably Gabriel) appeared before them, accompanied by "the glory of the Lord" (v. 9), which actually encircled (Greek, *peri*) the shepherds, causing them to fear. Naturally these poor men were "frightened with great fright." Shepherds were considered very common and even the lowest of the low. But it was through the prophet Nathan that the Lord revealed that through a shepherd boy, David, a great messianic covenant would be given (2 Sam. 7:8). God would use the idea of a shepherd to show His great care for His people. Jesus would be that ultimate Shepherd (Ps. 23:1; Isa. 40:11; Jer. 23:1–4; Heb. 13:20; 1 Peter 2:25; 5:2).

The question has often been asked why God would bring the message of the birth of the Messiah to lowly shepherds. Various reasons have been suggested. Shepherding was the lowest position on the economic and cultural ladder. Shepherds were seen as untrustworthy, and their work made them unclean by the standards of the Law. Therefore, the most obvious implication is that the good news about Christ's birth came first to the social outcasts of that period. Luke stresses such paradoxes often in his narration. Note also that in the Lord's instructions to Nathan about giving David the covenant, the Lord reminds David, who was to become the Messiah's ancestor, that he was called forth from the flocks in the fields (2 Sam. 7:8). Thus, in both testaments shepherds symbolize those who care for God's people, including the Lord himself. The shepherds of Luke 2 may, therefore, symbolize all the ordinary people who have joyfully received the gospel and have become in various ways pastors to others. Because the shepherds were out with their flocks in the fields at night does not preclude a December date, as the winter in Judea was mild. But, of course, the text says nothing about the time of year.

The angel calmed these men (Luke 2:9), as Gabriel had Mary upon his visit to her (1:30), and said, "Do not be afraid; for behold, I bring you good news of a great joy which shall be for all the people; for today in the city of David there has been born for you a Savior, who is Christ the Lord" (vv. 10–11). The shepherds had observed the hundreds or thousands who had come to Bethlehem for the census. They would quickly connect the fact that all the crowds of families were related to David, including the One who had just been born!

Where would the word *Savior* (Greek, *sōtēr*) come from as an Old Testament reference? Probably it is a reference to Isaiah 53 and the fact that the future Messiah would suffer for the sins of others as a sacrificial Lamb. The prophet wrote:

> All of us like sheep have gone astray,
> Each of us has turned to his own way;
> But the LORD has caused the iniquity of us all
> To fall on Him. . . . Like a lamb that is led to slaughter,
> And like a sheep that is silent before its shearers,
> So He did not open His mouth. (vv. 6–7)

The Greek word *Christos* is a translation of the Hebrew *hammāšîaḥ* used in Psalm 2:2. God will someday send His Anointed, whom the world will reject.

This One is God's Son (Ps. 2:7) who will break the nations of the earth "with a rod of iron" (Ps. 2:9). To refer to this One as "the Lord" is a reference to David's Son who will be the Lord (*Adonai*), who will someday ascend into the heavens and be told by *the* LORD (*Yahweh*) to "sit at My right hand, until I make Thine enemies a footstool for Thy feet" (Ps. 110:1). In most references in the Gospels, when Jesus is addressed as "Lord," many standing around understood that the term was pointing to this great and powerful messianic verse from Psalm 110!

While many infants may have been born when their parents were forced to go to Bethlehem on this census sojourn, the shepherds would identify the right child by "the sign" that He would be wrapped in cloths and "lying in a manger" (v. 12). With these words, there suddenly appeared "a multitude of the heavenly host praising God" (v. 13). This was a huge host (Greek, *plēthos*) of heavenly armylike troops (Greek, *stratia*) who were "constantly praising" (Greek, *aineō*, present active particle) the God of heaven. Their message was that the God who dwells in the highest part of the universe should receive perpetual glory and honor (v. 14). The last part of verse 14 needs to be explained. The NASB translates this, "And on earth peace among men with whom He is pleased." The word "pleased" is *eudokias*, a genitive case that is composed of two words put together, *eu* ("good") and *dokeō* ("to think, have an opinion about"). The idea is that men on earth who are well thought of by the Lord will have peace. This verse has been misinterpreted to promote the idea that there will be peace on earth if people simply try to get along with each other. Because of human sin, international peace is illusive. However, on the personal level, the Lord thinks in a positive way toward those who accept His Son as Savior. "The 'peace' here is that which the Messiah brings (cf. 1:79). Those whom Jesus healed or forgave on the basis of their faith could 'go in peace' (7:50; 8:48). Those on whom God's 'favor' (*eudokia*) rests are the 'little children' (10:21) to whom God graciously reveals truth according to his 'good pleasure.'"[5]

Visit of the Shepherds (2:15–20)

"The shepherds began saying to one another, 'Let us go straight to Bethlehem'" (2:15). When the heavenly host of angels departed, the shepherds decided to go to Bethlehem and "see this thing that has happened which the Lord has made known to us" (v. 15). If Jesus were indeed born in a cave, it must have been just outside the city. The shepherds were no longer afraid. They went quickly (Greek, *speudō*), or "with great speed," to see the Child just born (v. 16). Everything was confirmed just as had been described by the angel (v. 17). The

shepherds then "had satisfied themselves of the truth of the coming of the Messiah, and had ascertained that they could not have been mistaken in the appearance of the angels. There was evidence enough to satisfy them that what the angels had said was true, or they would not have gone to Bethlehem."[6]

While many probably saw Jesus shortly after the birth, the full meaning of the event was not shared in a public manner. Apparently only the shepherds confirmed the significance of what had happened, as seems to be indicated by verse 18. "And all who heard it wondered at the things which were told them by the shepherds." It can be assumed that Mary was exhausted from the delivery; she had some time to ponder in her heart what the birth of her child meant. She "treasured up" (Greek, *sunetērei*) or "kept on keeping together" all the things going on.[7] Using the imperfect or past tense here, Luke may be saying that she collected her thoughts over a period of time, trying to put them all together! As well, she constantly "pondered," or "kept throwing together" (Greek, *sunaballō*) in her heart what God was doing with her.

Returning to their flocks in the fields, the shepherds seemed to be the only ones who understood this glorious message of the birth of the promised Messiah. What had been told them by the angel happened precisely as "they had heard and seen" (v. 20). This verse seems to be a note of commentary by Luke to make sure his readers understand the accuracy of the events that took place around the birth of Christ.

Many have wrongly assumed that the magi appeared at the birth of Christ along with the shepherds. Actually, the family remained in Bethlehem, the town of their family origins, for about two years. During this time the magi traveled from Babylon. When these "wise men" arrived in Jerusalem and inquired where the Christ was (Matt. 2:1–12), Jesus was about two years old. Coming to Bethlehem by the miraculous guidance of the star (v. 9), the magi found Jesus and Mary residing in a house (v. 11). The family later returned to Nazareth.

Study Questions

1. Why was it important for Caesar Augustus's census to demand that all men return to the city of their birth?

2. What exactly is a manger and where can mangers be found?

3. Based on Luke 2:8, what arguments can be made concerning the date of Christ's birth?

4. Why do you think the angel told the shepherds in 2:11 that the Savior would be born in "the city of David" rather than saying, "in Bethlehem"?

5. How does the name Bethlehem relate to Jesus as Savior?

6. We often hear 2:14 translated, "Glory to God in the highest, and on earth peace, goodwill toward men." What is wrong with this translation?

7. When we look at 2:19, and consider Mary throughout this entire event, what does it tell us about her character?

CHAPTER 6

Presentation of Jesus in the Temple
Luke 2:21-38

Preview:
Throughout Jesus' life He was faithful to keep all of God's Law. Mary and Joseph also kept the Law by having Jesus circumcised eight days after His birth. At this ceremony the Holy Spirit led Simeon into the temple to proclaim Jesus as the Messiah. The prophetess Anna was also moved to speak of Jesus' identity, and His parents were amazed by what was being said.

Joseph and Mary, as pious Jews, would be expected to fulfill all the required ceremonies and stipulations of the Mosaic Law concerning the dedication of newborn infants. In the providence of God, the fulfillment of these requirements were necessary because Jesus would remind the Jews that He did not come to abolish the Law or the Prophets, but to fulfill what was written (Matt. 5:17). And this would certainly include certain ceremonial stipulations of His dedication as a Hebrew child. Jesus would undergo circumcision, the purification rites, and the parental presentation at the temple in a short period of time (Luke 2:21-24). By the revelation of the Holy Spirit, many in Jerusalem would recognize that the Messiah had been born!

The Circumcision (2:21)

"His name was then called Jesus" (2:21). This name was given to Him by the angel before He was conceived in Mary's womb (v. 21b). Luke wants to make

certain the reader sees all of the "fulfillments" that are going on in this narration. As in all pious Jewish families with baby boys, Jesus would be circumcised in compliance with the Law of Moses. The ceremony was to take place as prescribed in Genesis 17:12 and Leviticus 12:3. Circumcision was no small act, either ritually or hygienically. Such an operation, performed by a rabbi on the child's eighth day, would assure a degree of cleanliness for all Jewish males. But that physical benefit was part of a holy act that would make the children of Abraham unique in civilization. Circumcision made Jesus part of the covenanted people of God and placed Him under the Mosaic covenant (Gal. 4:4). It would make Christ a fulfiller of the Law in order to be able to redeem those under the Law. Besides being a requirement of the Mosaic covenant, circumcision would also connect the Lord to the Abrahamic covenant.

The Period of Purification (2:22–24)

"When the days for their purification according to the law of Moses were completed, they brought Him up to Jerusalem" (2:22). According to the Law of Moses, there would be a period of purification for the family, though the focus of such a ritual was for Mary (v. 22). The reason the text says "their" purification is because the couple was to abstain from sexual relations during this time. Some commentators feel that Theophilus, to whom this gospel was written, may not have been familiar with the law of purification, so Luke especially mentions it here. According to Leviticus 12:1 and the following verses, the mother who gave birth was unclean for seven days or until the circumcision of the infant, and then she could not touch holy things or come into the sanctuary for thirty-three days. After a total of forty days, she could come up to the temple to be made pure as the Law prescribed. As head of the household, Joseph is included to see that the act is carried out as intended and to carry out the proper rites with the sacrifices. Because of these laws, the family would travel from Bethlehem to Jerusalem and the temple, a trip of about fourteen miles, so that Jesus could be presented to the Lord. This was done to fulfill Exodus 13:2, 12. Luke quotes the Law, writing, "Every first-born male that opens the womb shall be called holy to the Lord" (v. 23). Such laws also include the first-born of animals. They are seen as "holy" or separated unto the service of the Lord.

Being poor, Joseph would offer a sacrifice of "a pair of turtledoves, or two pigeons" (v. 24; cf. Lev. 5:11; 12:8). The family could not afford a burnt sacrifice of a lamb. The birds cost only a few pennies in comparison to the price of a sheep. The one dove would act as a burnt offering and the second would take the place of the sin offering. One animal would be consumed in fire, the other was an offering of "substitution" for sin. These sacrifices were not for the Lord Jesus, who was perfect as the Son of God; they were for the sinfulness of Joseph and Mary.

The Prophet Simeon (2:25–35)

"Behold, there was a man in Jerusalem . . . this man was righteous" (2:25). Verse 25 begins with the exclamation "Behold" to arrest the attention of Theophilus and others who would be reading this account. The exclamation introduces Simeon, who is a "righteous and devout" man "looking for the consolation of Israel." One would think that God would announce the birth of the Promised One to the religious leaders in Jerusalem, but He did not. The revelation that the Messiah had been born would come to the lowly, such as the shepherds, this man Simeon, and then to the prophetess Anna (v. 36). Simeon was actually "looking for" or "waiting for" the Messiah, as best indicated in the word *prosdechomai.* "Consolation" is the Greek word *paraklēsis,* which is better translated "the comfort, help." It is related to the word that describes the coming work of the Holy Spirit as the "Helper" (John 14:16; 15:26). "The consolation of Israel" refers to the future help, the defeat of the nation's enemies when the Messiah comes to reign. The Jews did not know the Lord's timetable. To receive this kingdom of blessing, the nation of Israel had to repent of their sins. They of course did not, rejecting the witness of John the Baptist and then of Jesus Himself. A scattering would take place that would bring about a postponement of the promised Davidic rule of the Son of Man.

The Holy Spirit would also be upon Simeon (v. 25b), by whom it would be revealed that he "would not see death before he had seen the Lord's Christ" ("Anointed One", v. 26; cf. Ps. 2:2). Simeon was a common name among Israelites. Nevertheless, its etymology and significance are unknown. Simeon was in the temple "in the Spirit" (v. 27), that is, under the influence of the Holy Spirit or led or guided by the Spirit. Though Jerusalem was the center of Jewish worship and terribly corrupted by the leadership, even here there were many who were truly God's people. When Simeon saw the babe Jesus, he took Him into his arms (v. 28) and gave a hymn of blessing, certainly inspired by the Holy Spirit.

In his prayer and blessing he labels himself the "bond-servant" of the Lord who can die in peace (v. 29) because his eyes "have seen Thy salvation" (v. 30) which the Lord "hast prepared in the presence of all peoples" (v. 31). God's blessing with His Messiah would go beyond the Jewish nation, it would be "a light of revelation to the Gentiles, and the glory of Thy people Israel" (v. 32). These words come from Isaiah 52:10; 42:6; and 49:6. With the coming of Jesus, the fulfillment of and allusion to the prophetic Word tumble into place. Righteous Jews had studied these promises for centuries, and now they were coming about at this time in Israel's history.

Joseph and Mary were thoroughly amazed at what Simeon had said about Jesus (v. 33). One piece at a time, the full prophetic significance would fall into place. It would be wrong to assume that this godly couple understood instantly all that was coming about. Along with others, they had to learn and observe what the Lord was unfolding in regard to His divine Son! As Simeon continued to prophesy, he shared with Mary both the good and the bad. Mary's Son would be "appointed for the fall and rise of many in Israel" (v. 34), and her heart would be pierced as with a sword—"to the end that thoughts from many hearts will be revealed" (v. 35). Christ had come to divide people. While many would receive Him, many more would reject Him, and their hearts would reveal their lack of trust in God. After Joseph and Mary had heard the wonderful news about their Son's work, Simeon shared the painful part of the message. It is remarkable how the Spirit revealed to him that this child was the Messiah. Nothing was outwardly unusual about this mother and infant. He learned who Jesus was by the revelation of the Holy Spirit. What seemed so natural was actually the directing work of the Spirit of God.

The Prophetess Anna (2:36–38)

"A prophetess Anna . . . was advanced in years" (2:36). Anna was a prophetess as were Philip's daughters (Acts 21:9), and she must have used her gift in like manner to be a blessing to others. Her title does not mean that she went around predicting the future. And she does not seem to have pushed forward in an imposing manner but used her abilities in a limited and appropriate fashion. In the story of Anna, we see how dedicated to detail Luke was. He mentions Anna's father, Phanuel, and the family tribe, Asher (v. 36). Anna was much older than Zacharias and Elizabeth. "She was advanced in years, having lived with a husband seven years after her marriage." Her husband then died. She was a widow up to the age of 84, and "she never left the temple, serving night and day with fastings and prayers" (vv. 36b–37). If she married young, at around the age of 15, she could have been about 105 years old! But most commentators think her total age was only 84. Whatever, the point of the passage is that she must have been healthy, giving herself in continual service to the Lord at the temple. She was extremely pious, dedicating herself to fasting and prayer. Luke's use of plural forms indicates that her fasts were often and her prayers were many. Anna's communion with her God is the central fact about this remarkable elderly woman. That she served "night and day" may indicate that she arose early to clean the temple, polish the marble, and even help the priests in some way to prepare the oil lamps. Luke adds the astounding fact that she "never left the temple" (v. 37).

While Simeon was speaking his prophecy, Anna appeared "at that very moment" and began offering thanks to God (v. 38). She then "continued to speak of" the Lord, probably thanking Him that she had seen His promised Anointed One! She shared this great news with "all those who were looking for the redemption of Jerusalem." Because of the oppression of the Romans and the spiritual debauchery of the Jewish leaders, this hope was continually before all godly Israelites. "Looking for the redemption of Jerusalem" could better read in the Greek text, "Expecting Jerusalem's ransoming." The object is Jerusalem that is someday to be ransomed, and the ransomer is God. This hope seems to leap ahead to the second coming of the Messiah when He will redeem the great city of Jerusalem from its persecution by the nations of the earth. The prophet Zechariah prophesies that God "will set about to destroy all the nations that come against Jerusalem" (Zech. 12:9). The Jews will look upon the returning Messiah "whom they have pierced; and they will mourn for Him" (v. 10). But many of the people who live in the city will be spared and "there will be no more curse, for Jerusalem will dwell in security (14:11), with the Lord striking all who went against the city (v. 12). Then Zechariah writes about the end of the great world tribulation: "Then it will come about that any who are left of all the nations that went against Jerusalem will go up from year to year to worship the King, the LORD of hosts" (v. 16).

In summary, it is important to look more closely at the function of Anna as a prophetess. Luke's focus on the renewal of prophecy at the coming of the messianic age can be said to be highlighted with the introduction of Anna as a "prophetess" (v. 36). Zacharias also had been "filled with the Holy Spirit and prophesied" (1:67). Simeon, though not called a prophet, was filled with the Spirit and prophesied. Prophetesses were used of the Lord in both the Old and New Testament dispensations (Ex. 15:20; Judg. 4:4; 2 Kings 22:14; Neh. 6:14; Isa. 8:3; Acts 2:17; 21:9; 1 Cor. 11:5). Though it may not play on her prophetic role, Anna could trace her genealogy. She was from the tribe of Asher, which was not seen as an outstanding tribal people in the Old Testament (Gen. 30:12–13; 35:26). However, Luke thought it was important enough to show her as a true Jewish elderly woman.

Study Questions

1. What is the Hebrew origin of the name "Jesus," and what does it mean?

2. What, specifically, does the "law of Moses" say about the "days for their purification," spoken of in 2:22?

3. In 2:23, what does it mean that "every first-born male . . . shall be called holy to the Lord?"

4. What do we know about Joseph and Mary by the fact that they brought a "pair of turtledoves or two young pigeons" as a sacrifice?

5. What is the difference between John the Baptist being "filled with the Holy Spirit," and Simeon just having the Holy Spirit "upon him," as spoken of in 2:25?

6. In Simeon's prayer in 2:32, what was the basis for his referring to Jesus as "a light of revelation to the Gentiles"?

7. Luke 2:36 tells us that there was a woman named Anna who was a prophetess. What was the role of prophetesses in the Old Testament, and does their presence qualify women to be pastors in the New Testament church?

CHAPTER 7

Early Years of Jesus
Luke 2:39-52

Preview:

Jesus was raised in Nazareth, undoubtedly working with Joseph in carpentry and traveling with His parents every year to Passover in Jerusalem. Having grown in wisdom, at the age of twelve, Jesus decided to stay in the temple, conversing with the scholars of the Law. When Mary and Joseph noticed His absence on their way home, they returned to find Him in the temple, amazing the scholars with His knowledge.

In this short section, Luke tells about Jesus' early life. Although this section shares only one incident of His early years, it focuses on Jesus at age twelve letting it be known that He would be about His Father's business.

Jesus' Growing Years (2:39-41)

"They returned to Galilee, to their own city of Nazareth" (2:39). Luke begins this section by reminding the reader that Jesus' parents did everything according to the Law of the Lord in Jesus' early years. Luke on purpose leaves out the flight to Egypt recorded in Matthew 2:13–23 because he wants to get to his main purpose of introducing the ministry of John the Baptist and then of Jesus. Luke apparently wants to show the early rejection of the Lord as the promised Messiah. The holy family would, in several years, return to their home of residency in the city of Nazareth, which was about sixty-five miles north of Jerusalem (Luke 2:39b).

Luke tells nothing of the flight to Egypt and the reason for the return to Nazareth instead of Bethlehem, the place of the birth of Jesus as told in Matt. 2:13–23. But then neither Gospel gives all the details of this period. Luke has also nothing about the visit of the wise men (Matt. 2:1–12) as Matthew tells nothing of the shepherds and of Simeon and Anna (Luke 2:8–28). The two Gospels supplement each other.[1]

Luke points out how Jesus grew physically strong, and also increased in wisdom, with God's grace resting upon Him (v. 40). Luke is so impressed with Jesus' early development that he repeats in verse 52 how Jesus was "increasing in wisdom and stature" (v. 52). Luke shows how faithful Jesus' parents were by stating that they never missed journeying to Jerusalem for the Feast of Passover (v. 41).

Every Jewish male was expected to go up to Jerusalem yearly for Passover, Pentecost, and the Feast of Tabernacles (Ex. 23:14–17; 34:23; Deut. 16:16). But because the Jews had become scattered throughout the Middle East, this was not practical for most. Women were not so required to go, but Mary traveled each year with her husband. The Jewish Passover was the first of three annual feasts. It celebrated the exodus from Egypt under the leadership of Moses (Ex. 12:11, 21, 27, 43, 48; Lev. 23:5). Passover pictured redemption by the blood that was smeared on the doorposts of the houses of the Jewish slaves. An innocent lamb or kid secured their release, as Christ would someday redeem those who relied on His blood sacrifice. Pentecost was called the Feast of Weeks (Ex. 34:22; Deut. 16:10, 16), Feast of the Harvest (Ex. 23:16), and the day of the first fruits (Num. 28:26). It was a feast of rest and a joyful period following the spring harvest. (It was at the time of Pentecost that the Holy Spirit would be poured out on the early church [Acts 2]). The Feast of Tabernacles (tents, booths) celebrated Israel's rest when coming out of Egypt (Lev. 23:40–44). God said that living in tents for seven days was to be a reminder of "when I brought [My people] out from the land of Egypt" (v. 43). These three festivals were seen as evidences of the blessings of God on His chosen people.

Jesus in the Temple (2:42–52)

"And when He became twelve" (2:42). Luke picks up the story with the family going to the Feast of Passover when Jesus was twelve (v. 42). This would be the time that a young man would be as coming into manhood and would be seen as a responsible "son of the law" who would begin the process of learning to observe all the demands of the Law. As the family began the return trip (v. 43) in a caravan with other pilgrims (v. 44), it was discovered about a day

into the journey that the boy Jesus was not with his traveling relatives and acquaintances (v. 44b).

At this young age, Jesus could have been either with the women and children or with the men and older boys, if the families were grouped this way in the caravan. Each parent might have supposed He was with the other (v. 43). We need not assume that His parents neglected Him. It was after a day of travel that they missed Jesus (v. 44); another day would have been required for the trip back (v. 45); and on the next day ("after three days," v. 46) the successful search was made.

With some detail Luke describes the parents' emotions. Joseph and Mary were naturally taken back by Jesus' absence (cf. v. 33). Luke attributes surprise to those who should have known about the uniqueness of Jesus' person and future role. He observes and records the various responses of wonder at Jesus' words and works. His mother expresses her natural concern with a hint of scolding. She uses the word "anxiously" (the Greek participle *odunōmenoi*) to describe her and Joseph's feelings as they continually looked for Jesus. This Greek word is extremely emotional, often showing pain and suffering (16:24–25; Acts 20:38).

Jesus responded, "Why is it that you were looking for Me?" (v. 49). A theological point is being made here, for Jesus' question is similar to the question of the angels at Jesus' tomb in 24:5: "Why do you seek the living One among the dead?" The answer there is straightforward: "He is not here, but He has risen" (v. 6). In the present instance, the second part of the statement is of extraordinary significance. It is important to note Jesus' use of the phrase "my Father" (v. 49), with its designation of Jesus as the unique Son of the Father. This is amplified by the fact that Mary and Joseph did not understand what Jesus had really said (v. 50). There appears to be a subtle contrast between the words "your father" (v. 48) and "My Father" (v. 49).

Luke strongly intimates that Jesus is deity, and he assures the reader of Jesus' perfect humanity by noting that He was obedient to His earthly parents. Again, Mary reflected inwardly on the significance of what was now happening (cf. Gen. 37:11). Like the young lad Samuel (1 Sam. 2:26) and the responsible son in Proverbs 3:4, Jesus matured into a person both God and people approve.

The narration goes on to reveal that after three days of searching, Jesus was discovered in the temple "sitting in the midst of the teachers, both listening to them, and asking them questions" (v. 46). Ordinarily this would have been unacceptable for such a young lad, but Luke notes, "All who heard Him were amazed at His understanding and His answers" (v. 47). We must remember that Jesus was increasing in "the grace of God" (v. 40) and increasing in wisdom and "in favor with God and men" (v. 52). As a young man, Jesus was not simply a *learner*, He was *learned* beyond His years.

Jesus' parents were "astonished" at what they found, and they were anxious for Jesus' well-being (v. 48). Jesus answered, "Why is it that you were looking for Me? Did you not know that I had to be in My Father's house" (v. 49). While natural things are happening in this account, there is much that points to the supernatural—Jesus will be progressively coming forth as the Son of Man, the Messiah, and the Son of God, who has a divine relationship with the eternal God. While Jesus' parents did not understand what He meant at this time (v. 50), Jesus was not being smart or surly with them in His response. Jesus had never made an utterance like this. No wonder Joseph and Mary were confused. The mental and spiritual growth of Jesus were beyond human comprehension and experience. It might be said that at this moment, Jesus began to move toward that destiny of full obedience to His heavenly Father. He grew up in a natural fashion yet as a budding youth who was without sin. As a growing child, He was still deity and was in essence very God, or what is termed in theology, the God-Man!

Luke remarks that when Jesus returned home to Nazareth, "He continued in subjection" to His parents (v. 51a). This incident at the temple was a poignant and isolated happening that in no way was part of a pattern of adolescent rebellion. Mary pondered this event and "treasured all these things in her heart" (v. 51b).

Study Questions

1. Since Jesus is God, what did Luke mean when he said that "the Child continued . . . increasing in wisdom"?

2. What were the "full number of days" one had to spend in Jerusalem for the Feast of Passover?

3. How many feasts were actually involved?

4. Why were Joseph and Mary astonished that Jesus was in the temple?

5. Normally we consider north to be "up" and south to be "down." When we consider that Nazareth is north of Jerusalem, why does 2:51 say, "And He went down with them, and came to Nazareth"?

6. Although Mary saw Jesus interacting with the rabbis in the temple, what was her chief concern as revealed by her question in 2:48?

7. Why is it important that Jesus "continued in subjection" to His parents (2:51)?

CHAPTER 8

Baptism and Beginning Ministry of the Son of Man
Luke 3:1-22

Preview:

After just a short story from Jesus' childhood, Luke jumps forward to present Him and John the Baptist as adults. John is preaching a baptism of repentance and baptizing many in the Jordan River. He is a fiery orator, zealous for the Word of God and willing to confront those who abuse it. Jesus presents Himself to John for baptism, and the miraculous presence of the Trinity is revealed.

Preaching of John the Baptist (3:1-14)

"Now in the fifteenth year of the reign of Tiberius Caesar . . ." *(3:1)*. Luke starts his historical account here by mentioning Tiberius Caesar who ruled in Rome from around A.D. 30 to 37. Tiberius succeeded Caesar Augustus. He restrained the public from worshiping before the imperial statues, and he forbade votive offerings in his honor at the Roman temples. He did, however, allow his images of himself to be erected in public places if they did not show the likeness of the gods. He refused to be called "Lord" by the people. In A.D. 23 he finally gave in and permitted a temple to be erected to him at Smyrna.

At this time also Pontius Pilate governed the larger area of Judea. Representing Rome, with much power and authority, he acted as governor or procurator for ten years and was deposed after Passover of A.D. 36. Pilate would be significantly involved in the crucifixion of the Lord as described by Luke at the end of his gospel (ch. 23). Four other weak but influential personalities, some who were the sons of Herod the Great, ruled over other areas of the Holy Land. Herod Antipas was the tetrarch of Galilee from 4 B.C. to A.D. 39. A tetrarch was like a governor over one quarter of a given territory. His brother Philip was tetrarch of Iturea and Trachonitis, an area to the northeast of the Sea of Galilee. Lysanias, of whom little is known, was tetrarch over the region of Abilene, an area northwest of Damascus.

In Jerusalem the high priesthood included Annas and Caiaphas (v. 2). Annas was older and was considered high priest emeritus. He had reigned about twenty years during the time of Herod. His son-in-law named Josephus, or Caiaphas, was at this time the acting high priest who came to his position sometime between A.D. 18–26 and was deposed around A.D. 36. At this time John was abiding in the wilderness (Greek, *tē erēmō*, "the desert"), possibly in the area called El Ghor, the deep depression through which the Jordan flows toward the Dead Sea. There the "word of God' came to him. The wilderness mentioned here was probably an area on the southeast side of the Jordan River. Here he was thoroughly removed from civilization. There are many speculations about John. He probably could not stand the religious hypocrisy he saw in Jerusalem. God isolated him and taught him the truth, apart from all of the false impressions put forth by the religious parties in Israel at that time. John was a loner, but he would not remain as such. He would be summoned to the task of being the herald of the Messiah! He would bring many Jews to God, but he would also be hated by many because of his convicting message.

John began preaching up and down "all the district around the Jordan" a baptism of repentance (v. 3), that is, a *washing* that was marked by repentance. To the Jews such a ceremonial washing was a sign of cleansing. To become cleansed before God, the Jewish people had to look at their corporate and personal waywardness and sinfulness before the Lord. The perfunctory rituals at the temple in Jerusalem had lost their meaning. The hearts of the people were weary of sins that were destroying them. This "repentance" (Greek, *metanoia*) was a "change of the mind" about the spiritual and moral direction one had been going. The word implies a spiritual turning of the mind (and heart) from guilt and sin to receiving the cleansing forgiveness of God. Many Old Testament passages foretold of the Lord's great mercy and grace. He "pardons all your iniquities" (Ps. 103:3a), remembers sins no more (Isa. 43:25), and casts all "sins into the depths of the sea" (Mic. 7:19). And what loyal Jew could forget the pleading of the Lord as recorded in Isaiah 1:16, 18:

"Wash yourselves, make yourselves clean;
Remove the evil of your deeds from My sight.
Cease to do evil, . . .
"Come now, and let us reason together,"
Says the LORD,
"Though your sins are as scarlet,
They will be as white as snow;
Though they are red like crimson,
They will be like wool."

Luke reaches back into Isaiah 40:3–5 and shows how the ministry of John was prophesied (vv. 4–6):

The voice of one crying in the wilderness,
"Make ready the way of the Lord,
Make His paths straight.
Every ravine shall be filled up,
And every mountain and hill shall be brought low;
And the crooked shall be straight,
And the rough roads smooth;
And all flesh shall see the salvation of God."

These poetic words of Isaiah picture a path being made straight so that one can walk unhindered. Some have thought that the illustration of rough places made smooth describes a road being leveled in preparation for the arrival of a king who is coming into the region to visit his subjects. If this is so, how fitting for the presentation and arrival of the Lord Jesus in the company of His own people!

This "washing" administered by John would be both temporal and temporary, but the ultimate baptism of the Lord would be a permanent work performed someday in the future by the Spirit: "He will baptize you [Israel] with the Holy Spirit" (v. 16). While "baptisms" are similar in nature, in that they picture a cleansing, John's baptism will not pass on into the age of the church. When one trusts Christ as Savior, a water baptism is appropriate (Acts 8:26–39; 9:18), but it is a picture of the promised baptism of the Holy Spirit that places the believer into the spiritual body of Christ (1 Cor. 12:12–13; Eph. 4:5; Col. 2:11–13).

Many "multitudes" were coming to John (v. 7), from Jerusalem, all Judea, and throughout the Jordan area (Matt. 3:5). He baptized them as they confessed their sins (v. 6). But there were many legalistic Pharisees and Sadducees in the crowds who were openly critical of John's work, claiming they did not need to repent, arguing, "We have Abraham for our father" (v. 9). John turned on them and others who were unrepentant of their sins and said, "You brood of vipers, who warned you to flee from the wrath to come?" (Luke 3:7b). Their claim to be so secure as descendants of Abraham was answered by John: "I say to you that God is able from these stones to raise up children to Abraham" (v. 8). God is looking for flesh and blood to honor Him and have fellowship with Him; He is not simply seeking automatons to love. Many in Israel thought that their blood privilege as Jews was sufficient to merit God's blessings.

John warned the Jews that time was growing short; a judgment was coming. "The axe is already laid at the root of the trees; every tree therefore that does not bear good fruit is cut down and thrown into the fire" (v. 9). The axe was poised against the root to be cut down. And the fire of judgment would fall upon Israel less than forty years after the ascension of he Lord, in A.D. 70, when Jerusalem was destroyed by the Romans. Many in the crowd felt the sense of the lateness of the hour and asked, "Then what shall we do?" (v. 10). Tax-gatherers who had cheated the poor also asked, "Teacher, what shall we do?" (v. 12). John's answer seems strange at first, but the Jews got the point. "Let the man who has two tunics share with him who has none; and let him who has food do likewise" (v. 11). "Collect no more than you have been ordered to" (v. 13), "Do not take money from anyone by force" (v. 14). In so many words, John was saying, if you are truly repentant, it will come out in the way you treat others. What is inside will manifest itself outwardly!

Tax-gatherers were traitors to their own nation and thus were hated by the people and considered aides to the Roman oppressors. They were a disgrace to their families. "These tax gatherers are especially warned against the besetting sin of extortion. A mark of conversion is the honesty in all our dealings, but honesty for God's sake."[1]

There are three classifications of people to examine in this section: (1) the crowd, (2) the tax-gatherers, and (3) the soldiers.

1. *The crowd,* which was mixed, stood in contrast to the tax collectors and the soldiers (vv. 12–14). The crowd was urged to share what they had with those less fortunate, specifically their food and their clothing (v. 11). John the Baptist was not calling for a legalistic communal life similar to that at Qumran but "fruit in keeping with repentance" (v. 8; Gal. 5:22–23). The "tunic" or coat he was speaking about was the short coat (Greek, *chitōn*) worn under the outer robe (Greek, *himation*). Some who could afford it would have an extra tunic for warmth or for a change of clothes. This is why in 9:3 when Christ sent out the twelve disciples on their mission trip, He commanded them, "Do not even have two tunics apiece." Those who had ignored or forgotten the law of loving others needed to show their repentance in this kind of sharing.

2. *The tax-gatherers* (v. 12) were part of the despised and oppressive government system (5:27; 15:1). Of these three groups, they would have been considered most in need or repentance. The chief tax collectors (Greek, *architelōnēs*), such as Zacchaeus (19:2), put up bids and money for their position. They made their profit from collecting more than they paid the Romans. The chief among the tax collectors then turned around and hired others to work for them in robbing and extorting the people. Because their skullduggery and their associations with other crooked comrades rendered them ritually unclean and because they on an ongoing basis "stole" money from those who had less, they were alienated from Jewish society and linked with the grossest of sinners. John showed social concern, but he did not call for an overthrow of the system. Rather, he advocated a reform of the abuses. It can easily be said also that open social injustice shows that these men were spiritually without the Lord. Since these abuses arose out of individual greed, a radical change in the practice of the tax-gatherers themselves was required (v. 13).

3. Finally, *the soldiers* (Greek, *strateuomenoi*) were more than likely not Roman but Jewish, assigned to internal affairs (22:4). The nature of their positions and authority made it possible for them to have an opportunity to commit the sins that are mentioned here. Soldiers could use intimidation and reprisals to take money from the people. The soldiers' question suggests the seriousness of the moral problem by means of the added words *kai hēmeis* ("even we"): "What about us, what shall we do?"

The mob questioned whether such a forceful and bold prophet as John might be the Messiah (vv. 15). (Popular opinion about him is reported in greater detail in John 1:19–25.) Here in the book of Luke, John proclaims that the Messiah is "mightier" than he is (v. 16), so worthy of great reverence that even the task of tying His sandals is more than John feels worthy of (cf. John 3:30).

Questioning of John (3:15–18)

"The people . . . were wondering . . . whether he might be the Christ" (3:15). Because of the power of John's words and the conviction that followed for many, the people wondered in their hearts if he might be the *Christ* (Greek, *Christos*), the promised anointed King (v. 15). John sensed their thoughts and began pointing them to the soon arrival and presentation of Jesus. He answered, "I baptize you with water; but One is coming who is mightier than I, and I am not fit to untie the thong of His sandals; He will baptize you with the Holy Spirit and fire" (v. 16). The baptism of the Holy Spirit will be a

blessing, but the reference to fire implies judgment, and it is explained this way in the verse that follows: "And His winnowing fork is in His hand to thoroughly clear His threshing floor, and to gather the wheat into His barn; but He will burn up the chaff with unquenchable fire" (v. 17). The "floor" was actually a flat rock located in the harvest area. The "winnowing fork" looked something like a large snow shovel. With the shovel the grain is tossed into the air, with the chaff separating itself from the edible wheat. The worthless chaff is then consumed by fire. The three-and-a-half-year ministry of Jesus to Israel would be like a purging, a separating of those who accepted Him and those who would not. The teaching of Jesus, and the rejection of a great part of the Jewish people, would become an indictment to the nation itself. A vengeance would fall on Israel, the nation would be broken by Roman forces, and the Jews ultimately would be scattered worldwide.

Reproof of Herod the Tetrarch (3:19–20)

"Herod the tetrarch was reproved by [John]" (3:19). A crisis was now about to burst over the head of John that would ultimately lead to his death. Herod Antipas was incensed because of John's continual public rebuke of him. "Was reproved" is a durative participle that reads, "being repeatedly reproved." John did not let up with his criticism. The story is told in detail in Matthew 14:1–13.

Herod was married to Aretas, the daughter of the Arabian king of the Nabateans. He divorced her and took Herodias as his wife, who had been married to Philip, the son of Herod the Great and Mariamne II. Herodias was Antipas's sister-in-law and also his niece, the daughter of his half brother Aristobulus. John would not let up with his rebuke of Herod's incest: "It is not lawful for you to have her" (Matt. 14:4). Because of Herodias, John was thrown into prison (v. 3). But Herod was afraid to act against John because "he feared the multitude, because they regarded him as a prophet" (v. 5). At Herod's birthday party, Salome, the daughter of Herodias, danced before the king, bringing him pleasure (v. 6). He promised her whatever she asked. Prompted by her mother, she said, "Give me here on a platter the head of John the Baptist" (v. 8). Though grieved, Herod did as she asked and had John beheaded in prison. His head was presented to Salome, who then gave it to her mother (v. 11). The disciples of John came for his body and buried it (v. 12). Jesus must have been terribly grieved, because Matthew tells us, "When Jesus heard it, He withdrew from there in a boat, to a lonely place by Himself" (v. 13). John had served his purpose. He had spiritually convicted the nation of its sins and had presented Israel with their promised King.

While Luke does not go into all the details of John's death, he simply narrates for the reader John's reproof of Herod and Herodias and adds that his being thrown into prison was "on account of all the wicked things which Herod had done" (Luke 3:19).

Baptism of the Lord Jesus (3:21–22)

"Jesus also was baptized" (3:21). It is important to remember that Jesus would go through the baptismal process in these verses, not because He was a sinner in need of repentance, but to identify Himself with the people He came to redeem (Matt. 3:15). This is just one of several important happenings in Luke's gospel that took place when Jesus prayed (Luke 6:12; 9:18, 29; 22:41). While Luke's narration of the heavens opening is not as awesome in description as Mark's (1:10), it does make it certain that Jesus had a true vision of God the Father (cf. Ezek. 1:1; Stephen's vision, Acts 7:56; and Peter's, Acts 10:11). In contrast to these visions, the disciples on the Mount of Transfiguration were encircled by a mist or cloud. They actually heard the Lord's voice and saw Jesus accompanied by Moses and Elijah.

In the Old Testament God appeared through theophanies. Here the Spirit appeared as a dove. Only Luke uses the expression "in bodily form," giving more specific meaning to the manifestation of the Spirit's presence. The apostle does not write that anyone other than Christ was aware of the Holy Spirit. Possibly others standing there saw only a dove without realizing its significance. The manifestation of the Spirit was a reminder of Genesis 1:2, yet no specific parallel is pointed out.

"Thou art My beloved Son, in Thee I am well-pleased" (v. 22) shows Jesus as the unique Son of God. The words are similar to those heard at the Transfiguration (9:35; Matt 17:5; Mark 9:7). They are reminiscent of Old Testament christological passages such as Psalm 2:7 and Isaiah 42:1. With the Annunciation, Jesus was called the "Son of the Most High" (1:32).

With just two verses (vv. 21–22), Luke picks up the story with the presentation of the Lord Jesus to the people of Israel. He reminds us that Jesus was baptized (v. 21b) and that the heaven opened "and the Holy Spirit descended upon Him in bodily form like a dove, and a voice came out of heaven, 'Thou art My beloved Son, in Thee I am well-pleased'" (v. 22). "In bodily form" seems best explained by Isaiah's statement that "the Spirit of the Lord will rest on [the Messiah]" (Isa. 11:2). "In bodily form" has the better thought, "The Holy Spirit embodied Him." The coming of the Spirit here is actually a summary statement of what had happened earlier when Jesus came to John at the Jordan River. John seems to have had some kind of visual as well as verbal manifestation when the Spirit descended (John 1:33). He concluded, "And I have seen, and have borne witness that this is the Son of God" (v. 34). From Luke's standpoint, 3:21–22 begins his narration of the full ministry of Christ to His people.

> The mighty fact of the heavenly selection of the Son who now stands incarnate at the Jordan, ready of his own will to begin the work, is thus announced with the Father's supreme pleasure in having made the choice. That is why the Father now sends his Spirit upon Jesus.[2]

The Son who is eternal is clearly the Elect of the heavenly Father for His great task on earth. He is presented to the Jewish nation as God's "Beloved."

Study Questions

1. In 3:1, what is the difference between a "governor" and a "tetrarch"?

2. In 3:3, what specific area is meant by "the district around the Jordan"?

3. Explain John's "baptism of repentance for the forgiveness of sins."

4. Although Luke applies a passage from Isaiah to John the Baptist, in 3:4–6, what was the original meaning of Isaiah's prophecy?

5. In 3:7, when John says, "You brood of vipers, who warned you to flee from the wrath to come?" what was the "wrath" of which John spoke?

6. In 3:16–17 John speaks to the Jews of upcoming events. How far, chronologically is John looking ahead in these two verses?

7. Why did John reprove Herod regarding Herodias?

CHAPTER 9

Genealogy of the Son of Man Luke 3:23–38

Preview:

Of the four Gospels, only Matthew and Luke present genealogies of Jesus Christ. Matthew's starts with Abraham and comes through the line of Solomon; Luke's moves backward from Jesus, through the line of Nathan, all the way back to Adam and God.

Before Luke begins the details of Christ's ministry, he stops his narration to confirm for the reader the Lord's genealogical credentials. He mentions many names in Jesus' line with which we are unfamiliar. But it must be assumed that the earliest readers of Luke's narration would have some knowledge of this family line. Therefore, for those who counted, there was a corroboration of personalities in the genealogy that were probably well known. "It is not known how Luke secured his genealogy. Although we today cannot test its correctness in all details, there is no reason for calling any of its items into question."[1]

Introduction to the Genealogy (3:23)

"And when [Jesus] began His ministry . . ." (3:23). As Jesus began His ministry, at about the age of thirty, He was "supposedly the son of Joseph." "Supposedly" is the Greek word *nomizō*, meaning "to deem, think." It is in an imperfect, or past, tense with a passive voice. It could be translated "the people used to continually think about Him as Joseph's son." Luke adds, "the son

of Eli." The word "son" is not in the Greek text. Without the word "son," the text is simply telling us that Jesus came through one called Eli. Since the apostle Matthew tells us that Joseph's father was actually a man by the name of Joseph (Matt. 1:16), who is Eli? The most logical answer is that Luke is giving us the genealogy of Jesus through Mary. Eli then would be the grandfather of Jesus through her. The claim by some that Mary ought to have been presented as Eli's daughter is more than clarified by Luke's narration as to how she became the mother of the Lord. Jesus was not the natural son of Joseph! Every reader could tell that this verse best reads, "being a son . . . of Eli," and this could mean only one thing: Jesus was Eli's son through Mary. Jesus was simply supposed or thought to be Joseph's son. Therefore, Matthew's genealogy was of Joseph, and Luke's record was about Mary!

Genealogy (3:24–38)

"The son of Matthat, the son of Levi, . . ."(3:24). As Luke records the genealogy of Eli, he consistently writes simply "of Matthat," etc. The word "son" is not in the original text throughout this lineage. This means that he is just writing that "whoever" is in this line, not necessarily the specific "son of. . . ." Luke's genealogy goes all the way back to the patriarchs (Abraham, Isaac, Jacob) but also includes Shem, Noah, Methuselah, Enoch, Enosh, Seth, and Adam. The point seems clear: Jesus is a distinct part of humanity yet without sin. Many of the names closest to Eli cannot be identified.

3:24–27. These names take the reader from Jesus up to the period of the Babylonian captivity. The names most easily identified are Zerubbabel and Shealtiel. *Zerubbabel* means "seed of Babel." He was the grandson of King Jehoiachin, who was taken to Babylon in the deportation of 597 B.C. by Nebuchadnezzar (2 Kings 24:10–17). Shealtiel was the father of Zerubbabel (Ezra 3:2), the second son of Jehoiachin (1 Chron. 3:16–17). Ezra mentions him (2:1–67) as one of the leaders who came back from the Babylonian exile. His name means "I have asked of God."

3:28–31. This includes the period of the captivity down through King David. The most important names are Eliakim, Nathan, and David. Eliakim means "God will raise up." Eliakim was the son of Hilkiah the servant in charge of the household of King Hezekiah of Judah (2 Kings 18:18). Nathan means "gift [of God]." Nathan was a son of David and Bathsheba (1 Chron. 3:5). It is with David that the royal dynasty began. While Saul was the first reigning king, he was not the father of the legal kingly household (1 Sam. 15:23, 35; 16:1). God denied the reign to Saul's children and, following Saul's death, set on the throne the "anointed" David. Though David was an imperfect ruler with many faults, God destined him and his descendants to be the royal household. David ruled over both Israel and Judah. His son Solomon continued the dynasty, though after him the nation was split by civil war. The name David means "beloved." Solomon was also the son of David and Bathsheba, a Hittite. David killed her husband, Uriah, in order to take her as his wife. This ugly story shows vividly how sinners and those who are not of the family of Israel entered the physical line through which Jesus was ultimately be born.

3:32–38. The most well-known personalities are Jesse, Obed, Boaz, Perez, Judah, Jacob, Isaac, Abraham, Terah, Peleg, Cainan, Shem Noah, Methuselah, Enoch, Jared, Enosh, Seth, and Adam. Jesse (meaning "man, manly") was David's father (1 Sam. 16:1). He had eight sons of whom David was the youngest. Jesse was the son of Obed (meaning "serving"), and the grandson of Boaz (meaning "lively") and Ruth (Ruth 4:17). Ruth was a Moabitess who came into the lineage of Christ through her second husband Boaz. Perez was one of the twins born as the result of Judah hiring his daughter-in-law, Tamar, whom he assumed was a prostitute (Gen. 38). After her husband had died, her brother-in-law Onan refused to marry her, in what was called a levirate marriage. To keep the name of her dead husband alive, she tricked Judah into an adulterous affair (vv. 13–30). Perez means "breach." Judah is the fourth of twelve sons of Jacob (Gen. 29:35), and his name means "praise Yahweh." It is through him that future kings will come. "The scepter shall not depart from Judah" (49:10a), until "Shiloh ['peace-maker,' thought to be a reference to the Messiah] comes."

The name Jacob is built on the Hebrew word for "heel." Coming forth from the womb of Rebekah, behind his twin brother, Esau, the infant Jacob grasped his heel, as if to be the first-born of the two. He became labeled the "cheat" or "supplanter" (Gen. 25:26; 27:36). Jacob would become the father of the twelve sons who would sire the twelve tribes of Israel (25:26—Ex. 1:5). After wrestling all night with the Angel of Jehovah, his name was changed to Israel, meaning "he who wrestles with God" (Gen. 32:28; 49:2). Isaac was the son of Abraham through whom the promised Abrahamic covenant would pass. Isaac's half brother Ishmael, who was born to the servant girl Hagar, was excluded from the covenant line (Gen. 17:18–21). Isaac means "he who laughs." Abraham fell on his face and laughed when God informed him that he and Sarah would have a son (17:17). Terah was the father of Abraham (11:26), who had come out of Ur of the Chaldees with a migration of others who left Babylon. Terah died at Haran (vv. 31–32). Abram means "the exalted father," but his name was changed to Abraham meaning "father of a multitude" (17:5). He would be the recipient of God's covenant that would change the direction of world history. The Abrahamic covenant would include promises about the land of Canaan, the

propagation of a great number of descendants, and a blessing that would benefit all families of the earth (12:1–3). Canaan, or what is now called the Holy
Land, is deeded forever to Abraham's children through Isaac and Jacob. It is
theirs in perpetuity. Abraham's children will continue through the end of history. And through them, the promised Messiah would come. The nations would
ultimately be blessed through the death and sacrifice of the Messiah.

Next in the list comes Peleg (meaning "division, watercourse"), who is a
descendant of Shem (Gen. 10:25), and related to Abraham (11:16–19). Peleg
is seen as the ancestor of most all of the Semitic peoples of Mesopotamia.
Cainan (Kenan, meaning unknown) is an ancestor of Noah (5:10–14). Shem
(meaning "name") is Noah's oldest son and is also considered an original
ancestor of the Semitic nations, including Israel (5:32; 6:10; 7:13).
Methuselah means "worshiper of Selah." He was a son of Enoch (who walked
with God) and the grandfather of Noah (5:21, 25–27). He was the oldest
human being to live, dying at the age of 969 (5:27). Enoch, because of his
trust in and fellowship and walk with the Lord, was taken up into heaven
without dying (5:21–24). He is listed in the Hebrews hall of fame of believers
(Heb. 11:5). Enoch means "dedication"; he was the son of Jared (meaning
"slave") (Gen. 5:15–20). Enosh's name means "man." He was the son of Seth
and the grandson of Adam. Following his birth, the book of Genesis says people began to worship the Lord (vv. 6–11). Seth means "replacement" because
he was born to Adam and Eve after Cain had murdered his brother Abel (4:25;
5:3). Finally, we come to the first parent of the human family, Adam (meaning "man"). Adam and Eve brought sin into the realm of human experience.
God, however, placed the responsibility for the fall on Adam, who was first
created by the Lord. Paul reminds us that while it was Adam who brought
humans down to judgment, it would be his far distant son, the Lord Jesus,
who would provide deliverance and salvation (Rom. 5). Luke takes the reader
finally to Adam to show that Christ is part of the human family. He would be
able to die for people because He is part of the human race.

Luke had two purposes for this genealogy: (1) to show the place of
Jesus in the family of Israel and (2) to reveal how He is a member of the
human race.

Study Questions

1. Luke's genealogy is thought to deal with which parent of Jesus?
   Why?

2. Since Luke undoubtedly knew the exact age when Jesus started
   His ministry, what is the significance of him saying, "Jesus
   Himself was *about* thirty years of age"?

3. Chronologically, how does Luke's genealogy differ from Matthew's?

4. Why do Luke and Matthew's lists differ in the period from David to Shealtiel?

5. A controversial figure in Jesus' genealogy in Matthew is Jeconiah. Why is he not mentioned in Luke's genealogy, and what is the controversy surrounding him?

6. Matthew's genealogy goes back only to Abraham. What is the significance of Luke's genealogy of Jesus going all the way back to Adam and to God?

7. All of the statements in this genealogy except the last one tell of one man being related to another. What major significance is related in the statement, "Adam, the son of God"?

CHAPTER 10

Temptations of the Son of Man
Luke 4:1-13

Preview:

Shortly after His baptism Jesus was led by the Spirit into the wilderness where He was confronted by Satan. Since Jesus didn't have a sin nature like other men, there was really nothing to which Satan could appeal. Nevertheless, he persisted in making offers to and demands upon the Lord. Being the true Servant of His Father and the ultimate keeper of His Father's Word (as well as being the actual Word Himself!), Jesus used Scripture to rebuke and rebuff Satan until he departed.

Luke starts his story of the ministry of the Lord from the Jordan area to the place of His temptation. Some commentators do not believe it is possible to know where the temptation events took place, but a persistence of tradition says they started on the west side of the Jordan near the high cliffs outside of Jerusalem. Matthew gives the three temptations in their historical order (Matt. 4:1-11), while Luke brings out the highlights in their geographical locations: desert, mountain, Jerusalem, and the temple area.

First Temptation (4:1-4)

The twin themes in the story of the baptism of Jesus are taken up in the story of his temptation, so that there is no doubt that this narrative was derived from a source in which the baptism and temptation stood together. On the one hand, the story demonstrates how the Spirit, who had come upon Jesus, guided and empowered him in his new task; on the other hand, it shows how Jesus, as the Son of God, was obedient to God. The new factor in the situation is the devil, who attempts to deflect Jesus from obedience to God and hence from the fulfillment of the messianic task laid upon him by God.[1]

"Jesus, full of the Holy Spirit, returned from the Jordan and was led about by the Spirit in the wilderness" (4:1). As the ministry of Christ began, He was operating under the guidance of the Holy Spirit, the third person of the Trinity. While the Lord, as the God-Man, is always faithful to God the Father, this fact only amplifies the truth that Jesus was doing the perfect will of the Father in full obedience. Verse 1 says that Jesus was "full of" (controlled by) the Holy Spirit. The verse then says that He "returned from the Jordan and was led about by the Spirit in the wilderness." A better translation is, "Christ turned back from the Jordan" from the place where John the Baptist had baptized Him. Jesus would be under the direction of the Holy Spirit for forty days (v. 2). That is about the limit a human can go without food. The passage even notes that "He ate nothing during those days." This does not mean He would have died at the end of this period, because God had another task for Him— that is, He would die for the sins of the world on the cross. Since Jesus was human, it is certainly understandable that when these days were completed, "He became hungry"!

The temptation (Greek, *peirazō*, "to try, test") has often been misunderstood. It was an attempt to trip up the Son of Man on the part of Satan; but being very God, the Lord Jesus never would have fallen. Some have argued that, if this is the case, it was not a true temptation. Because a temptation is placed before Christ does not mean that He was disposed to sin. An old illustration seems to make the point: Can a rowboat attack a battleship? Yes. But can a rowboat sink a battleship? No. Satan could place temptations before the Lord, but this does not mean that He would fall. In fact, it demonstrates once and for all that Christ was indeed the sinless One who would not fail in His mission.

While Jesus may have been under siege with many temptations by the devil, only a few are mentioned here. In the desert the first one mentioned related to physical hunger. "If You are the Son of God, tell this stone to become bread" (v. 3). In verse 4 the Lord answered by using the words of Deuteronomy 8:3: "Man does not live by bread alone, but man lives by everything that proceeds out of the mouth of the LORD." These words were recorded by Moses in reference to Israel's forty years of wandering in the desert. The refugees from Egypt were not to forget the Lord their God; they were to keep His commandments, "His ordinances and His statutes which I am commanding you today" (v. 11). In like manner, Jesus was being obedient to His heavenly Father!

Second Temptation (4:5–8)

"[Satan] led Him up and showed Him all the kingdoms of the world" (4:5). In the next temptation the devil "took Him to a very high mountain" (Matt. 4:8a) and "showed Him all the kingdoms of the world in a moment of time" (Luke 4:5). Satan said, "I will give You all this domain and its glory; for it has been handed over to me, and I give it to whomever I wish" (v. 6). Both Isaiah 14 and Ezekiel 28 seem to be a poetic but accurate account of the fall of Satan from his place of fellowship with God in heaven. After the devil had said, "I will make myself like the Most High (Isa. 14:14), he was cast down, with the result that at some future time he would "make the earth tremble" and shake kingdoms (v. 16). The apostle seems to pick up this idea when he writes that Satan is "the god of this world" who has blinded the minds of the unbelieving (2 Cor. 4:4). At present Satan has great power and authority, though he cannot act without the divine permission of God.

Satan continued with his temptation of Jesus, adding, "If You worship before me, it shall all be Yours" (Luke 4:7). Jesus again used Scripture (v. 8) and answered from Deuteronomy 6:13: "You shall fear only the LORD your God; and you shall worship Him, and swear by His name." In quoting this passage, Jesus added, You shall "serve Him only." This seems to come from Deuteronomy 6:14, which reads, "You shall not follow other gods, any of the gods of the peoples who surround you." In trying to usurp God and drive Jesus from His rightful future throne, Satan thought he could achieve the victory by causing Jesus to worship him. The devil certainly knows Christ as the second person of the Godhead in eternity past. To bring on such disloyalty would mean that he would have succeeded in his evil plans. But with full obedience to the Father, the Lord Jesus never would have capitulated to such a demand.

Third Temptation (4:9–13)

"said to Him, 'If You are the Son of God, throw Yourself down from here'" (4:9). Satan led Christ back to Jerusalem and the temple (v. 9a). He had Him stand on the highest point of the wall, the pinnacle on the southeast corner. Satan said, "If You are the Son of God, throw Yourself down from here" (v. 9b). This is the second time, including verse 3, that the devil referred to the rela-

tional position of Jesus with His heavenly Father—the Son of God! Satan, maybe sensing that he was losing in his arguments with Christ, in verses 10–11 quotes Scripture back to Him (Ps. 91:11–12). "For it is written," the devil adds, "He will give His angels charge concerning You to guard You," and, "On their hands they will bear You up, lest You strike Your foot against a stone." Psalm 91 is about God our refuge and fortress, "My God, in whom I trust!" (v. 2b). He protects and shields His own and "will be with him [who is] in trouble" (v. 15). Often His instruments of safekeeping are His angels whom the Lord will use to "deliver [His] own" (v. 14). But Satan used these comforting verses to try to cause Jesus to "test" God by flaunting His protective goodness. This would have made a spectacle and circus of the Lord's care. God does not have to prove anything by His wonderful providential workings in His universe!

In Luke 4:12 Jesus put an end to the words of Satan by quoting Deuteronomy 6:16: "It is said, 'You shall not put the Lord your God to the test.'" At this point in this spiritual encounter, God was indeed being tested by Satan. Lenski writes:

> It would be a caricature of humble trust to take a gracious promise of God and by some foolhardy act to challenge Got to see whether he will, indeed, do what he has said, or still say. As the first temptation tries to lead, under the plea of acting like a true son, to distrust of the Father, so this temptation tries to lead, under the same plea, to *a false trust* of the Father.[2]

And,

> The essence of this temptation is that of presuming on God (v. 12) and displaying before others one's special favor with him. In this instance the devil quotes a passage of Scripture (Ps 91:11–12) out of context—notice that the mere use of Bible words does not necessarily convey the will of God (v. 10). Further, Satan omits the words "in all your ways" (Ps 91:11), possibly to facilitate application to an act inconsistent with the normal "ways" of the godly person.[3]

The Lord Jesus was not setting one passage of the Bible against another in His answers. He was simply placing one Scripture passage alongside another. The Tempter is finally vanquished by the Son of God and by the Word of God. When "every temptation" was completed, Satan "departed from Him until an opportune time" (v. 13). Satan would come again to try to defeat Christ. This could be the prediction that Judas, one of the Lord's own disciples, would act as "a devil" (John 6:70) and come against Him "to betray Him" (v. 71).

Study Questions

1. Jesus' temptation, lasting for forty days, is reminiscent of some Old Testament events also involving a period of forty (be it days, years, etc.). Name some of these Old Testament events.

2. Where, geographically, is it assumed that this forty-day wilderness trek took place?

3. What does Jesus' use of Scripture tell us about our witnessing to the world?

4. What is noteworthy about Satan's quotation of Scripture in 4:10–11?

5. The order of the second and third temptations are reversed in Matthew's gospel. What significance may this have?

6. Concerning the responses by Jesus to Satan, taken from Deuteronomy, what were their original meanings when given by Moses, and how do these meanings relate to Jesus' ordeal?

7. If we study the first two chapters of the book of Job, what does it tell us about the temptation of Jesus?

SECTION III

Early Ministry and Miracles of the Son of Man

Luke 4:14—9:50

The Lord Jesus would now begin His great works among His own people, the Jews. His words would cut deep into the fabric of Jewish life and teaching. The proof that He was Israel's Messiah would be His great works and manifestations of miracles. But while many of the Jewish people would receive His words and believe, many others would reject Him with a deep and burning spiritual anger. Jesus would touch every class of people. He would show His authority over nature and even over demons. This section closes with the Lord's prediction of His suffering, final rejection, death, and miraculous resurrection.

CHAPTER 11

Teaching in the Synagogues
Luke 4:14–30

Preview:

After His time in the wilderness, Jesus returned to His home in Nazareth to begin His public teaching ministry. He immediately proclaimed His deity by claiming to be the fulfillment of a messianic passage in Isaiah. In response, those in the synagogue tried to kill Him.

The first part of this section seems to be a bridge between the time of Jesus' baptism and His temptation and the beginning of the full manifestation of His ministry in Galilee. Luke separates the mention of the imprisonment of John the Baptist (3:19) from the work of Christ in Galilee.

Start of Christ's Ministry in His Hometown of Nazareth (4:14–15)

"Jesus returned to Galilee in the power of the Spirit" (4:14). Following the final temptation of Jesus by Satan in Jerusalem, the Lord "returned to Galilee," which was several days journey from Judea. Now in His earthly work, Jesus was fully ministering "in" or "by" the power (Greek, *tē dunamei*) of the Spirit (v. 14a). Luke seems to connect this manifestation with the fact that "news about Him spread through all the surrounding district" (v. 14b). In the Galilee area, "He began teaching in their synagogues and was praised by all" (v. 15). "Praised by all" (Greek, *doxazō*) could read, "glorified by all." Since the passage indicates more than one synagogue, excluding the one at Nazareth,

79

He apparently moved about the area where He was raised, with the result that the people were greatly blessed by His words of wisdom.

The Lord's Teaching in Nazareth (4:16–27)

"And He came to Nazareth" (4:16). When Jesus arrived in His hometown of Nazareth, He was invited to read the appointed passage of Scripture in public in the local synagogue, "as was His custom" (v. 16).

> After the liturgical services which introduced the worship of the syna-
> gogue, the "minister" took a roll of the law from the ark, removed its case
> and wrappings, and then called upon someone to read. On the Sabbaths,
> at least seven persons were called on successively to read portions of the
> law, none of them consisting of less than three verses. After the law fol-
> lowed a section from the prophets, which was succeeded immediately by
> a discourse. It was this section which Jesus read and expounded.[1]

Verse 17 tells us that Jesus stood up on that Sabbath and began to read Isaiah 61:1–2:

> "The Spirit of the Lord is upon Me,
> Because He anointed Me to preach the gospel to the poor.
> He has sent Me to proclaim release to the captives,
> And recovery of sight to the blind,
> To set free those who are downtrodden,
> To proclaim the favorable year of the Lord."

Luke has already referred to the Holy Spirit working through the Lord Jesus four times so far in this gospel (3:16, 22; 4:1, 14). Jesus read this great messianic passage that reminded Israel that the Spirit of the Lord would be upon the Anointed One (the Christ) (Luke 4:18). He would be "anointed" by God to do marvelous things for the Jewish people: preach the good news, release captives, give sight to the blind, and lift up the downtrodden. Proclaiming the favorable year of the Lord would be the announcement that the king was in the presence of Israel and the kingdom was about to come (v. 19). Were the Jews ready spiritually to receive Him as their promised ruler? For the most part, repentance was far from the minds of the people of Israel. They were hardened in their sinful ways.

The audience in the synagogue got the point. When Jesus closed the scroll of Isaiah "the eyes of all in the synagogue were fixed upon Him" (v. 20). Jesus pointed to Himself when He said to those present, "Today this Scripture has been fulfilled in your hearing" (v. 21). Those who heard Him were "wonder-ing at the gracious words which were falling from His lips" (v. 22a). They asked among themselves, "Is this not Joseph's son?" (v. 22b), meaning "Why is He so special; He is Joseph's son and was raised here in our midst?" Knowing that they were thinking, "If He is the Messiah, why doesn't He perform great works here as He did in Capernaum?" Jesus added, "You will say to Me the proverb, 'Physician, heal yourself!'" (v. 23), meaning "Why can He not do the same wonders around here that He performed elsewhere?"

Jesus knew the people wanted some more great miraculous manifestations to benefit their "home town as well" (v. 23c). He answered, "Truly I say to you, no prophet is welcome in his home town" (v. 24). In other words, "You do not see what I do as special. You want even more for your personal sake." To make His point, Jesus tells the story of Elijah and of the widow of Zarephath (v. 25) found in 1 Kings 17. Because of the idolatry of King Ahab and the people, the Lord brought about a three-and-a-half-year drought (v. 1) by which "a great famine came over all the land" (Luke 4:25–26). The Lord shielded Elijah in the desert and fed him by the ravens (1 Kings 17:6); however, he was finally instructed to go to the widow of Zarephath who was about to die for lack of bread (v. 12). By performing a miracle through the prophet, oil and flour were not exhausted until the famine abated (vv. 14–16).

The Reaction in the Synagogue (4:28–30)

"And all in the synagogue were filled with rage" (4:28). In verse 27 Jesus also reminded those in the synagogue that some years later, under God's judgment during the time of the prophet Elisha (2 Kings 5:1–14), there were few miracles, except the healing of the leper Naaman. All of those listening to Christ got the point: they "were filled with rage as they heard these things" (Luke 4:28). By telling these Old Testament stories, the Lord was showing the Jews that there was a spiritual dryness in the land. God was not speaking to the nation, and no miraculous signs were being performed. By giving the accounts of how God revealed Himself to two pagans, Jesus was saying that His generation was not deserving of seeing the Lord act.

Jesus had not come to His hometown of Nazareth nor ministered in nearby Capernaum simply to be acclaimed. He performed miracles and taught the people because of who He was! However, the Lord could do no more miracles where He was raised "because of their unbelief" (Matt. 13:58). Where hostile arrogance and unbelief met Jesus and his followerss, nothing else was left but for them to turn away (Matt. 10:14–15; Acts 13:46–47). The men in the synagogue rose up from their seats and threw Him out of the city. They led Him to a brow of a hill to cast Him over (Luke 4:29), but by a miracle He passed "through their midst, [and] He went His way" (v. 30). "This escape was very remarkable. It is remarkable that he should escape out of their hands when their very object was to destroy him, and that he should escape so peaceful a manner, without violence or conflict. A similar case is recorded in Jn. viii.59."[2]

This incident gives a strong indication of how far away the Jewish people were from God. They could not recognize their own promised Messiah though He was ministering in their presence. Belief had hardened into formal religion, and there is nothing more deadly to the human soul. The rejection by those who knew Him best was not simply a neutral or passive response; it was abject hatred to the point of attempting to murder Christ! And that attempt was taking place on the most holy of days, the Sabbath! Did Jesus use His great powers to pass through the murderous crowd of people? Did He run or walk calmly out of their presence? The Lord apparently walked right through the mob and left Nazareth unmolested. Did such a miracle bring fear and even repentance to the people? It did not!

During the three-and-a-half-year ministry of the Lord, many would turn to Him as their Messiah and Savior, but as a whole, the nation of Israel would reject Him. The majority would refuse to repent of their sins. The hearts of most of the people would remain hardened, and they would fail to listen to the evidence that God's Son was among them.

Study Questions

1. What does 4:14 mean? Didn't Jesus have any power of His own?

2. When Jesus read from Isaiah 61, He did not complete the prophecy given to Isaiah. Why did He "close the book" before reading the whole prophecy?

3. How do Jesus' words in 4:23–27 relate to faith healers today?

4. Relate Jesus' teaching in Nazareth, specifically 4:22 and 24, to a believer's efforts to witness to his or her own family.

5. What is unique about the two examples of healing Jesus speaks of in 4:25–27?

6. Why were the people in the synagogue enraged by Jesus' words?

7. Did Jesus use miraculous power to walk away from the crowd wishing to kill Him, or is there some other plausible answer?

CHAPTER 12

Healing Miracles of the Son of Man
Luke 4:31–6:11

Preview:
Jesus moved His home to Capernaum and began His healing ministry as well as His preaching of the kingdom of God. He also chose His first disciples. Luke names Simon (Peter), James, John, and Levi (Matthew) in this segment of His gospel. He also records Jesus' first confrontations with the Pharisees over the Law of God.

"And He came down to Capernaum, a city of Galilee" (4:31). Luke highlights two miracles that Jesus performed on one day in Capernaum (cf. Mark 1:21). He uses the word "and" to keep the narration flowing. Luke says, "came down" because the Sea of Galilee is set in a bowl with mountains on all sides, and Capernaum is a city of that area. Luke had to mention this information because Theophilus did not know much about the geography of the region.

The Lord's Command over Demons (4:31–37)

"[Jesus] was teaching them on the Sabbath" (4:31). At Capernaum Jesus was again teaching on the Sabbath as He had done in Nazareth (v. 31). At Nazareth Luke says the people in the synagogue "fixed" their eyes on Jesus (v. 20), and here at Capernaum they "were amazed at His teaching, for His message was with authority" (v. 32). "Amazed" is an extremely strong word

(Greek, *ekplēssō*) meaning "struck by a blow" or "being dumbfounded." His message in Greek actually is "the word" (Greek, *ho logos*). What was equally astounding was that He delivered His teaching "with authority" in contrast to the legalistic ramblings of most of the priests. "Authority" actually means "power" (Greek, *exousia*). In the crowd at the synagogue was a man "possessed" *by* a demon (Greek, *daimonion*) who suddenly cried out with a loud voice (v. 33). The words that follow are not simply the words of the man himself, but show that he was controlled by the demon. He screamed, "Ha! What do we have to do with You, Jesus of Nazareth? Have You come to destroy us? I know who You are—the Holy One of God!" (v. 34).

Demons are the fallen angels who now roam the earth doing Satan's bidding. At some point in eternity past when Lucifer fell from the presence of God, the rebellious angels went with him. Isaiah 14:12–13 seems to be a poetic description of what happened: "How you have fallen from heaven, O star of the morning, son of the dawn! . . . You said in your heart, 'I will ascend to heaven, I will raise my throne above the stars of God.' " The "stars of God" probably is a reference to the fallen angels who joined Lucifer (the star of the morning) in his revolt.

The demons know they have but a limited period to do their evil deeds. They spoke to the Lord through the man living in the tombs: "What do we have to do with You, Son of God? Have You come here to torment us before the time?" (Matt. 8:29). The time will come when they are cast "into the eternal fire which has been prepared for the devil and his angels" (25:41).

In Luke 4:34, when the possessed man, under the influence of the demons, called Jesus "the Holy One of God," he was referring to Psalm 16:10 where the resurrection of the Messiah is prophesied. There, the Messiah says to God: "Thou wilt not abandon my soul to Sheol; neither wilt Thou allow Thy Holy One to undergo decay." Jesus wasted no time in responding and instantly rebuked the demon with the words "Be quiet" (Greek, *phimaō*), literally meaning "Be muzzled" (Luke 4:35a). The demons had thrown the man to the ground, and the Lord commanded, "Come out of him!" The demons obeyed and came out without doing the man further harm (v. 35b). The crowd in the synagogue was shocked and began discussing what had happened, saying, "What is this message?" (v. 36a) or "What is this word [*logos*] we are supposed to receive?" "For with authority and power He commands the unclean spirits, and they come out" (v. 36b). From a present-day perspective, it is hard to understand why the people seeing such miraculous manifestations through Jesus did not realize He was their promised King. "So these people after all fell short of apprehending what stood forth so plainly before them that Sabbath day in their synagogue."[1]

The message and report about the Lord was traveling fast "into every locality in the surrounding district" (v. 37). While many would turn to Him and believe in Him, many more thousands would either reject Him or pay no attention to His words and deeds. It cannot be said that the nation of Israel was left without a witness and a testimony. Their rejection of Jesus would make them even more culpable and due judgment. Later the Lord would warn Israel of the coming condemnation. He told the people that their enemies would "level you to the ground and your children within you, and they will not leave in you one stone upon another, because you did not recognize the time of your visitation" (19:44), meaning the time of the arrival of the Son of God to bless the Jewish people.

The Lord's Command over Disease (4:38-44)

"[Jesus] arose and left the synagogue" (4:38). Leaving the synagogue, Jesus went to the house of Simon Peter whose mother-in-law was suffering with a fever (v. 38a). A request was made of the Lord to heal her. Jesus "rebuked" (Greek, *epitimaō*) the fever, and it left her immediately (v. 39). When Jesus healed someone, it was an instant and permanent healing. Peter's mother-in-law was so completely restored that she "waited" on Jesus, meaning she fixed Him food (v. 39b). Some illnesses Jesus encountered were caused by demonic physical oppression, but not all. In the next chapter we will see cases of leprosy (5:12-14) and paralysis (vv. 18-23). Since Jesus rebuked the fever, some argue that this must mean there is a "demon of fever." But there is no such evidence for this. Christ was the Master over nature, with the wind and waves obeying Him when the storm came up on the Galilee (Mark 4:35-41). Most illness come about because of the curse on nature following Adam's fall. Paul reminds us that we groan to be delivered and that "the whole creation groans . . . until now" (Rom. 8:22). Only the final resurrection and redemption of the body will free those who trust Christ from the curse of disease and the finality of death. Believers wait for the ultimate redemption of their bodies (1 Cor. 15:35-50).

By evening, many who were sick were brought to Christ, who laid His hands on "every one of them, [and] He was healing them all" (Luke 4:40). Demons were coming out of some, and they were crying out, "You are the Son of God!" (v. 41). They were attesting to the great truth found in Psalm 2:7 that God has a Son. But Jesus rebuked them and silenced them "because they knew Him to be the Christ" (the Anointed One) as revealed in Psalm 2:2. Why did He command that they be quiet? The demons probably would have continued shouting out this great truth of Christ's deity and messiahship. While other testimonies as to who He was were important, the people needed to compute for themselves that He was the promised Messiah. But also, the testimony of the spirits would be suspect and considered by some invalid. For whatever reason, the Lord commanded them to remain silent.

At daybreak Jesus departed from the area in order to retire to a quiet place of rest, but the crowd tried to stop Him (Luke 4:42). They apparently wanted more healings and possibly another miraculous display of feeding. But He answered, "I must preach the kingdom of God to the other cities also, for I was sent for this purpose" (v. 43). He continued preaching in the cities of Judea (v. 44). However,

> it is not surprising that after such a strenuous day, Jesus felt the need of quiet communion with his Father (cf. Mark 1:35). Therefore at daybreak he left and went to a lonely place. The crowd—including Simon, perhaps preceded by him—went out to look for him. When they found him, they tried to prevent him from leaving them. But he said, "Also to the other towns I must preach the good news of the kingdom of God." He started to do just that.[2]

The kingdom of God was the great earthly hope of the Jewish prophets. Because all of Israel will fail to repent, the kingdom will be postponed.

> The writer of the book of Hebrews also reinforces the idea of postponement. He writes, "So Christ also, having been offered once to bear the sins of many, shall appear a second time for salvation without reference to sin, to those who eagerly await Him" (9:28). It already has been established that the suffering had to come before the reign as king. Even the Jewish orthodox rabbis understand those events apart from the New Testament point of reference.

> So the author of Hebrews refers to a "second" earthly appearance, labeling this coming a "salvation without reference to sin." He can be referring only to Jesus' messianic reign as the Davidic king. . . . It follows, then, that the kingdom has been set aside until this present time of personal salvation—the church age, or age of grace—has ended.[3]

The Lord's Command over His Disciples (5:1–11)

"The multitude were . . . listening to the word of God" (5:1). Luke in 4:44 tells us that Christ went south from Galilee and continued preaching in the larger district or region of Judea. These next few chapters could be a flashback of happenings just before Jesus traveled to Judea, or it could be describing events when He returned to the area of the Galilee. Whichever, it is clear that the

crowds are growing in their clamor to hear Him. They "were pressing around Him and listening to the word of God" (5:1). The Lord was being shoved toward the shore of Lake Gennesaret (or Galilee). This is a corruption of the Hebrew word Chinnereth describing the configuration of the shoreline, "harp-shaped." Seeing two boats at the waters' edge where men were washing their nets (v. 2), Christ got into a boat that belonged to Simon Peter (v. 3a). While we often think of the disciples continually walking with the Lord after they first met Him, this passage may indicate that this was not so. The disciples may have come and gone, going back home for a time to take care of pressing business. Simon may have done just this, and now Christ found him working out of a fishing boat. Jesus tells Simon to push out a little way from the shore so he could speak more amply to the crowds standing near the water's edge (v. 3b).

When Jesus was finished addressing the multitude, He told Peter to move out into deeper water and "let down your nets for a catch" (v. 4). (That Peter had to temporarily leave the Lord and come home to Capernaum to fish seems to be implied in v. 5.) Simon answered, "Master, we worked hard all night and caught nothing, but at Your bidding I will let down the nets." Peter seemed to be a bit frustrated, and he certainly did not seem to be expecting a miracle from the Lord! When the nets were cast out, "they enclosed a great quantity of fish; and their nets began to break" (v. 6). Other boats came near, and they were filled with so many fish that they were beginning to sink (v. 7). Both Peter and his companions were emotionally shaken (Greek, *thambos*), or "absolutely terrified" because of the catch (v. 9). But the impact upon Peter seems to have been even greater. He experienced a rush of conviction and cried out to Jesus, "Depart from me, for I am a sinful man, O Lord!" (v. 8). Some contend that sin in Peter's life is what caused him to go back and forth in his following of Christ. This great cry of anguish may demonstrate that theory.

Clearly, the Lord had Peter's attention. He said to him, "Do not fear, from now on you will be catching men" (v. 10b). Peter's fishing partners were the sons of Zebedee, James, and John (v. 10a). Because this miracle was so overwhelming and poignant to these men, when they landed ashore, "they left everything and followed Him" (v. 11). This may tell us that they had been vacillating in their convictions; but no more! These disciples would never be the same and would not stop following Him.

The Lord's Healing of the Sick (5:12–26)

"There was a man full of leprosy; and when he saw Jesus . . ."(5:12). Healings have already been described in the book of Luke (4:38–40), but each episode

mentioned in the Gospels has a unique twist. Because of this it is important to examine each recorded incident and see the lesson the Holy Spirit wishes to give. Here, Luke will describe the healing of a leper (vv. 12–16) and the healing of a paralytic (vv. 17–26). The setting for the healing of the leper is probably one of the cities of the Galilee area. The man deformed with leprosy must have heard about the healing ministry of Christ. When the man saw Him, he fell on his face and cried, "Lord, if You are willing, You can make me clean" (v. 12b). The question was not the ability of Jesus. This poor man was convinced that He had the power to heal him of his terrible disease. But the question is, would the Lord desire to do so? This man's conviction about the authority of the Lord says volumes about how he and many others saw Jesus. They recognized that He was the Messiah who would bear our griefs and carry our sorrows (pains) (Isa. 53:4). The apostle Matthew quotes this verse to show that the Messiah would be a healer and would cast out evil spirits (Matt. 8:14–17).

Jesus touched the leper, which no one else would dare do! He said, "I am willing [to heal you]; be cleansed" (Luke 5:13a). Luke records, "And immediately the leprosy let him." In keeping with the law of healing for a leper (Lev. 14:1–57), Jesus ordered the man to "go and show yourself to the priest, and make an offering for your cleansing, just as Moses commanded, for a testimony to them" (Luke 5:14). Jesus added that He did not want the man to tell anyone else about the miracle, probably so that he would go straight to the priests to let them know a divine blessing had taken place in their midst. Mark tells us that the man could not keep quiet but freely spread the news with the negative results "that Jesus could no longer publicly enter a city, but stayed out in unpopulated areas" (Mark 1:45). Others continued to tell of this happening and gathered to hear Him teach, and also to receive healings from their sicknesses (Luke 5:15). Because of the great rush of people, "He Himself would often slip away to the wilderness and pray" (v. 16). This verse may imply that Jesus even left the company of His disciples and went to rest and pray alone.

Verse 17 indicates a great explosion of interest in what Jesus was saying and doing. "Pharisees and teachers of the law" came to hear Him "from every village of Galilee and Judea and from Jerusalem." The word about Christ had blanketed the land from north to south and east to west. The divine power of His heavenly Father was upon Him. Luke records, "The power of the Lord was present for Him to perform healing" (v. 17b). The paralytic in the story was brought on a cot by some of his friends. They wanted to set the crippled man down in front of Jesus (v. 18), but because of the crowd, and because of their dogged determination, they went up on the roof, cut through the ceiling tiles, and let the man down with his stretcher "right in the center [of the room], in front of Jesus" (v. 19). Seeing a demonstration of the faith of all of these men, Christ said to the crippled man, "Friend, your sins are forgiven you" (v. 20). This statement was a shock to the scribes and Pharisees present who began to reason among themselves, "Who is this man who speaks blasphemies? Who can forgive sins, but God alone?" (v. 21).

It is interesting to note throughout the Gospels, that the Pharisees teamed up with the scribes to attack Christ. The scribes (Greek, *grammateus*, "the writers") were the recorders, custodians, and interpreters of the Mosaic Law. They were the "theologians" of the Jewish religious hierarchy. These men had figured correctly—only God can indeed forgive sins! And Jesus is very God. He is the God-Man! Knowing their thoughts, Jesus questioned them: "Why are you reasoning in your hearts?" (v. 22), for "Which is easier, to say, 'Your sins have been forgiven you,' or to say, 'Rise and walk'? But in order that you may know that the Son of Man has authority on earth to forgive sins, I say to you [the paralytic], rise, and take up your stretcher and go home" (vv. 23–24). Jesus was speaking forward toward the cross and His coming death as the Lamb of God. Isaiah had earlier prophesied in chapter 53 of his prophecy that God said, "My Servant, will justify the many, as He will bear their iniquities. . . . He Himself [will bear] the sin of many" (vv. 11–12). Christ was making it clear that He had full earthly authority to do the same works that God does, including the forgiving of sins.

The Jewish Scribes

Scribes came into existence during the Babylonian captivity.

Scribes are almost always seen with the Pharisees (Luke 5:21).

Scribes are seen conspiring against Christ with the elders and the chief priests (Luke 9:22).

Scribes generally identified with the Pharisaic party (Mark 2:16; Acts 23:9).

Like Ezra, the scribes were often the teachers of God's Word (Ezra 7:6).

The scribes led in the plans to kill Jesus (Luke 19:47).

The scribes pretended to honor Christ as a Teacher (Luke 20:39–40).

Jesus warned the people to beware of the scribes (Luke 20:46).

The paralytic leaped up at once, picked up his bedding, and went home glorifying God (Luke 5:25). The miracle touched everyone who witnessed it. "They were all seized with astonishment and began glorifying God." The crowd, consisting of both the common people and the religious rulers, said,

"We have seen remarkable things today" (v. 26b). All three of the synoptic Gospels report slightly different words of praise. The differences show that the gospel writers sometimes focused on different issues when they wrote down this story. This is one indicator that the apostles did not follow some document, for they would then have reported these expressions of praise in a similar form or at least in forms that have the same meaning. The writers give us the same story, but the flavor of the account is enhanced by the witnesses who in their own words, "were all seized with astonishment."

Call of Matthew (5:27–39)

"[Jesus] said to [Levi], 'Follow Me'" (5:27). The above story must have happened in Capernaum because the tax collector Levi, or Matthew, was the tax officer for this area. To show this, verse 27 reads, "And after that He went out [of the city], and noticed a tax-gatherer named Levi, sitting in the tax office." Levi in Hebrew means "a joining." The name comes from the third son of Jacob and Leah (Gen. 29:34) who was the original ancestor of Israel's priests. Matthew means "the gift of Yahweh." He would become one of the twelve disciples (Matt. 9:9; 10:3). When Jesus saw him in the tax office at the city gate, He said two words: "Follow Me" (Luke 5:27b). Matthew is said to have "left everything behind, and rose and began to follow Him" (v. 28). This more than likely indicates that the rumors of what Jesus was doing and saying were spreading everywhere. Matthew was probably pondering in his heart, "Is this the Messiah?" He responded instantly, which may tell us that he was on the verge of such an action.

Levi seemed to be so thrilled with his new faith in the Messiah that he threw a banquet for the Lord and invited in all of his friends, other tax-gatherers and people who were known as sinners (Matt. 9:10–11). In biblical days, when a wealthy man held a party, his friends would come, recline on couches, and sometimes stay for days. The common people would appear at the windows and stare at the event taking place. The Pharisees and the scribes from Jerusalem, always looking for cause to accuse Christ of lawbreaking, grumbled out loud to the disciples who would hear and see them through the windows, "Why do you eat and drink with the tax-gatherers and sinners?" (Luke 5:30). "Grumbled" could be better translated "murmured" since it comes from the Greek word *egogguzon*. This is a onomatopoetic word that sounds like the meaning. It is

> a late word used of the cooing of doves. It is like the buzzing of bees. . . . [Jesus' critics] were not invited to this feast and would not have come if they had been. But, not being invited, they hang on the outside and criticize the disciples of Jesus for being there.[4]

The disciples seemed stumped with the question, but Jesus answered their charge with, "It is not those who are well who need a physician, but those who are sick. I have not come to call the righteous but sinners to repentance" (vv. 31–32). Matthew adds that Christ referred to Hosea 6:6 in regard to needing a physician: "Go and learn what this means, 'I desire compassion and not sacrifice'" (Matt. 9:13). To the Pharisees the ritual of sacrifice was the great sign of one's salvation. Jesus challenged this by noting that God desired to be compassionate and merciful toward sinners. He was not first interested in ceremony. When the Lord said, "Learn what this means," He used the Greek word *manthanō*, which means to "learn by doing, practicing." Christ was saying, "To know what Hosea was saying, you need to go out and exercise compassion and mercy and not act so judgmental!" Christ Jesus came as a spiritual healer, a spiritual physician who desired to save sinners. The "pious" Pharisees did not grasp this.

The Jews continued their attack and noted how both the disciples of John the Baptist and of the Pharisees often fasted and prayed, but Jesus' disciples were not so pious and ate and drank with vile people (Luke 5:33). Jesus gave a lengthy answer by using the illustration of a Jewish wedding to set forth a key principle that explained what was happening with the Jews. What He said helped to explain their explosive hatred toward Him (vv. 34–39). He pointed out that the attendants of the bridegroom do not fast while the bridegroom is with them (v. 34), but they can fast when he leaves the wedding party with his bride (v. 35). He was telling them in so many words that He was Israel's groom and someday would depart and return back to the Father.

Jesus then added two parables—one about how an old coat is patched and another about what has to be done to preserve new wine. One cannot patch an old garment with a new piece of cloth (v. 36), nor can one put new wine into an old wineskin (v. 37). The new piece of fabric, being stronger, will tear out from the coat. The new fermenting wine will expand the old wineskin that has already been stretched to the maximum. It will burst, and the wine will be lost. "New wine must be put into fresh wineskins" (v. 38) that have elasticity to expand. What the Lord was bringing to old Jewish thinking was like an old coat repaired with a new piece of cloth. And, what He was teaching was like new wine put into an old wineskin that could not survive the stretching! In other words, He could not teach old dogs new tricks! The Jews were locked into their works salvation, their legalistic and judgmental ways. The Lord closed His remarks by adding, "No one, after drinking old wine wishes for new; for he says, 'The old is good enough'" (v. 39). The Jews were saying, "We do not want to hear anything new this man has to say!"

This entire section of verses makes clear that although John's disciples and the Pharisees had certain agreement, they also had vast differences. Jesus told the Pharisees later on that John came in certain ways they understood, but it was a case of extremes meeting; for no two religious parties could be more remote in some respects than the two just named. The difference lay rather in the motives of the Pharisees and John's followers. Both did the same things. They fasted, practiced ceremonial ablutions, and made many prayers, but they did them with different mind-sets. John and his disciples carried out their religious duties with godly sincerity and moral earnestness; the Pharisees, as a class, did all these works ostentatiously, hypocritically, and as matters of mechanical routine.

It is important to look more deeply at the issue of the bridegroom. Jesus made reply to the question, remarkable at once for originality, setting forth in lively parables the great principles by which the conduct of His disciples could be vindicated. Jesus did not blame John's disciples for fasting but contented Himself with defending His own disciples for abstaining from fasting. He took up the position of one who virtually says, "To fast may be right for you, the followers of John: not to fast is equally right for My followers" (v. 34).

His reply is to this effect: "I *am* the bridegroom, as John said; it is right that the children of the bridal chamber come to Me; and it is also right that, when they have come, they should adapt their mode of life to their altered circumstances. Therefore, they do well not to fast, for fasting is the expression of sadness; and why should they be sad in My company? As well might people be sad at a marriage festival. The days *will* come when the children of the bridal chamber will be sad, for the bridegroom will not always be with them (v. 35).

Though it is not stated here, the bridegroom is the Messiah (Matt. 25), and His going away will take place at His ascension. And He will return to establish His messianic kingdom at some unknown point in the future. He will then come back as "the bridegroom." Christ's point is that fasting in any other circumstances is forced, unnatural, and unreal, a thing that people may be made to do as a matter of form, but which they do not with their heart and soul. "Can you make the children of the bridal chamber fast while the bridegroom is with them?" He asked, virtually asserting that it was impossible.

The Lord's Authority over the Sabbath (6:1–11)

"On a certain Sabbath He was passing through some grainfields" (6:1). Luke adds two more happenings that illustrate how the scribes and Pharisees continued to hound Jesus. While the Lord and His disciples were passing through a grain field on the Sabbath, they were hungry and began picking handfuls of grain to eat (v. 1). The incidental mention of the hunger of the disciples, which they

were seeking to satisfy by plucking and eating the ripe grain, is very telling (Matt. 12:1). Jesus' justified their "working" on the Sabbath by appealing to the necessity of eating. This degree of poverty was a new experience for the disciples since they had forsaken all to follow Jesus. Two of them at least, James and John, seem to have belonged to the higher strata of society—they had had servants and were on intimate terms with the high priest. Matthew had followed the lucrative calling of a tax-gatherer, and the other apostles had probably not been in such straits before. Nevertheless, they probably considered the sacrifices they made in obeying Jesus light and the hardships they occasionally had to endure trivial in comparison with the blessedness of walking with Him. No life can be called destitute in which there is true fellowship with Christ. The Pharisees observed this and accused them of working on the Sabbath because they had picked some grain: "Why do you do what is not lawful on the Sabbath?" (v. 2).

Strict Sabbath observance had become the hallmark characteristic of the Jews since the Babylonian exile. After their return it had become interwoven with national determination and religious fervor so that the measure of freedom Jesus took in connection with the observance of the day greatly offended the Jewish people throughout the land. The great number of rules and the hair-splitting legalisms associated by the Jews with Sabbath observance were well known. They made life miserable and intolerable. A devoted Israelite was afraid to bat an eye or lift his finger for fear of breaking some rabbinical precept or regulation.

Sabbath subrules were brutal, and they were for the most part not biblical. For example, almost any action that would appear normal or necessary was against the law. A false tooth could not be worn. A person with a toothache could not rinse his mouth with vinegar, but he could hold it in his mouth and swallow it. Spitting would be interpreted as "a work," and there was to be no labor on the Sabbath! No one could write down two letters of the alphabet. The sick could not send for a physician. A person with lumbago could not rub the infected part of the body. A tailor could not go out with his needle on Friday night (Sabbath eve) lest he should forget it and so break the Sabbath by carrying it about. The very purpose of the Sabbath had been lost. The Lord God had given it through Moses as a blessing to the Jewish people, and it had been made into a burden.

And upon an observance of these fantastic and self-imposed rules devotees thought they could build up a holiness that would justify them in the sight of God. However, the Jews forgot that the Lord had said that if one was hungry and needed to be satisfied, he could pick grapes from the neighbor's vineyard and eat his standing grain when passing through his fields (Deut. 23:24–25).

To relieve hunger in these ways was not considered stealing or breaking the law. In fact, Christ mentions that David and his men did something similar when hungry (Luke 6:3–4). The priest Ahimelech gave him and his men the consecrated tabernacle showbread to eat when they were hungry (1 Sam. 21:1–6). David "entered the house of God, and took and ate the consecrated bread which is not lawful for any to eat except the priests alone" (Luke 6:4). It must have made the Pharisees furious when Christ completed the discussion by adding, "The Son of Man is Lord of the Sabbath" (v. 5). Since the Sabbath was the rest prescribed by God Himself, Jesus was proclaiming His deity. He is God, and the Sabbath was made by Him and for Him, and He can do with it as He pleases! The Sabbath was known as "the Sabbath of the LORD your God" (Deut. 5:14). Jesus' right to claim the Sabbath is in line with the same truth that He could also forgive sins (Luke 5:20), which was a right of God alone.

At the beginning of this section, Jesus brought the Pharisees up short when He began speaking: "Have you not even read what David did when he was hungry, he and those who were with him . . . ?" (v. 3). This question brings on a great theological question: "Is 'religion' manmade or does it come from the Word of God? The Pharisees *had* read the history of their great national hero David, but they had not grasped the principle from the Word of God that undergirded and legitimatized His action and that of the high priest on this occasion. The Lord Jesus did not answer the petty Pharisees as to whether plucking ears of grain and rubbing out the kernels were virtually the same as reaping and threshing. Instead, He settled the dispute by setting forth the great principle that the Word of God, which instructed and proclaimed the legal regulations, laid greater stress on moral duties than upon ceremonial activities and taught that mercy was better than sacrifice.

In the story of David and his hungry companions from 1 Samuel 21, the bread consecrated to God in the holy tent was not profaned when given to relieve the hunger of His children. Jesus also implied that Scripture, to be of use, must be interpreted by Scripture, in order that its true spirit and teaching might be learned. A single text of God's Word must be seen in context to be authoritative.

Christ vindicated the feeding of His disciples on two grounds: (1) there were occasions when the ordinary rules of Sabbath observance might without blame be set aside; and (2) He, as Son of Man, had power to modify those very rules. His decisions were to be taken as authoritative, and the same weight was to be attached to them as to the law concerning the Sabbath given through Moses. The title Son of Man meant that Jesus was the Messiah, the king of Israel. He is the final arbiter of the revelation of His heavenly Father. Because the Sabbath day of rest was an ordinance given for the use and blessing of the

Jews, the Son of Man, who had taken upon Himself full manhood, was now the sovereign over the nation of Israel and had the Sabbath institution under His own power.

The healing on the Sabbath (vv. 6–11). On another Sabbath occasion Jesus was teaching in a synagogue where there was a man with a withered hand (v. 6). The scribes and Pharisees were watching for Jesus to heal again on the Sabbath "in order that they might find reason to accuse Him" (v. 7). Their accusation would be that He had broken the Law, and He could even be stoned. Being deity, "He knew what they were thinking, and He said to the man with the withered hand, 'Rise and come forward!'" (v. 8). Turning to these men, Jesus then asked, "Is it lawful on the Sabbath to do good, or to do harm, to save a life, or to destroy it?" (v. 9). The Lord stared at the religious leaders and then turned to the man, and said, "Stretch out your hand!" The hand was instantly restored (v. 10). The men were furious and "filled with rage, and discussed together what they might do to Jesus" (v. 11).

The great sorrow of this story is how the leaders could ignore the great miracle that had just taken place before their eyes. Their religiosity and animosity toward Christ was so great that they were blinded with hatred. This moral and emotional tragedy permeates the gospel stories.

Study Questions

1. Why did Jesus not want the unclean spirits to reveal that He was the Christ?

2. In 4:42, why did the people try to detain Jesus? Were they fervently desirous of His teaching?

3. Was leprosy routinely healed in the Old Testament? How many examples of the healing of leprosy are we given in the Old Testament?

4. Why does 5:17 tell us that "the power of the Lord was present for Him to perform healing"? Didn't Jesus always have the power to heal?

5. Does 5:17 support faith healing today?

6. What is the meaning of Jesus' parable in 5:36–39?

7. Why, in 6:11, were the Pharisees filled with rage? Had Jesus misquoted the Law?

CHAPTER 13

Call of the Disciples and the Great Sermon by the Lake Luke 6:12–49

Preview:

Jesus continued healing all who came to Him and chose the rest of the twelve disciples who would later be known as apostles. He then taught the multitudes on a mountainside starting with a series of blessings and woes. Luke's version of this sermon differs from Matthew's because of his audience. Matthew's version includes Jesus' restatement of the Law since it was written to a Jewish audience. Luke forgoes this section, giving mainly Jesus' instructions for living a righteous and loving life, since Luke's audience was predominantly Gentile.

The Son of God Communes with His Father (6:12)

"[Jesus] spent the whole night in prayer to God" (6:12). Luke seems to imply that the confrontation with the religious leaders was the reason the Lord went into a far-off mountain to pray to His heavenly Father. This theory would stand to reason. Jesus, the God-Man, had feelings, became tired, and felt the pain of the accusations of those who detested Him. The account as given in Matthew 14:23 tells us that the disciples did not go with Him. His time with His Father was intense (see Heb. 5:7, 8). Luke tells us that He "spent the whole night in prayer to God" (v. 12). On many occasions the Lord so communicated with His heavenly Father.

97

Choosing of the Twelve Disciples (6:13–16)

"He called His disciples to Him; and chose twelve of them" (6:13). The prayer of the Lord may have been about the selection of the men who would walk with Him until His final days. Verse 13 begins, "And when day came. . . . " At this point, Jesus firmed up the list, to twelve, of those who would travel with Him. He was the one doing the choosing, and He would designate them as "apostles" (Greek, *apostolos*, "one sent forth with a message"). These men would be ambassadors or couriers who would carry the message that the King had come. They would later confirm this truth, both individually and as a group. Examining other passages of Scripture these men qualified as witnesses because: (1) they had seen Christ's resurrection (Acts 1:22; 1 Cor. 9:1), (2) were given the power to do signs and wonders (Acts 5:15–16; Heb. 2:2–4), and (3) were chosen by the Lord and by the Holy Spirit (Matt. 10:1–2; Acts 1:26). Paul would be added to this company of "the most eminent apostles" because he saw the resurrected Jesus and was called by Him (Acts 9:1–19). He had the ability to do signs, wonders, and miracles as "a true apostle" (2 Cor. 12:11–12). While it is true that Judas was asked to be part of the company of the apostles and "received his portion in this ministry" (Acts 1:17), his apostolic calling was not sealed with his personal faith and dedication to Christ. After he went out into the dark at the final Passover meal to betray the Lord (John 13:30), Jesus turned to the eleven remaining and said, "I chose you, and appointed you, that you should go and bear fruit" (15:16a). Satan had entered Judas (13:27) in order that he would carry out his wickedness (Acts 1:18). Judas did not follow Christ out of a love, but for personal gain. His betrayal was foretold in Psalm 41:9. Following Judas's death by hanging (Acts 1:18–19), and after much prayer (v. 24), the apostles cast the lot that fell on Matthias (vv. 23–26). By the providence of God, Matthias "was numbered with the eleven apostles" (v. 26). Luke 6:14–16 lists the twelve disciples:

- Simon Peter
- Andrew, Peter's brother
- James
- John
- Philip
- Bartholomew

- Matthew
- Thomas
- James, the son of Alphaeus
- Simon, called the Zealot
- Judas, the son of James
- Judas Iscariot

Luke strings these names together the same way Mark does in his list (Mark 3:13–19). Luke makes no divisions, but Matthew puts the names in pairs. In Acts 1:13 Luke places the names in groups of four, plus two, plus two, plus three, yet omits Judas Iscariot. Peter is always listed first, with Judas listed last. These men would be known as "the Twelve." Omitting Judas (but adding

Matthias), they would change the course of human history as the first-line witnesses of the works and words of Jesus!

The Coming of the Multitude (6:17–19)

"There was a great multitude of His disciples" (6:17). Often called the Sermon on the Mount, or the Great Sermon, most believe this series of spiritual instructions was given on the west shore of Capernaum, a city on the northern shore of the Sea of Galilee. Actually, Jesus did not stand on a mountain; He "stood on a level place" (v. 17) that was probably the brow of a hillside. At the traditional site, the hillside slopes down toward the lake. This is probably where the "great multitude" of a larger body of disciples stood or sat, along with "a great throng" of people from all Judea and Jerusalem and the costal region of Tyre and Sidon (v. 17). From the most distant regions of the Holy Land people came to hear the Lord. His feedings of the multitudes earlier were also an incentive for the people to gather. Luke is careful to note that they came from the far west coast of the land, from Tyre and Sidon, which at that time was pagan Greek territory where many Jews mingled with the idolaters of Asia Minor. These verses tell how far and wide Christ's words were spreading.

Before going further it is important to ask whether this section is a repeat (with some differences) of the Sermon on the Mount recorded in Matthew 5–7 or is a similar message that took place at another location.

Those who have traveled to Israel know that the traditional site of the Sermon on the Mount is a gradually sloping hill that could fulfill the description that Jesus "stood on a level place." Scholars are divided. All admit that the message here in Luke is similar yet different in some of the elements. Hendriksen holds that the Sermon recorded in Matthew and now in Luke is the same event, with variations that are unique to the two apostles.[1]

All realize that Luke focuses on the fact that the sermon was preached on "a level place" (v. 17), while Matthew records that it took place on a mountain, actually a hillside. There is no discrepancy, because the "problem" goes away when one realizes that the level place could have been the slope of the mountain. Christ "stopped here" and "remained standing" when the throng approached Him. Luke says that the Lord turned His gaze on His disciples, while Matthew simply says He opened His mouth and began to teach. The train of thought is basically the same in both Gospels.

The two reports are not identical. Matthew's quoting of the sermon is actually three times as long as Luke's. This makes it clear that the two men were not simply copyists, but that each was reporting Christ's words from his own background, personality, and interests—all orchestrated through the inspiration of the Holy Spirit. It should not be surprising that Matthew focuses on what would be of special interest to the Jews he was attempting to touch for the sake of Christ. Luke was not writing specifically for the Jews, but more, or equally so, for a Gentile audience. More than likely, much that Jesus said in His sermon was repeated many times as He traveled about the countryside. This message was the beginning of His core thoughts to the nation of Israel.

As this message was given, it was first for the ears of Christ's disciples, but also had great practical meaning for the crowds that were so thirsty for a spiritual word from God! Thousands came from the south (Judea and Jerusalem) but also from the north, northwest, and coastal regions of Tyre and Sidon. They came to hear Jesus and to be healed of many diseases. It would be hard to say how much of what He said was instantly absorbed. Yet it could be said for certain that they pondered His message for some time and began to understand the things of God more clearly. What Jesus said would last forever and be repeated throughout the ages. It would be recorded in dozens of dialects and languages!

As people pushed forward to hear Him, He healed and cured their diseases "and those who were troubled with unclean spirits" (v. 18). Because of the healing power coming from Him, "the multitude were trying to touch Him" (v. 19). Some have interpreted this to mean that certain healing "electricity" was coming forth from Him. Luke 8:43–48 mentions the woman suffering from twelve years of hemorrhaging who said, "If I only touch His garment, I shall get well" (Matt. 9:21). When she did, the Lord Jesus felt healing "power had gone out" of Him (Luke 8:46). When she touched Him, "she had been immediately healed" (v. 47b). But it was her faith that had made her well, not simply the physical touch (v. 48). As mentioned in chapter 8 as well as here in chapter 6, people recognized that these were unusual and dramatic cases that accentuated the fact that Jesus was Israel's Messiah. While both stories seem miraculous, 5:17 may supply a clearer answer as to what is happening. There we read that as Jesus performed miracles, "the power of the Lord [God the Father] was present for Him [Jesus] to perform healing." While in many places Christ did not heal every sick person He encountered, it seems that He did here at Galilee. Luke writes that He was "healing them all" (6:19).

The Great "Blessings" (6:20–34)

"Blessed are you who are poor, for yours is the kingdom of God" (6:20). When the Lord began speaking, He was addressing His comments to His disciples (v. 20), but when He finished His teachings, a crowd had gathered to listen to His discourse (7:1). The Gospels vary a little in recording this sermon. Luke lists some

of the "blessed" sayings and mentions four "woes." He shows how Jesus taught by contrasts in that He would give a prohibition ("Do not") and then give a positive moral action ("Do this or that").

A question often asked is, what was the Lord trying to accomplish with these moral and spiritual sayings? Was He presenting the idea of salvation by a system of works? It seems as if Christ was attempting to drive the Jewish people to a point of conviction, that is, that they were sinners who needed something besides failing efforts of trying to keep the Law. In quoting the same sermon, Matthew seems to focus on the words of the Lord that may give a clue as to His ultimate purpose. He told the people, "I say to you, that unless your righteousness surpasses that of the scribes and Pharisees, you shall not enter the kingdom of heaven" (Matt. 5:20). Since the people conceived of these men as living perfect Law-keeping lives, they would respond, "Oh, I need God's mercy because I am not as perfect as the scribes and Pharisees!" And that was Jesus' point. They needed to accept something from God that was beyond human effort. The Lord added, "But seek first His kingdom and His righteousness . . . " (6:33). In other words, they needed His *imputed* or *applied righteousness* that saved their father Abraham by faith (Gen. 15:6). Some of the Jews began to understand this; some of them did not!

The blessings. When Christ began giving His *blessed* teachings, He used the noun *makarios* and not the verb. The word *makarios* means that one is *happy* or *fortunate.* It may have the idea here of "being content, at rest, at peace" within oneself. Notice how Jesus uses these words in contrast:

> Blessed are you who are poor—yours is the kingdom of God (6:20). Having peace of soul, yet living in poverty has its reward—the promised messianic kingdom!

> Blessed are the hungry—you shall be satisfied (v. 21a). This satisfaction may not come from having more food, but from living in peace while having little.

> Blessed are you who weep now—you shall laugh (v. 21b). If you are in pain or under persecution, God will someday bring about relief and joy.

> Blessed are you when men hate you and ostracize you—for the sake of the Son of Man (v. 22). What you endure for the name and service of the Anointed One, the Messiah, God will someday honor. At that time you will have joy just like that of the prophets who were persecuted by the ancestral fathers (v. 23).

A single characteristic of these blessings is that there is a day of reckoning. While relief may not come instantly, it is certain because God is faithful to keep His promises.

The Woes. Woe (Greek, *ouai*) is a call for mourning and sorrow for mistakes made.

> Woe to the rich—you are now receiving your physical comfort in full (v. 24). "You are getting yours now," Christ is saying. Pleasure lasts but for a season, and material plenty can be fleeting.
>
> Woe to the well-fed now—for you shall be hungry (v. 25a). The Lord may be going beyond the physical here. The person who spends most of his time securing his well-being will be judged and be in spiritual hunger.
>
> Woe to you who laugh now—you shall mourn and weep (v. 25b). Jesus was aiming His words at those who live a frivolous and shallow life, who do not think of God and eternal issues. There is nothing wrong with laughter per se. The Lord is addressing the issue of priorities and criticizing those who live for pleasure. Someday they will be drowned in a sea of regrets.
>
> Woe to you when all men speak well of you—this is the same way the ancient fathers treated the false prophets (v. 26). In other words, flattery may be honoring that which was wrong or actually evil about you. Christ then adds not to seek flattery but to "love your enemies, do good to those who hate you" (v. 27). It is better to be cursed for what is right and to "pray for those who mistreat you" (v. 28). In the realm of spiritual truth, that which is contrary to the human way of thinking is actually from God, and that which is natural may really be what is carnal and deceptive.

On verse 24 Marvin Vincent writes:

When, therefore, Christ says, "they that mourn shall be comforted," he speaks in recognition of the fact that all sorrow is the outcome of sin, and that true comfort is given, not only in pardon for the past, but in strength to fight and resist and overcome sin. The atmosphere of the word, in short, is not the atmosphere of the sick-chamber, but the tonic breath of the open world, of moral struggle and victory; the atmosphere for him that climbs and toils and fights.[2]

The Lord then speaks of turning the other cheek, giving the one who hurts you your coat and even your shirt (v. 29). The Lord is not talking about not defending yourself when personally attacked physically, nor is He giving a pacifistic sermon that does not allow a nation to defend itself from invading enemies. He is addressing the ins and outs of human relationships. The Jews at this time were living selfishly and were not applying the principles of graciousness, love, and patience toward each other. Jesus is using hyperbole, or exaggeration, to convey a deeper principle. His point: remain kind and generous toward those who dislike you. Go the extra mile with them in order to win them and make peace (Matt. 5:41). What Jesus is saying here was contradictory to the way the Jews lived. R. C. H. Lenski well writes:

> These precepts have an astounding sound, and that is exactly what Jesus wants them to have. They do teach the complete reverse of what the unregenerate call right. . . . On the other hand, those misunderstand Jesus' meaning who regard him as teaching the doctrine of absolute "nonresistance" which would ignore and overthrow all justice and all righteousness. The law of love is not intended to encourage lawlessness nor to open the floodgates of cruelty and crime.[3]

Christ then adds "Just as you want people to treat you, treat them in the same way" (Luke 6:31). What credit is there to love only those who love you (v. 32)? Even sinners return good to those who are good to them (vv. 33–34).

The Lord then gives a series of commands.

Love and Be Merciful (6:35–38)

"Love your enemies, . . . and you will be sons of the Most High" (6:35). Love your enemies (v. 35), be merciful, just as your Father is merciful (v. 36), do not judge and do not condemn, pardon and you will be pardoned (v. 37). By doing these things you will be "sons of the Most High" (v. 35). This is the first time in the New Testament this concept is introduced. In this context, the Lord is referring to the fact that as the sons of God they would be practicing mercy because their heavenly Father is merciful (v. 36). Concerning "judging" (Greek, *krinō*), Jesus uses a present tense in Greek. He is telling the people not to be living on a daily basis in a judgmental mood, criticizing motives and actions without evidence. A judgmental attitude opens the door to be condemned, but one who has a pardoning spirit will find mercy and be pardoned.

In verse 38 Christ uses the illustration of the merchant who is generous and not stingy with his measuring out a measurement of grain. The good merchant shakes the container and presses down the grain, so that the buyer gets even more than he bargained for. Those who practice such kindness will find "it will be measured to you in return," that is, kindness for kindness. Apparently this is not what the majority of the Jews were practicing in their daily living.

The Parables (6:39–49)

"And He spoke a parable to them" (6:39). If the people are blind to these matters, how can they lead the blind (v. 39), or how can they be a moral example

to someone else? "Will they not both fall into a pit?" They need to be pupils because they cannot lead as teachers (v. 40). Only after one has been fully trained can he or she be a teacher of others.

> Tenderly and lovingly the Master now assures them that although they will never be able to outrank or surpass him, yet thorough training under his direction will, if they accept it, cause them to become like their Teacher; that is, like him not in degree of knowledge or wisdom but in truly reflecting his image to the world, so that people instructed by them will begin to say, "We can notice that these men have been with Jesus."[4]

Jesus points out that often one cannot see his own faults. It is easy to criticize the speck in a brother's eye "but . . . not notice the log that is in your own eye" (v. 41). Because the Lord had a way of teaching with hyperbole, there had to be a ripple of laughter with this statement. One has to take the log out of one's own eye, to see clearly to remove the speck from the eye of a brother; otherwise one is acting like a hypocrite. A good tree does not produce bad fruit (v. 43); "each tree is known by its own fruit" (v. 44). One cannot gather figs from thorns or find grapes on a briar bush. What comes out of a person reveals what he is in his very nature. It is impossible to claim to be a son of God, a faithful follower of the precepts of the heavenly Father, when there is contrary evidence in the way one relates to others. Out of the good treasure of the heart is brought forth what is good; "and the evil man out of the evil treasure brings forth what is evil" (v. 45a). For his mouth speaks from that which fills his heart (v. 45b). It is only a matter of time before the heart motives become obvious.

The soul and spirit of a person must be transformed by the Holy Spirit in order for that individual to become a transparent and whole person. It is not what people claim in their piety that counts. They can say, "Lord, Lord," and still not do what He says (v. 46). By coming to Christ, hearing His words, and then acting upon them, Jesus says He "will show you whom [that person] is like" (v. 47). He is like a wise builder who dug a deep foundation down to bedrock. Then, "when a flood rose, the torrent burst against that house and could not shake it, because it had been well built" (v. 48). The one who has heard Christ's words and failed to act on them will be like a man who built a house on the ground without any foundation. When the water rushed against the house, "immediately it collapsed, and the ruin of that house was great" (v. 49).

In His teaching, the Lord Jesus used situations, objects, common events, and happenings to teach spiritual truths. If one is not stabilized spiritually and refuses to listen to His thoughts and commands, chaos and failure will follow.

Study Questions

1. The Sermon on the Mount is recorded in Matthew as well as Luke, but Luke's version is shorter. What is significant about the sections Luke left out of his version?

2. What does the word *apostle* mean?

3. In the first blessing (Luke 6:20; Matt. 5:3), Luke refers to the "kingdom of God," while Matthew references the "kingdom of heaven." Why are two different terms used?

4. List the seven aspects of unconditional love given in 6:27–38.

5. Since 6:37 tells us, "Do not judge and you will not be judged; and do not condemn, and you will not be condemned," on what basis can we tell unsaved sinners that without Christ they are condemned to hell? Is that not judging and condemning them?

6. Luke 6:43–45 speaks of the good man producing good fruit. Does this mean then, if you do not see good fruit being produced in the life of a professing Christian, that he or she is not saved?

7. Compare this sermon in Luke and in Matthew. Is the Sermon on the Mount a set of rules for believers to live by today?

CHAPTER 14

Continuation of Miracles and Healings
Luke 7:1–9:50

Preview:
Jesus traveled much throughout Israel, teaching primarily in parables, driving out demons, and healing. He gave the Twelve power to do the same and sent them out to proclaim the kingdom of God. Other recorded miracles include Jesus calming the storm and feeding the five thousand, and the Transfiguration.

In this section Luke gives a running narration of a series of events in Christ's ministry. These passages cover part of what is called Jesus' great Galilean ministry and continue on until the time when He began in earnest with the special training of the twelve disciples. To a degree, the disciples had observed similar works and miracles that He would perform here. They would hear again and again His great words of divine wisdom. They would witness the reactions of those who hated Him, and they would see the rush of joy when so many would embrace what He was all about. Many would come to believe He was the promised Messiah, the Son of the living God!

Healing the Centurion's Servant (7:1–10)

"When He had completed all His discourse . . . He went to Capernaum" (7:1). To understand this section of Scripture, it is important to first understand the relationship between masters and slaves and the context of the story of the

centurion. When Luke writes that the "centurion's slave . . . was highly regarded by him" (v. 2), this gives a clue that the story is unusual. Generally slaves were not held in such high esteem as to make their masters concerned about their lives unless by their extraordinary labor or some other virtue they had secured the favor of their masters. Luke is thus indicating that this person was a faithful servant, distinguished by good qualities and highly esteemed by his master. The master exhibits a certain love and kindness not usually found in such relationships.

Master and slave. This outpouring of affection from the master to the slave is very touching, particularly when the brutality that so often marked the slavery of the ancient world is considered. We can safely conclude that the piety, love, faith, and humility that were so prominent in the character of the centurion had been a good influence on one who had long been in daily servitude to him and had called forth the slave's good qualities.

One of the greatest demonstrations of trust recorded in Scripture would come not from a Jew but from a Roman centurion. A centurion traditionally was a commander over one hundred soldiers; however, he could be in charge of even more troops. This wealthy officer was stationed in Capernaum. He must have studied the Old Testament Scriptures to acquaint himself with the culture and religion of the Jews. In that process he apparently became a believer in Jehovah, for the Jewish elders testified that he loved the Jewish nation and had even built the people a synagogue in the city (v. 5). Having a sick slave who was near death (v. 2), he had begged the Jewish elders to appeal to Jesus for a healing. Coming to the Lord, the elders confirmed that the centurion "is worthy for You to grant this to him" (v. 4). The soldier's faith was so great he reasoned that Christ did not have to trouble Himself to come to His house.

"Jesus started on His way" (v. 6a), is reminiscent of another occasion when Jesus had a similar request made to Him. A certain nobleman besought him to come and heal his son who was at the point of dying (John 4:46–47). Jesus did not go but simply said a word by which the child was healed. That Jesus did not go to the bedside of the nobleman's son but did accede to the request to come to heal the centurion's slave may have special significance. Perhaps the greater faith of the centurion explains our Lord's procedure. In the nobleman's case Jesus' course of action was calculated to strengthen weak faith.

When the centurion sent a message to Christ saying, "Lord, do not trouble Yourself further" by coming (v. 6b), the phrase could better be translated, "Don't worry yourself," a colloquial expression that could be describe as "slang."

By saying he was not worthy, the centurion not only contrasted his own sinfulness with Jesus' perfect holiness, but implied that he was an alien to the race to which Jesus belonged and to which He largely confined Himself (v. 7). The man counted himself unworthy that Christ should enter into his doors, yet he argued that all the Lord had to do was "just say the word, and my servant will be healed." *If* the Lord Jesus had been a mere man, could He have allowed such views of Himself to be uttered and left uncorrected? Instead, Christ allowed the statement to stand because it did indeed reflect His very deity and sovereignty to do whatsoever He wished!

The centurion gave two reasons why Christ need not take the trouble of entering his house: the first was based on his own unworthiness to receive so great a guest; the second was based on the power he believed Christ possessed. It was needless for Him to come in person; He had but to speak the word and the servant would be healed.

As the centurion had the right to command someone to do whatever he wanted done, he realized that whatever Christ desired would come to pass (v. 8). The faith of the centurion was childlike yet absolutely "right on" in the spiritual insight it manifested. He argued from the less to the greater: "Though I am only a military commander with limited authority, I can yet give orders to slaves and know that they will be carried out. Much more You are able to heal my servant by bidding the disease to depart." The centurion had learned from his authority as a military officer of the divine authority Christ held as the King of the Jews! He also must have known that Jesus had come with all of the authority of the Father in heaven.

When Jesus heard the centurion's words, He "marveled at him, and turned and said to the multitude that was following Him, 'I say to you, not even in Israel have I found such great faith'" (v. 9). When the Jewish elders and others who came to Christ went back to the centurion's house, "they found the slave in good health" (v. 10).

While Luke does not say so, it is likely that this man had studied the Old Testament passages about the coming of the Messiah and had reasoned that Jesus was the One. His faith in the Lord's healing ability may have come from his reading of Isaiah 53:4, where the prophet says that the Messiah will bear our griefs and carry our sorrows.

Raising the Dead Son (7:11–17)

"He went to a city called Nain" (7:11). Following His time at Capernaum, the Lord traveled west toward the village of Nain, located about ten miles south and east of Nazareth. He was accompanied by His disciples and "a large

multitude" (v. 11). A funeral procession was coming out of the city. The man who died was the only son of a widow (v. 12a). The mention of her widowhood is important because she was now in a helpless state with the death of her son who was probably her sole provider. The woman must have been pious and well respected, for Luke says "a sizeable crowd from the city was with her" (v. 12b). Jesus was touched with compassion for her and said, "Do not weep" (v. 13). With this He halted the bearers, touched the coffin (v. 14a), and commanded, "Young man, I say to you, arise!" (v. 14b). The man immediately sat up and began to speak. Jesus, probably taking his hand, presented the man back to His mother (v. 15). To this great crowd, this event must have appeared spooky, for Luke says that "fear gripped them all" (v. 16a), but they began glorifying God, saying, "A great prophet has arisen among us!" (v. 16b). This miracle was told throughout the western Galilean region and everywhere toward the south, in Judea (v. 17).

In terms of time, this bringing of the young man back from the dead seems to have happened before the resurrection of Lazarus (John 11:1–44). Besides Lazarus and the young man in this account, the Lord also raised the daughter of Jairus (Mark 5:41). What happened at Nain must have made a permanent impression on almost the entire nation. The writer of Hebrews seems to be referring to the great compassion of Christ that is available even now for those who trust Him when he writes, "Let us therefore draw near with confidence to the throne of grace, that we may receive mercy and may find grace to help in time of need" (4:16).

Why did Luke add this story to his Gospel? Some have seen this story as symbolizing something of the entire ministry of Christ on earth. The funeral procession is coming one way, while the Lord and those with Him are traveling another way. They come in contact, and the Lord stops the procession by saying to the widow, "Do not weep" (v. 13). The Lord then brings the dead back to the living. This encounter and meeting might stand for a symbol of Christ's whole coming and work on earth. Why had this poor widow been chosen? Could the Lord Jesus have touched someone else? There is no final answer. In any case, God used this incident to demonstrate the great resurrection authority of His Son!

Comforting John the Baptist (7:18–35)

"The disciples of John reported to him about all these things" (7:18). Though John the Baptist was a great servant of the Lord, he was only human and he had his share of doubts. John sent his followers to Jesus with the question, "Are You the Expected One or do we look for someone else?" (vv. 19–20). "The

Expected One" is a present participle in Greek, *ho erchomenos*, meaning "the one coming, the one on the way." At this time the Lord was healing multitudes and driving out many evil spirits (v. 21). He urged John's disciples to report back to John the great messianic prophecy of Isaiah 61:1: "The blind receive sight, the lame walk, the lepers are cleansed, and the deaf hear, the dead are raised up, the poor have the gospel preached to them" (v. 22).

The crowds hearing the words of Christ may have perceived the weakness of John in asking these questions. Jesus knew their thoughts and replied with forceful words: "What did you go out into the wilderness to look at? A reed shaken by the wind? But what did you go out to see? A man dressed in soft clothing? Behold, those who are splendidly clothed and live in luxury are found in royal palaces. But what did you go out to see? A prophet? Yes, I say to you, and one who is more than a prophet" (v. 24–26). While John for the moment seemed to be doubting, he was one of the greatest of all prophets. Jesus reminded them that John's ministry was predicted in Malachi 3:1: "Behold, I send My messenger before Your face, who will prepare Your way before You" (v. 27). This could only refer to the coming of the Messiah! Though Luke does not quote it, Malachi adds, "And the Lord, whom you seek, will suddenly come to His temple" (Mal. 3:1b). On this Old Testament verse Merrill F. Unger notes:

> The Lord **shall suddenly come to his temple** evidently includes the presentation of the baby Jesus to the Lord in the Temple after His circumcision (Luke 2:21–24), as well as His coming at other occasions, such as when He cleansed the Temple (John 2:13–22). In this passage the Messiah's deity and His oneness with God are revealed. He comes to the Temple as "his temple," marking His divine lordship over it, contrasted with all His creatures, who are [to be] but servants *in* it (Hag. 2:7; Heb. 3:2, 5–6).[1]

With what may have been a fiery response to the people, the Lord added, "There is no one greater than John" (v. 28a). Though John is great, the one who trusts in the Messiah and may be the least in the kingdom is considered "greater than he" (v. 28b). The point the Lord was making is that those who come after John and exercise faith will someday see the Davidic kingdom and be recognized as the ones who believed all that was said about the Messiah.

Many who had earlier been baptized by John, the tax-gatherers who often were considered as crooks, and others standing around who heard these words "acknowledged God's justice" (v. 29). They realized by what Jesus had said that the vilest of sinners and those who were the least of the citizens could still receive the mercy of God. God was just and had sent Christ to reach beyond the great prophets, such as John, and save unworthy sinners! Luke adds an astounding commentary about the thinking of some of the Pharisees and the lawyers who heard what Jesus had just said: "But the Pharisees and the lawyers rejected God's purpose for themselves, not having been baptized by John" (v. 30). When John began his ministry, the entire nation was challenged to repent of its evilness and its coldness toward God. The rejection of John's message would be the backdrop for the rejection of Jesus as the Messiah throughout His ministry to the people.

Jesus continued His discussion and asked: "To what then shall I compare the men of this generation, and what are they like?" (v. 31). He answered His own question by saying that they are like children who sit in the market place and pout. They refuse to dance or even "play" funeral and pretend to weep when they hear the sound of a flute (v. 32). John the Baptist came eating no bread and drinking no wine, and they said, "He has a demon!" (v. 33). The Son of Man came eating and drinking, and they said, "Behold, a gluttonous man, and a drunkard, a friend of tax-gatherers and sinners!" (v. 34). In other words, in no matter what mode the truth was presented, the people remained contrary and stubborn, just like children who refuse to play with each other. But there would be some who would see the light and realize that God was speaking to the nation through John and through Christ, because "wisdom is vindicated by all her children" (v. 35), "by all who are themselves wise, not foolish and unreasonable like the 'generation' described."[2]

Ministering to Sinners (7:36–50)

"[Jesus] entered the Pharisee's house, and reclined at the table" (7:36). Surprisingly, one of the Pharisees named Simon, who probably lived in Capernaum, asked Jesus to come and dine with him (v. 36). Simon's motive for inviting Jesus is unclear. While Jesus was reclining at the meal, an unsavory woman, probably a prostitute, came into the room with an alabaster vial of very expensive perfume (v. 37). This woman had heard the words of the Lord, possibly on several occasions, and was deeply moved with conviction. Weeping, she began wiping His feet and with her hair and kissing them, and then she followed up by anointing them with the perfume (v. 38). It was customary to cleanse the feet of the dinner guests with a bowl of water and a towel. And often, because of the heat of the sun, the head was rubbed with anointing oil. The Pharisee did not provide either of these niceties. When he saw what the woman was doing, the Pharisee was dumbfounded and reasoned that if Jesus was truly a prophet, He would realize this woman touching Him was a sinner (v. 39). Knowing the man's thoughts, the Lord told him the following story: A moneylender had two debtors who could not pay what

they owed. He graciously forgave the one who owed five hundred denarii and the other who owed fifty denarii (v. 41). (A denarii was a Roman silver coin that was about a day's wage for an average laborer.) Jesus asked, "Which of them therefore will love him more?" (v. 42). Simon answered correctly, "I suppose the one whom he forgave more" (v. 43). Pointing to the woman, the Lord then said to the man: "I entered your house; you gave Me no water for My feet, but she has wet My feet with her tears and wiped them with her hair. You gave Me no kiss; but she, since the time I came in, has not ceased to kiss my feet. You did not anoint My head with oil, but she anointed My feet with perfume. For this reason I say to you, her sins, which are many, have been forgiven, for she loved much; but he who is forgiven little, loves little" (vv. 44–47). Jesus then turned to Mary and said, "Your sins have been forgiven" (v. 48). By a simple decree spoken, as He sat at the table, Jesus blotted out the record of this woman's sins. Christ's divine knowledge of her sincere repentance was absolute, and His authority to act in God's holy name was supreme and absolute. The people at the table were shocked and said to themselves, "Who is this man who even forgives sins?" (v. 49). The shock and astonishment shown by those who were present at Jesus' claim to forgive sin was most natural, for the majority of those there evidently hesitated to regard Him as the penitent woman did. These witnesses cannot be accused of wholesale and malignant unbelief, for they were astonished at a claim which without a doubt many of them soon came to see was fully justified. The answer to their question would have been, "He is the Son of Man, the promised Messiah!"

The Pharisees

Pharisee means "the separated ones."

The first reference is by Josephus.

They are dated in the time of the military general Jonathan (160–143 B.C.).

Their prominence ended during the time of John Hyrcanus (134–104 B.C.).

They returned to power when Salome Alexandra became queen (76 B.C.).

They were the spiritual descendants of the Hasidim, the religious fighters during the time of Judas Maccabeus.

They developed extensive oral laws and traditions.

They moved Israel away from the sacrificial system to a system of legalism.

This encounter is similar to Jesus' healing of the paralytic when He restored the man and said to him, "Friend, your sins are forgiven you" (5:20). Both incidences proved "the Son of Man has authority on earth to forgive sins" (v. 24). Jesus told the woman, "Your faith has saved you; go in peace" (7:50). Christ mercifully ascribes to *faith* those blessings that are due to Himself because of who He is! Faith for salvation is based on the recognition of the awfulness of sin. This woman was struck with great conviction, and her emotional acknowledgment of Jesus as the Christ was exhibited before everyone. The awareness of sin causes one to rush to Jesus!

Many older Bible scholars have identified this woman as Mary Magdalene of 8:2. But there is no evidence that this is the same person. The woman of 7:37 was residing in the city of Capernaum and was apparently known as a sinner by everyone (v. 39). The events of chapter 8, which include the mention of Mary Magdalene, "came about soon afterwards" when Jesus "began going about from one city and village to another" (8:1).

Ministering with Parables (8:1–21)

"[Jesus] began ... proclaiming and preaching the kingdom of God" (8:1). Luke sets the scene for the teaching of these parables. With His twelve disciples, Jesus was going through each village "proclaiming and preaching the kingdom of God" (v. 1). In the process "some women" were healed of "evil spirits and sicknesses." This included Mary who was called Magdalene, "from whom seven demons had gone out" (v. 2). That more than one demon is identified shows the strong grip these spirits had on her. Around the larger Galilee area there seems to have been greater demonic activity than elsewhere. Magdalene is a spinoff of the name for the village Magdala, a small fishing community on the coast between Capernaum and Tiberius. Among the other women who were liberated from the demons were Joanna, the wife of Chuza, Herod's steward, and a woman named Susanna. Later they "were contributing to the support out of their private means" of the Lord and His disciples (v. 3). As Jesus and these men moved about the land preaching the Word of God, funds were needed to supply basic necessities. Mary saw the crucifixion of Jesus (Mark 15:40), attended His burial (v. 47), went to the empty tomb (16:1), and was a witness to His resurrection (v. 9).

From various cities throughout the Galilee region, a great multitude was coming to hear Jesus speak (v. 4). He used parables because they simplified spiritual concepts the crowds could identify with. The word *parable* comes from two Greek words: *para* meaning "alongside," and *bolē* from *ballō*, meaning "to cast, throw." A parable then is a story cast alongside a specific truth that one wishes to communicate. If the parable can be understood, the spiritual point should become apparent. Because of the hardness of the hearts of the Jews, this did not always happen!

Luke does not record here all of the Lord's parables. He focuses on two: the seed cast forth on the ground (vv. 5–15) and the light from a lamp (vv. 16–18).

The seed (vv. 5–15). The sower throws his seed out, with some falling on the road where it was trampled underfoot and some getting eaten by birds (v. 5). Other seed fell among the rocks and dried up (v. 6), with additional seed falling among the thorns and being choked out (v. 7). But some of the seed fell on good soil, flourished, and produced a great hundredfold crop (v. 8a). As was His practice, when He finished with this story, He called out, "He who has ears to hear, let him hear" (v. 8b). With this challenge, Jesus was seeking a spiritual connection with the people. Yet even the disciples did not get the point and asked "as to what this parable might be" about (v. 9). Jesus answered that to them was granted "to know the mysteries of the kingdom of God, but to the rest it is in parables in order that seeing they may not see, and hearing they may not understand" (v. 10). The Lord quoted a heavy judgment prophecy from Isaiah 6:9 that showed how someday the Jews would be blinded and would never be able to understand the deeper spiritual truth about "the kingdom of God" (Luke 8:10).

Since the Messiah was in the presence of the Jewish people, the literal Davidic earthly kingdom of God (or kingdom of heaven) was being offered. Nevertheless, His blessed reign would not come about at this time. What was Jesus referring to when He spoke about "the mysteries of the kingdom of God"? Some think the Church age is the present mystery form of that promised millennial reign of the Son of God. But it seems best to believe that the mystery aspect of the millennial rule refers to the deeper spiritual qualities of that kingdom that the Old Testament could not fully explain. "This view is most consistent with normal and literal hermeneutics and allows the continuity of words and thoughts to continue through the Gospels, without suddenly having to shift to a new meaning for the idea of the kingdom of [God]."[3] Stanley Toussaint adds:

> This view states the kingdom promised to the Jews is giving new revelation concerning the kingdom promised to the Jews. The truths relate to the time of the establishing of the kingdom, the preparation for it, and other such material which had never before been revealed. . . . This view has the further advantage of being consistent with the New Testament concept of a mystery. Because of the Jewish rejection of the Messiah, the promised kingdom [will] now be held in abeyance. The parables . . .

reveal new truths involving the preparation for the establishment of the kingdom.[4]

Jesus then proceeded to explain the parable: "The seed is the word of God" (v. 11). Those who are beside the road are like those who hear the truth in their hearts, but the devil comes and takes the truth away, "so that they may not believe and be saved" (v. 12). Those on the rocky soil are like those who hear and receive with joy, but without a deep root, they fall away when temptation comes (v. 13). When the seed falls in the thorns, those who hear go their way and are choked with worries "and riches and pleasures of this life, and bring no fruit to maturity" (v. 14). And when the seed falls on good ground, "the ones who have heard the word in an honest and good heart, and hold it fast" are able to bear fruit with steady patience (v. 15). While these thoughts apply specifically to the teaching concerning the kingdom of God, the principle is applicable in all of the dispensations of Scripture. Spiritual truth must fall in receptive, spiritually good soil, or it will dry and wither.

The light from a lamp (vv. 16–18). The light of a lamp is not to be covered and hidden; instead it is to be placed on a lampstand "in order that those who come in may see the light" (v. 16). Nothing should be hidden or kept in secret away from the light (v. 17). Jesus then makes the point: take care how you listen. The one who possesses that which is of value, to him "shall more be given; and whoever does not have, even what he thinks he has shall be taken away from him" (v. 18). R. C. H. Lenski explains the verse this way:

> [God sent His Son] to give his Word, and they who keep hearing aright grow richer and richer. God can give to them, and thus God does give because giving and enriching us for eternity are his delight. But they who hear amiss prevent God from giving thus to them so that the more they continue hearing thus, the worse their state becomes. They may think that they have, i.e., sufficient or even superior knowledge, without this Word of Jesus, but this, they will find, is valueless, and they will thus end in everlasting poverty.[5]

Though the people may not have been able to understand what Jesus was teaching, the crowd was pressing upon Him so that His mother and brothers, who wanted to see Him, had to stand outside. Their presence was reported to Him (v. 19). The fact that they were "outside" may mean that the Lord had moved indoors as He continued to teach. To draw the crowd more closely to Him emotionally to make known that He deeply cared for them, He answered, "My mother and My brothers are these who hear the word of God and do it" (v. 21). The family of the Lord had probably come from their hometown of Nazareth, which was not too far off. Joseph is not mentioned, and this may support the notion that he had already died and that Mary was now a widow who was cared for by her other children. Matthew records: "Is not His mother called Mary, and His brothers, James and Joseph and Simon and Judas? And His sisters, are they not all with us?" (13:55–56). More than likely the writing apostles James and Jude (Judas) are referred to here. Nothing is known of His brothers Joseph and Simon; nor are there other references to His sisters. These would be half siblings, with Mary as their mother and Joseph, their father.

Giving Comfort in the Storm (8:22–25)

"[Jesus] and His disciples got into a boat, . . ."(8:22). During this same time, "on one of those days," the Lord and His disciples put out into a boat on the sea of Galilee (v. 22). They planned to cross over to the far side of the lake, probably to find rest from the crush of the crowds. Being terribly tired, Jesus fell asleep in the boat. Suddenly "a fierce gale of wind descended upon the lake, and they began to be swamped and to be in danger" (v. 23). Awakening Jesus, the disciples called out, "Master, Master, we are perishing!" Coming awake, "He rebuked the wind and the surging waves, and they stopped, and it became calm" (v. 24). He then said to the disciples, "Where is your faith?" (v. 25a). Being fearful and amazed, the men said to one another, "Who then is this, that He commands even the winds and the water, and they obey Him?" (v. 25b).

The disciples had seen the Lord cast out demons, heal, and even raise the dead, but experiencing firsthand His authority and instant command over nature was quite something else. This power reflected His deity; the Son of God had the same control over the elements as His Father! The apostle John would later write, "Apart from Him nothing came into being that has come into being" (John 1:3), and Paul would affirm, "In Him all things hold together" (Col. 1:17). The writer of Hebrews would add that God had appointed His Son "heir of all things, through whom also He made the world" (1:2), and He "upholds all things by the word of His power" (v. 3).

Power over Demons (8:26–39)

"And they sailed to the country of the Gerasenes" (8:26). Having ended up on the eastern shore of the Sea of Galilee in an area called the Gerasenes, Jesus and the disciples had a powerful encounter with demonism. The area of the Gerasenes was named after the prevailing city of Gadara. This entire area was the outpost of the Jewish lands, a place of spiritual and moral darkness; and the inhabitants had been widely influenced by Greek paganism.

Demon possession was prevalent. Near Gadara was a man "possessed with demons," more accurately "having demons" (v. 27). This man was living naked among the tombs. Seeing Jesus, he ran toward Him and cried aloud, "What do I have to do with You, Jesus, Son of the Most High God? I beg You, do not torment me" (v. 28). The reason this was said was because the Lord began commanding the unclean spirit to come forth. In this struggle, the demon kept seizing the man over and over. The man had been shackled with chains and even guarded, but to no avail. He tore the chains and was tormented by the demon who controlled his body and drove him into the nearby desert (v. 29). This spirit was vicious! It could torment (torture) him (v. 28), seize him repeatedly (v. 29), and impart unnatural strength (v. 29b). But the demon was actually many demons (Legion, meaning "many") speaking with one voice, "for many demons had entered him" (v. 30).

In this terrible drama, it is important to notice that the demon recognized that Christ was the Son of God, and that He had the power to ultimately judge him (them). "I beg You, do not torment me" (v. 28b). Matthew 8:29 records that the demon added "before the time." All the demons, along with Satan, face "the judgment of the great day" (Jude 1:6). When Jesus the King, the Son of Man, comes to establish His millennial kingdom, He will say to the lost, "Depart from Me, accursed ones, into the eternal fire which has been prepared for the devil and his angels" (Matt. 25:41). These angels are apparently those that fell with Satan (Isa. 14; Ezek. 28), with some roaming the earth now as demons.

The demons begged Jesus to send them "into the abyss" (Luke 8:31). The word "abyss" is *abussos* and is sometimes translated "the bottomless pit," "bottomless depth," or "shift of the abyss." This is where some of the fallen angels are now confined and "kept in eternal bonds under darkness (Greek, *zophos*, "gloom, blackness") (Jude 1:6). Some of these creatures will come forth from this place to torment people on the earth during the tribulation (Rev. 9:1–12). Jesus apparently did not grant their request. Instead, they asked to leave the man they were tormenting and be cast into a herd of swine feeding nearby (Luke 8:32). When the Lord allowed their request, they left the man, entered the swine, and caused the herd to rush headlong into the lake and drown (v. 33). When this remarkable event happened, the people in the town came out and asked the Lord to leave their area (v. 37). Nevertheless, they found the man who was possessed well and sitting at Jesus' feet (vv. 35–36). As Christ and His disciples were leaving in the boat, the man asked that he might go with them. But Jesus replied, "Return to your house and describe what great things God has done for you" (v. 39a). In this spiritually dark area of the land, this man's testimony went far and wide. He went about and proclaimed "what great things Jesus had done for him" (v. 39b). In this verse, the construction of the verbs is the same: both are aorist tenses with articles attached to the nouns. The clauses read: "What for you He *did*, the God"; "What for him He *did*, the Jesus." It is impossible to escape the implication: Jesus performed the very same work that was done by God the Father!

This fact is reinforced in John 10:27–30. Jesus had said that no one can snatch His sheep from His hand, and no one can snatch them from the Father's hand! He then added, "I and the Father are one" (v. 30). In other words, He was saying, "My Father and I do the very same work because of our Father/Son relationship of divine essence." Jesus is God the Son! He is the very God!

Power Over Death (8:40–56)

"As Jesus returned, the multitude welcomed Him, for they had all been waiting for Him" (8:40). Coming back from the Gerasene region, The Lord encountered another situation involving death. In this case, it was the death of a twelve-year-old girl whose father was the official of the local synagogue in Capernaum. This man began begging Jesus to come and heal his daughter (v. 41). As Jesus was coming the crowds pressed against Him (v. 42). A woman with a twelve-year hemorrhage came up to touch His clothes. When she did, "immediately her hemorrhage stopped" (v. 44). Because of the surge of the crowd, Peter was surprised when Jesus asked, "Who is the one who touched Me?" (v. 45). The Lord then added, "Someone did touch Me, for I was aware that power had gone out of Me" (v. 46). The woman came forward and confessed before the multitude that she had touched Jesus, believing she would be healed. And immediately, she testified, she was healed (v. 47). While this miracle was unusual in that Christ was generally frontal with the healings He performed, He was still the one enacting the cure. His clothes were not magical, for He said to her, "Daughter, your faith has made you well; go in peace" (v. 48). By "go in peace," Jesus probably had in view that now she would have peace of mind over this matter that had caused her stress for twelve long years.

Meanwhile, a friend of the synagogue official came to him and to Christ and said, "Your daughter has died; do not trouble the Teacher anymore" (v. 49). The Lord responded, "Do not be afraid any longer; only believe, and she shall be made well" (v. 50). Coming to the house of the man, only Peter, John, James, and the girl's parents entered where the girl was (v. 51).

By now the weeping and lamenting had begun by the servants, neighbors, relatives, and maybe even the professional mourners, but Jesus said, apparently forcefully, "Stop weeping, for she has not died, but is asleep" (Luke 8:52). Knowing that she was dead, they all began mocking and laughing at Him (v. 53). When the Lord took the girl's hand and commanded, "Child arise!" (v. 54), her spirit returned and "she rose immediately; and He gave orders for something to be given her to eat" (v. 55). Her parents were "amazed," or astounded (Greek, *existēmi*), a word Luke generally uses when the supernatural has taken place. Why did the Lord then instruct them "to tell no one what had happened" (v. 56)? One answer may be that the crowd would have rushed immediately into the house to see this great miracle firsthand. When the little girl would finally come out of the house, there would be plenty of time for the people to witness, and to have verified in their own minds, the mighty work of the Messiah!

Sending out the Disciples (9:1–17)

"[He] gave [the disciples] power and authority over all the demons" (9:1). The time came for the disciples to practice what they had seen their Master doing. They would be sent forth to cast out demons, heal diseases, and proclaim the kingdom of God (vv. 1–2). They could do nothing on their own authority. They were just simple men whom the Lord was instructing and grooming for the day when He would no longer be with them. Therefore, He had to grant them "power and authority" to accomplish their mission. To demonstrate their dependency on God, they were instructed to travel with nothing, taking "neither a staff, nor a bag, nor bread, nor money, . . . not even . . . two tunics apiece" (v. 3). This would show that they went out to serve God alone and that they were indeed helpless and dependent on this journey. They apparently could be fed by those with whom they stayed, but they were not to take any supplies given them by their hosts. And as for those who did not receive them, Jesus added, "Shake off the dust from your feet as a testimony against them" (v. 5).

The entire nation had heard of the ministry of John the Baptist and now also of the words and miracles of Christ. The apostles were not going into areas that were in the dark concerning the ministries of John and of Christ. Far and wide in the land the Jews were receiving the message of the kingdom of God. The disciples were simply following up, performing miracles like their Master, and "preaching the gospel, and healing everywhere" (v. 6). Note that "the gospel" mentioned here is not that of personal salvation brought about by the death, burial, and resurrection of Jesus. In the context of the Gospels, this "good news" is about the arrival of the King and His kingdom. The repentance of the nation was what was needed next.

Meanwhile, Herod Antipas, the tetrarch over Galilee and Perea, was hearing "all that was happening" (v. 7a). He was greatly perplexed because some were saying that Christ was John the Baptist who had come out of the grave (v. 7b), and others thought He might be Elijah or one of the other "prophets of old [who] had risen again" (v. 8). Herod must have been feeling some tinge of guilt ordering John's death. John was on his mind! He said, "I myself had John beheaded; but who is this man about whom I hear such things?" (v. 9a). Luke adds, He kept trying to see Him" (v. 9b). Was Herod experiencing spiritual conviction or just wanting to see a miracle worker? The answer is found in Christ's appearance before Herod before His crucifixion. Since Jesus was from Herod's jurisdiction in Galilee, He had to come before him. Luke tells us that Herod "wanted to see Him for a long time, because he had been hearing about Him and was hoping to see some sign performed by Him" (23:8). When Christ refused to answer, Herod had his soldiers treat Him with contempt, "mock Him," dress Him "in a gorgeous robe," and send Him back to Pilate (v. 11). There was no conviction in Herod's heart!

When the disciples returned to Jesus, "they gave an account to Him of all that they had done." The Lord then took these men and withdrew to the town of Bethsaida (Luke 9:10b) on the north shore of the Sea of Galilee. This meeting may have been for the purpose of debriefing them as to what happened on their journeys. Still, the crowds continued to follow. With compassion the Lord continued to speak about the blessings of the coming kingdom and to cure those who needed healing (v. 11). At evening, the disciples urged Him to send the people away for food and lodging (v. 12), but He said, "You give them something to eat!" (v. 13a). They responded by saying that they had only five loaves of bread and two fish (v. 13b), and this to feed five thousand men (v. 14). Many have calculated that if there were women and children in the crowd, the numbers could have been double (Matt. 14:21). Jesus told His disciples to have all of these people recline in groups of about fifty each. In proper Jewish fashion, He blessed the food, broke the bread and fish into portions, and instructed the disciples to pass out the meal. "And they all ate and were satisfied; and the broken pieces which they had left over were picked up, twelve baskets full" (Luke 9:17).

This was another kind of miracle different from what went before. It was a "multiplication" work that defied logic. Earlier hundreds had witnessed the great works of Christ, but now thousands would be participants of His divine and messianic manifestations.

The Confession and the Transfiguration (9:18–37)

"Who do the multitudes say that I am?" (9:18). Luke 9:18–50 covers events that occurred during what is sometimes called Jesus' "retirement ministry." The

shift to this ministry from the one that preceded it is not abrupt and radical but rather a matter of emphasis. For example, during the lengthy period which Jesus had primarily spent in Capernaum and vicinity (Luke 4:14—9:17), he was often surrounded by crowds. Even now (9:18–50) he did not escape those multitudes.[6]

The Prayer Life of Christ

Jesus prayed in the wilderness (Luke 5:16).

Jesus prayed on a mountain (Luke 6:12).

Jesus often spent the entire night in prayer (Luke 6:12).

Often He prayed alone (Luke 9:18).

The disciples asked Him to teach them to how to pray (Luke 11:1).

Jesus drove the money changers from the temple because it was to be "a house of prayer" to the Father (Luke 19:46).

In the end, Jesus prayed that the disciples' faith would not fail (Luke 22:32).

Before His crucifixion, Jesus prayed in agony and very fervently (Luke 22:44; Matt. 26:42).

Sometime later, when Jesus was alone with the disciples, He asked them, "Who do the multitudes say that I am?" (v. 18). The disciples revealed the confusion of many of the people: "[Some say,] John the Baptist, and others say Elijah; but others, that one of the prophets of old has arisen again" (v. 19). Pressing them, He asked, "'But who do you say that I am?' And Peter answered and said, 'The Christ of God'" (v. 20). Peter, as was often the case, did not hesitate to answer first. And so often he had the right answer. While his faith sometimes appeared to be slim, it was firm as to who the Lord was. Jesus used this occasion to tell them where His life and ministry were going. It was aimed for the cross where "the Son of Man must suffer many things, and be rejected by the elders and chief priests and scribes, and be killed, and be raised up on the third day" (v. 22). Did the disciples comprehend what the Lord was talking about? Many doubt that they did. They said little, showing that they may have paid scant attention to what He had just said. Only Peter spoke out, saying, "God forbid it, Lord! This shall never happen to You" (Matt. 16:22). What Peter had then uttered was the wish of Satan—that the journey to the cross not happen. With some of His strongest words of rebuke, Jesus said, "Get behind

Me, Satan! You are a stumbling block to Me; for you are not setting your mind on God's interests, but man's" (v. 23). God's plan had to do with the cross, whereby Jesus would become a sacrifice for the sins of the world.

Jesus then set forth the challenge: anyone following Him must deny himself and take up his cross daily (Luke 9:23), not wishing to save his life, but to lose it for His sake (v. 24). "For what is a man profited if he gains the whole world, and loses or forfeits himself?" (v. 25).

> The contrast is between the brevity of this world and the eternality of the human soul. To strive after the goods of this world to the neglect of the values of eternity is no profit; it is only a tragic loss (cf. Luke 12:13–34 and Ps. 49). In other words, to follow the way of the world, instead of the footsteps of Jesus, is to invite the judgment of God.[7]

Jesus then interjected the issue of the future messianic kingdom; with straightforward words, He reminded the disciples that He is the Son of Man who someday would come "in His glory, and the glory of the Father and of the holy angels" (v. 26b). Would they be ashamed of Him at that time? (v. 26a).

He then told them, "There are some of those standing here who shall not taste death until they see the kingdom of God" (v. 27). Eight days later He took Peter, John, and James to a high mountain to pray. And there while praying "His face became different, and His clothing became white and gleaming" (v. 29). Suddenly, Moses and Elijah appeared, talking with Him about His departure "which He was about to accomplish at Jerusalem" (vv. 30–31). The departure would be His crucifixion that He had recently talked about. The apostles Matthew and Mark call this event the Transfiguration (Matt. 17:2; Mark 9:2). The Greek word *metamorphoō* means "against form." In other words, the Lord Jesus was changed from His present physical form to the glorified body that would be His permanently when He came to reign on earth. These apostles were given a preview of the Lord in His glory, as He would be seen when He sat on the throne of David in the kingdom, in Jerusalem. Paul uses the same word, *metamorphoō*, when describing how believers should "not be conformed to this world, but be *transformed* by the renewing of your mind" (Rom. 12:2, italics mine). Why did God allow Moses and Elijah to appear with Christ? Moses was recognized by the Jews to be the greatest prophet who ever lived, and Elijah is the prophet who will herald the final tribulation judgments, the second coming, and the messianic reign. Through Malachi, God told Israel, "Behold, I am going to send you Elijah the prophet before the coming of the great and terrible day of the LORD. And he will restore the hearts of the fathers to their children, and the hearts of the children to their fathers" (Mal. 4:5–6). Elijah's prophetic role continually placed him in confrontations with the Jewish people and polytheism. Elijah stood valiantly for the Lord before the 450 prophets of Baal and the 400 prophets of Asherah (1 Kings 18:19–40). It stands to reason that he would have the blessed privilege of introducing the nation of Israel to its promised King!

Though they had been asleep, the disciples became "fully awake" and were witnessing this great visual prediction that would someday come to pass in full in the pages of prophetic history. Wanting to stay and take in this glorious event, Peter said, "Let us make three tabernacles [tents]: one for You, and one for Moses, and one for Elijah" (Luke 9:33). God the Father again spoke from heaven: "This is My Son, My Chosen One; listen to Him!" (v. 35). With that, Moses and Elijah returned to heaven.

> The voice of God came from the cloud, reminiscent of Jesus' baptism (3:22), except that here the voice was directed more to the onlookers (the disciples), than to Jesus. Three things were said about Jesus, each of which identified Him with an Old Testament title indicative of His intimate relationship with God. First, the divine voice called Jesus "My Son," a reference to Psalm 2:7. The title as applied to Jesus communicated His heavenly origin and deity. Second, God announced that Jesus was His "chosen one," an allusion to the Suffering Servant of Isaiah 42:1. . . . Third, the heavenly voice commanded the disciples to "hear Him," with reference to Jesus.[8]

The three disciples must have been stunned, because they told no one of the event, apparently as long as Christ was still with them (v. 36). John may be referring to this event when he comments in his Gospel, "And the Word became flesh, and dwelt among us, and we beheld His glory, glory as of the only begotten from the Father, full of grace and truth" (John 1:14). Peter certainly writes about it when he says, "We were eyewitnesses of His majesty. For when He received honor and glory from God the Father, such an utterance as this was made to Him by the Majestic Glory, 'This is My beloved Son with whom I am well-pleased'—and we ourselves heard this utterance made from heaven when we were with Him on the holy mountain" (2 Pet. 1:16b–18).

The Young Man Seized by a Spirit (9:37–45)

"When [the disciples] had come down from the mountain, a great multitude met Him" (9:37). On the very next day, after coming down from the mountain, Jesus and the disciples encountered another demonic spirit seizing a young man and throwing him into convulsions (vv. 38–39). The youth could get no relief from the demon's torments. The father begged Jesus to cast out the spirit because His disciples earlier could not (v. 40). Jesus said, "O unbelieving and

perverted generation, how long shall I be with you, and put up with you?" (v. 41). Lenski believes Jesus was talking to His disciples specifically and to the nation in general. The disciples were a product of their times and of their day. They continually showed how little they comprehended. The father of the boy was not guilty of disbelief. He believed Christ could heal His son. This account may reveal that the disciples were only partly successful in their earlier ministry journey (vv. 1–6).

Jesus "healed the boy, and gave him back to his father" (v. 42). While everyone was amazed and marveled (vv. 43–44), Jesus, using this exorcism, turned to His disciples and reminded them, "the Son of Man is going to be delivered into the hands of men" (v. 44b). In other words, "Do not think this will continue to go on. It will not!" But as was so common, they did not understand what He was talking about because the statement "was concealed from them so that they might not perceive it" (v. 45a). In a mysterious way, God's providence works together with the natural stubbornness and blindness of men. The time was not right for these followers to fully get it!

The Disciples Argue over Position (9:46–50)

"An argument arose among [the disciples] as to which of them might be the greatest" (9:46). With all the great things happening around them, the disciples show their true spiritual colors when they begin arguing "among them[selves] as to which of them might be the greatest" in the coming kingdom of heaven (v. 46; Matt. 18:1).

> In very different frames of mind did Jesus and the twelve apostles return from the Mount of Transfiguration to Capernaum. His thoughts were fixed upon the cross, theirs upon places of honour in the kingdom which they believed He was about to establish on earth. This difference came out in their respective utterances. Jesus spoke for the second time about His coming sufferings, while the disciples disputed among themselves which of them should be the greatest.[9]

Knowing of their inner selfishness, Jesus picked up a child and said to them, "Whoever receives this child in My name receives Me; and whoever receives Me receives Him who sent Me; for he who is least among you, this is the one who is great" (Luke 9:47–48). John, who later would become one of the most prominent of the apostles, answered, "Master, we saw someone casting out demons in Your name; and we tried to hinder him because he does not follow along with us" (v. 49). Jesus replied that they were not to hinder him, "for he who is not against you is for you" (v. 50). Competition, status, and position seem to be on John's mind. In other words, "We are the only ones who have the right to do good or perform signs!" With His response, and in so many words, the Lord leveled everyone by His answer. "Do not be so high and mighty! Everyone doing good is with us!" It was easy for these men to think that they were the only ones serving Christ. Too often their spirituality revolved only around themselves. Jesus reminded them that He had many other servants, even some whom these disciples did not know.

Study Questions

1. It was highly unusual for a Roman centurion to build a Jewish synagogue. Would such an act get the centurion in trouble with his commanders in Rome?

2. John the Baptist had been filled with the Holy Spirit from the womb. He knew Jesus and baptized Jesus, yet 7:18–22 tells us of a delegation sent by John to Jesus to inquire if He indeed was "the Expected One." Was John really in doubt of Jesus as Messiah?

3. What did Jesus mean in 7:28 when He said, "Among those born of women, there is no one greater than John; yet he who is least in the kingdom of God is greater than he"?

4. What does 8:1 mean when it says that Jesus went about "proclaiming and preaching the kingdom of God"?

5. What is significant about the fact that the Gerasenes had a herd of swine?

6. Why, after Jesus' great miracle of healing, were the Gerasenes "gripped with great fear," and why did they ask Jesus to leave?

7. Luke 9:18–21 has its parallel in Matthew 16:13–20, but Luke leaves out a whole section concerning Peter that we find in Matthew (vv. 17–19). Why did Luke leave this section out of his gospel?

SECTION IV

Beginning of the Rejection of the Son of Man

Luke 9:51 – 19:27

Through most of this section the rejection of Jesus as the Messiah grows stronger. As the nation, and even those who are outside of the nation, such as the Samaritans, turn away from His person and message, the Lord begins with more fervor to train the disciples. This is the longest and most detailed division in Luke, and it comes all the way down to His final week in Jerusalem. Christ's teaching about the promised messianic kingdom is prominent. But behind this teaching is the growing rejection by the nation as a whole.

CHAPTER 15

Samaritans Reject the Son of Man
Luke 9:51–62

Preview:

Jesus decided to go to Jerusalem in a most un-Jewish manner—He would go south, through Samaria. The Samaritans, however, did not welcome Him, so He continued traveling. During the journey, Jesus had to correct an improper view held by some of His disciples and explain true discipleship to some who would follow Him.

"He resolutely set His face to go to Jerusalem" *(9:51)*. The Samaritans did not receive Jesus (vv. 51–56). This section begins with Jesus setting "His face to go to Jerusalem" because the days of His crucifixion and ascension were approaching (v. 51). He and His disciples would be passing through a Samaritan village on the journey and planned to stay there (vv. 52–53), but the Samaritans rejected Jesus. Still, in the providence of God, coming to this town was not an accident. Because the people did not receive Jesus or appear to want Him to stay with them, James and John said, "Lord, do You want us to command fire to come down from heaven and consume them?" (v. 54). Rebuking them, Jesus replied, "You do not know what kind of spirit you are of; for the Son of Man did not come to destroy men's lives, but to save them" (vv. 55–56). With that, they went on to another village.

The Samaritans were half Jewish and half Assyrian. When the Assyrians invaded the northern kingdom Israel (722 B.C.), they destroyed the nation, killed many, and took most of the people back to Assyria as slaves. However, they left some of their own in the land as farmers, who in time intermarried with the few remaining Jews. The Samaritans were seen as half-breeds and were rejected by those who were of purer Jewish stock. They acknowledged only the first five books of Moses, the Law, and repudiated the prophetic Old Testament books. Pious Jews did not travel through the Samaritan territory that lay to the north of Judah. The Lord had journeyed through their area over a year before, with the result that many believed on Him (John 4:1–42). But here in Luke 9:51–56, He passed through another village where the people apparently were not interested in what He had to say.

James and John must have had grand allusions that they now had authority like Elijah of old. When that great prophet encountered the religious paganism of the prophets of Baal, he set up an altar, drenched it with water, and then called upon the Lord. God heard him! "Then the fire of the LORD fell, and consumed the burnt offering and the wood and the stones and the dust, and licked up the water that was in the trench" (1 Kings 18:38). The Israelites called out, "The LORD, He is God; the LORD, He is God" (v. 39).

The half-hearted followers (vv. 57–62). On the road two men rushed up to Jesus and proclaimed their loyalty. The first man said, "I will follow You wherever You go" (v. 57). The man must have melted away into the crowd when Jesus responded, "The foxes have holes, and the birds of the air have nests, but the Son of Man has nowhere to lay His head" (v. 58). To another the Lord said, "Follow Me," but the man used the excuse, "Permit me first to go and bury my father" (v. 59). Knowing the man's true motives and the weakness of his resolve, Christ answered, "Allow the dead to bury their own dead; but as for you, go and proclaim everywhere the kingdom of God" (v. 60). Another man comes up and says, I will follow you, "but first permit me to say goodbye to those at home" (v. 61). Jesus answered, "No one, after putting his hand to the plow and looking back, is fit for the kingdom of God" (v. 62).

On the surface it seems that the Lord was not tolerant enough with what these men were saying. But it must be remembered that He knew the hearts and minds of everyone. He knew that they were but offering excuses to either forgo or delay following Him. Their direction was not focused on the fact that He was indeed the Messiah, the Son of Man! They liked His "religious" sermons, and they were fascinated with His healings, but they could not bring themselves to give their lives totally to His mission. Commitment is not cheap, and it requires the resolve of the total person. Spiritual priority entails sacrifice and may even lead to martyrdom and death.

When Jesus told the one man, "Allow the dead to bury their own dead" (v. 60), what did He mean? More than likely He was referring to those who were spiritually dead: "Let those who are not interested in spiritual things take care of the normal obligations of life! If you follow Me, you have a higher cause—to proclaim the kingdom of God everywhere!" Some commentators believe the man's father had not yet passed away and was only sick and waiting for death. While this cannot be proved, clearly Christ knew that his request was merely an excuse.

Study Questions

1. Who were the Samaritans? What made them different from the Jews?

2. Why did the Samaritans reject Jesus for heading to Jerusalem?

3. Earlier in chapter 9 Jesus gave his apostles great power. How had this power affected James and John?

4. What was Jesus attempting to teach the person who came up to Him in 9:57?

5. In 9:59, is the man's father already dead, or was he asking Jesus to wait until his father died before he followed Jesus?

6. What does 9:59–60 teach believers about their required commitment to Jesus?

7. What does 9:61–62 teach believers about following Jesus and the importance of His message?

CHAPTER 16

Sending Forth of the Seventy Disciples
Luke 10:1–24

Preview:

Jesus decided to expand His ministry by empowering seventy of His disciples to go before Him, into cities and towns, to announce the coming kingdom of God and cast out demons. The seventy returned to Him with a good report, for which Jesus gave a prayer of praise to His Father.

The Sending of the Seventy (10:1–16)

"The Lord appointed seventy others, and sent them two and two ahead of Him" (10:1). After His discussion with the three men who came to him on the road, it was time to send forth "everywhere" some from the larger circle of disciples, the "seventy others" (v. 1). He instructed them to go out two by two to each city (in the northern Galilee area) until He arrived, because "the harvest is plentiful, but the laborers are few; therefore beseech the Lord of the harvest to send out laborers into His harvest" (v. 2). God uses human instruments to reach the lost. These men were instructed to go and speak the truth to the spiritually blind who were like a field of grain ready to be harvested. The northern Galilee had already heard much that the Lord had said and had seen many of His miracles. These men would be following up on His previous visits and would present again the message of the kingdom of God. Jesus

would then come where they had been. These disciples were instructed like the twelve apostles when they were sent out (9:1–6): they were not to take purse or shoes (10:4). They would be like lambs in the midst of wolves (v. 3). They were to offer "Peace" to the house where they are taken in (v. 6), and they were to stay in one place and teach, just as if they were a laborer "worthy of his wages" (v. 7). Jesus told them to fellowship and "eat what is set before you" (v. 8), and "heal those in [the house] who are sick, and say to them, 'The kingdom of God has come near to you'" (v. 9).

If the kingdom of God is not the soon arrival of the Church, then what does Jesus mean when He says his followers are to say the kingdom "has come near"? When the Lord was among His people, He, as the King, was presenting to the nation of Israel the promised messianic reign of the Son of David. The Greek text actually reads, "The kingdom of God has been in the process of approaching, and that approaching has stopped! The kingdom has come up to this point!" "Has come near" in the Greek text is a perfect tense of *engizō*, which means something has been in the process of coming and has now ceased in that coming.

> Based on the grammar and context of a given passage, *engus* may simply mean that something is *coming near, approaching,* or *being brought near.* But does this guarantee that the referred-to event will take place immediately? If John the Baptist and Christ said the "kingdom of heaven *is at hand*" (Matthew 3:2; 4:17; 10:7), is it inherent in the verb that the kingdom will come right then? Could the kingdom be *near* or *certain* but not *actually arrive* because of some other factors? As well, could the verb tense simply be telling us that the kingdom *is certainly on its way?* Could it be that the Jewish rabbis understood that the kingdom would not be announced yet not arrive because the nation of Israel was unworthy—that it was not inaugurated because of the sins of the nation? Can it be shown by the writings of the church fathers that they understood this problem? The church fathers indicate that the kingdom was yet to arrive—perhaps in their day, or beyond.[1]

If the disciples were not received in a particular city, they were to shake the dust from their feet because the people had rejected the kingdom message (vv. 10–11). Jesus then pronounced a curse on and a woe to certain cities near the lake of Galilee—Chorazin and Bethsaida! These and other cities were those "in which most of His miracles were done" and yet they did not repent (Matt. 11:20). Chorazin sat on a high mountain ridge on the west of the lake. Its nightlights could be seen throughout the region. It is traditionally known as "a city set on a hill" that could not be hidden (Matt. 5:14). Bethsaida ("house of fish") was located on the northeast side of the lake and was the home of Andrew, Peter, and Philip (John 1:44; 12:21). It's people also refused to repent when the Lord ministered there. Many converts came from Capernaum; nevertheless, it exalted itself to heaven and would "be brought down to Hades!" (Luke 10:15). Using hyperbole, Jesus then added that if Tyre and Sidon would have seen what these Galilean cities had seen, they would have repented in sackcloth and ashes (v. 13). Christ may be referring to the fact that the coastal cities of Tyre and Sidon were told by Joel that their sons and daughters would be sold into the hands of the pagan Sabeans (Joel 3:8). This was fulfilled in 345 B.C., when Artaxerxes III invaded, and the same thing happened again when Alexander the Great punished the city in 332 B.C. But these pagan cities were not so blessed as to hear the words of Jesus.

The Lord added that in the judgment, the people of Sodom will receive more mercy than these Galilean cities (cf. Gen. 19). The Lord then adds, "It will be more tolerable in that day for Sodom," than for these cities (Luke 10:12). Through the ministry of Christ, and now through the preaching of the seventy disciples, the truth had been made known. And this truth focused on Jesus, Israel's promised King and Anointed One! The evidence was overwhelming, and the truth was repeated over and over. "The one who listens to you [Seventy] listens to Me, and the one who rejects you rejects Me; and he who rejects Me rejects the One who sent Me [i.e., My Father]" (v. 16).

Return of the Seventy (10:17–24)

"The seventy returned . . ., saying, 'Lord even the demons are subject to us in Your name'" (10:17). When the Seventy came back, they rejoiced saying, "Lord, even the demons are subject to us in Your name" (v. 17). Jesus responded by saying that He "was watching Satan fall from heaven like lightning" (v. 18). He was probably tying the fall of Satan, at some point in time past, to the "angels who did not keep their own domain, but abandoned their proper abode" (Jude 1:6). Some are now confined to darkness awaiting judgment, but others became the demons and evil spirits who are serving Satan. Many scholars believe these fallen beings are the "stars of God" and the "clouds" who rebelled with Lucifer when he plotted to "make [him]self like the Most High" (Isa. 14:13–14).

These seventy, along with the twelve disciples, were given authority over all the power of the enemy, and Jesus told them, "nothing shall injure you" (Luke 10:19). While it was miraculous that the spirits were subject to them, even greater, He reminded them, was that their names were recorded in heaven (v. 20). Such deep truths are hidden from "the wise and intelligent,"

He added. Then He rejoiced "in the Holy Spirit" that the "Father, Lord of heaven and earth," revealed them to babes (v. 21a). This is God's purpose, that His Son was doing what was well-pleasing in His sight (v. 21b). Jesus then revealed His special relationship as Son with God the Father. Only the Father truly knows the Son; and only the Son truly knows the Father (v. 22b). "All things have been handed over to Me by My Father" (v. 22a), He said. As well, it is the sovereign prerogative of the Son of God to reveal the Father to whom He wishes. These seventy were blessed because of what their eyes had witnessed (v. 23). They had seen and heard at firsthand what many prophets and kings had wished to know (v. 24).

Study Questions

1. Some Christians today quote Luke 10:2 when speaking of sharing the gospel with unbelievers. Is that what Jesus was talking about?

2. What did Jesus mean in 10:9 when He said, "The kingdom of God has come near to you"?

3. Why, in 10:11, after leaving a rebellious town, were the disciples, "to be sure," that they knew "the kingdom of God has come near"?

4. In 10:12, which specific "day" was Jesus referring to when He said, "in that day"?

5. We know from Genesis 19 of the terrible sin of Sodom. Why does Jesus say in Luke 10:12 that it will be more tolerable for Sodom in that day?

6. In 10:19 Jesus reflects on the powers He had given His disciples. Is there biblical evidence to show that these powers have been passed down to believers today?

7. Who are some of the prophets and kings that Jesus referred to in 10:24?

CHAPTER 17

The Lawyer's Question
Luke 10:25–42

Preview:

Jesus was confronted by a scholar of the Mosaic Law who challenged Him on how to gain eternal life. Jesus questioned him then answered his question down to the last detail through the parable of the good Samaritan. He then visited Martha and Mary (the sisters of Lazarus) and counseled Martha to reevaluate her priorities. Jesus explained that the most important thing in life is to listen to Him.

The Kind Samaritan (10:25–37)

"'Teacher, what shall I do to inherit eternal life?'" (10:26). A supposed theological authority came to put Jesus to a test (v. 25). The Jewish lawyer (Greek, *nomikos*, from the Greek word for "law"), was a scribe (Greek, *grammateus*), "the copier and keeper of the Old Testament manuscripts." Such a scholar was known in the Old Testament as a *sôpēr* (writer), such as Ezra (c. 450 B.C.), who was "a scribe skilled in the law of Moses which the . . . God of Israel had given" (Ezra 7:6). By the time of Christ, the scribes were seen as above the people. They were legalistic, or "religious," and considered themselves the only interpreters of the Law.

In his test, the lawyer asked the Lord, "Teacher, what shall I do to inherit eternal life?" To this man, and to the orthodox Jews, nothing Jesus said would be enough. They believed that law keeping was the way to God. They also saw

Christ as a rebel, one who was not doing enough that was "religious" to ful-fill the Mosaic code for salvation.

But being a master teacher, Jesus answered a question with questions: "What is written in the Law? How does it read to you?" (Luke 10:26). The scribe answers by citing the second greatest commandment: "You shall love the Lord your God with all your heart, and with all your soul, and with all your strength, and with all your mind; and your neighbor as yourself" (v. 27), taken from Deuteronomy 6:5 and Leviticus 19:18. Christ commended the man, saying, "You have answered correctly; do this, and you will live" (v. 28). Was the Lord simply saying that by so loving the Lord and the neighbor one could be saved? The Old Testament Law was meant to bring forth conviction in sinners. No one, however, could so love God, much less one's neighbor! Therefore, the one who was sincere about the Law would have to say, "Oh, God! I cannot keep it! Be merciful to me, a sinner, and save me!" But the reli-gious and legalistic Jews thought they were doing enough to keep the Law. In truth they were into pious mind games. They were actually evil in thought and deed, but they had the common people fooled by how they carried them-selves, as if they were holy!

In the lawyer's verbal encounter with Jesus, he was actually trying to jus-tify himself when he asked, "And who is my neighbor?" (v. 29). He probably reasoned that he completely loved God, but he sought to technically pinpoint who his neighbor would be. The Lord answered by citing the lengthy story of the man who was waylaid by robbers on the road from Jerusalem to Jericho and left stripped, beaten, and half dead (v. 30). A priest, probably just finish-ing his service at the temple in Jerusalem, saw the man but went so far as to pass by on the other side of the road (v. 31). A Levite came along and did the same thing (v. 32). Both men were of the priestly tribe of Levi. The priest more than likely had just finished his tour of temple duty. The other man, desig-nated as a Levite, more than likely was not active in his priestly work. Lenski, however, believes this man would be active in his priestly service, doing heavy work in the temple, rather than officiating at the sacrifices. Whichever, both men were supposed to be religious and compassionate, showing love to all the people of Israel.

Nevertheless, the priest showed how terribly unfeeling he was passing by on the opposite side of the road. This supposedly holy man of God should have acted differently, especially in light of the fact that he had probably just completed his sacred temple responsibilities and was on his way home to Jericho, where possibly many priests and Levites resided. This same priest of course was a Jew. He knew the law of kindness, yet he refused to render assis-tance to a fellow Jew. He turned away from his responsibilities, and instead of "rescuing the perishing" who needed his charity and care, crossed over to the opposite side of the road.

There is no excuse for such horrible neglect. It is impossible to absolve him by arguing that by coming into contact with a dead body he would incur ritual impurity, making it impossible for him to function in his priestly role. The reason is clear because, first of all, he was going away from the temple and would not have to return to the temple for some time. Furthermore, showing mercy to someone in need is a basic tenet of the Law of Moses (see Mic. 6:8). Leviticus 19:34 makes it clear that the Jews were required to show charity and grace to strangers and even to enemies (Ex. 23:4, 5; 2 Kings 6:8–23). Most certainly then they were to show the same care to fellow Israelites! Thus, there was no justification for the priest's sinful neglect. He simply did not want to "get involved."

The fate of the injured man changes dramatically with Jesus' introduction of the Samaritan. Who were the Samaritans? Did not the Israelites and the Samaritans have a longtime mutual hatred? Did not the enemies of Jesus who hated Him call him a Samaritan when they wished to insult Him (John 8:48)? And as well, was it not true that the Samaritans themselves returned hatred for hatred and insult for insult (Luke 9:53)? As soon as the Samaritan saw the sorely afflicted one, his heart went out to him (10:33). This compassion is a reminder of what Jesus Himself would do (Matt. 9:36); however, it would not be correct to say that the Samaritan represents or symbolizes Jesus, as some have tried to say. It is impossible to read this Bible story and not be made aware of the similar works of compassion and deeds of mercy other people have done.

Without doubt this story dramatically changes when Christ with some detail describes the Samaritan who saw the man and "felt compassion" (10:33). He attended the man's wounds and placed him on his own animal "And brought him to an inn, and took care of him" (v. 34). The Samaritans were half-breeds, part Jewish and part Assyrian. They lived to themselves just north of Jerusalem, and they were considered outcasts and "dogs" by the pious Jews. Yet here this Samaritan had compassion and sympathy for this nearly dead Jew! The Samaritan saw the wounded man as a "neighbor," someone who had been planted near him in a helpless state. The man left the money for two days of care (two denarii) and instructed the innkeeper to watch over him, and "whatever more you spend, when I return, I will repay you" (v. 35).

Jesus asked the lawyer, "Which of these three do you think proved to be a neighbor to the man who fell into the robbers' hands?" (v. 36). The lawyer got it right: "'The one who showed mercy toward him.' And Jesus said to him, 'Go and do the same'" (v. 37). The answer the lawyer had to admit to probably was a sting to him and to all who were standing around hearing this conversation. This was not the normal way Jews behaved toward other people. And too, they had narrowed their view of who the neighbor was. They had thus often escaped responsibility for caring for many other people when they had the opportunity.

Reception of Mary and Martha (10:38–42)

"He entered a certain village; and a woman named Martha welcomed Him" *(10:38).* The hosting of Jesus at the home of Mary and Martha in Bethany is not recorded in the other Gospels, but to Luke it is an important story. These two sisters would be key players in the story of the raising of their brother Lazarus (John 11:1–44). Their faith and trust in the work of Christ would become a lasting testimony of confidence in God. It was Martha who said near the gravesite, I know my brother "will rise again in the resurrection on the last day" (v. 24). Here in Luke's gospel we find a study in personalities and in how people grow spiritually. Mary could not get enough of Jesus' teaching. She spent her time "listening to the Lord's word, seated at His feet" (Luke 10:39). Martha was distracted with the physical preparation of the meal. She became angry and said, "Lord, do You not care that my sister has left me to do all the serving alone? Then tell her to help me" (v. 40). Jesus gently responded, "Martha, Martha, you are worried and bothered about so many things" (v. 41), but "Mary has chosen the good part, which shall not be taken away from her" (v. 42). From this we learn:

> That the cares of this life are dangerous, even when they seem to be most lawful and commendable. Nothing of a worldly nature could have been more proper than to provide for the Lord Jesus and supply his wants. Yet even *for this*, because it too much engrossed her mind, the Lord Jesus gently reproved Martha. So a care for our families may be the means of our neglecting religion and losing our souls. 2d. It is of more importance to attend to the instructions of the Lord Jesus than to be engaged in the affairs of the world.[1]

The Lord saw the immaturity and limitation of Martha, but He focused on the spiritual thirst that kept Mary listening at His feet.

Study Questions

1. The lawyer in 10:25 is what we know as a "scribe." How did the scribes relate to the Pharisees and Sadducees?

2. Why do you think Jesus placed His parable on the road between Jerusalem and Jericho?

3. The parable of the good Samaritan has both its literal meaning and a symbolic meaning relating directly to Jesus. In this symbolic meaning, who was the "priest" in 10:31 meant to represent?

4. Who was the "Levite" in 10:32 meant to represent?

5. Who was the "Samaritan" in 10:33 meant to represent?

6. After reading the parable of the good Samaritan, who would you say is your neighbor? More important, are you living in accord with your answer?

7. What does the story of Martha and Mary say about being a hard worker?

CHAPTER 18

Teaching on Prayer
Luke 11:1–13

Preview:
In reply to a request from His disciples, Jesus gave them the elements that should be included in every prayer to the Father. He then explained the need for constant prayer and the love of His Father to answer prayer in His children's best interests.

Question about Prayer (11:1)

"One of His disciples said to Him, 'Lord, teach us to pray just as John also taught his disciples'" (11:1). Commonly called The Lord's Prayer, this is Jesus' response to his disciples' request that He teach them to pray, "as John also taught his disciples" (v. 1). This may show two things about the disciples: (1) they did not know how to pray to their heavenly Father, and (2) they show a tinge of competition with John's disciples. Apparently they were operating in the flesh, looking at religious expression rather than the issues of what makes honest spiritual substance.

Luke reports on only a few of the parts of this pattern for prayer. Jesus said, when you pray, say:

> Father, hallowed be Thy name.
> Thy kingdom come.
> Give us each day our daily bread.
> And forgive us our sins,
> For we ourselves also forgive everyone who is indebted to us.
> And lead us not into temptation. (vv. 4–5)

Matthew records the final words of the prayer: "And do not lead us into temptation, but deliver us from evil. For Thine is the kingdom and the power, and the glory, forever. Amen." (Matt. 6:13).

What to Pray (11:2–13)

"'Father, hallowed be Thy name . . .'" *(11:2)*. The prayer begins by acknowledging the holiness of God. His name is to be sanctified! He is to be approached with reverence. That His promised kingdom should come to earth ought to be on the minds of all who love Him: "Thy kingdom come." This is followed by a humbling thought: we do not feed ourselves; God supplies our daily rations. "Give us" is a Greek present imperative of *didōmi*. "Daily and continually be giving us" what we need for survival. This is really more of a statement of recognition in that God provides our food whether we ask or not. However, we should not fall into presumption. We do not eat unless He supplies! To "forgive" us our sins is an aorist imperative of *aphiēmi* that means "to release, dismiss." This may have the force of, "Right now, please dismiss our sins," or "Take them off of our record!" Christ adds, "You should also do likewise to those who are indebted to you!" "What you need on the divine plane, others need also on the human level!"

The Lord adds, "And lead us not into temptation" (Luke 11:4b). A. T. Robertson comments: "'Bring us not' is a better translation than 'lead us not.' There is no such thing as God enticing one to sin (James 1:13). Jesus urges us to pray not to be tempted as in Luke 22:40 in Gethsemane."[1] Technically, "lead us not" is in Greek what is called a prohibitive, ingressive aorist subjunctive that should be translated, "'You should not bring us' into temptation." This is not to say that God would lead any of His children into spiritual and moral harm's way, but the passage acts as a heart appeal for the Lord to keep those who belong to Him safe, to steer them away from wrong!

Jesus then reinforced the power of prayer by telling the story of a man who went to his friend at midnight asking for the loan of three loaves of bread to feed an acquaintance who had come in from a trip (Luke 11:5). The man inside his house shouted out for his neighbor to go away because his children were asleep, yet he gave what his persistent friend needed because he was being bothered (v. 8). Christ concluded, "Everyone who asks, receives; and he who seeks, finds; and to him who knocks, it shall be opened" (v. 10).

Asking implies humility and a consciousness of need. The verb is used with respect to a petition which is addressed by an inferior to a superior. The Pharisee of the parable (Luke 18:10–13) asks nothing. He *tells* the Lord how good he is. The publican *asks*, that is, *pleads*, "God be merciful to me, the sinner." . . . Seeking is *asking plus acting.* It *implies* earnest petitioning, but that alone is not sufficient. A person must be active in endeavoring to obtain the fulfillment of his needs. For example, one should not only *pray* for a deep knowledge of the Bible but should also diligently *search* and *examine* the Scriptures (John 5:39; Acts 17:11). . . . Knocking is *asking plus acting plus persevering.* One knock again and again until the door is opened. In reality, however, perseverance is probably already implied in all three imperatives, since all are in the present tense; hence, a possible rendering would be "continue to ask, to seek, to knock."[2]

To further get the point across, Jesus told a story of the boy who was hungry and asked his father for a fish or an egg to eat (vv. 11–12). Would he be so cruel as to give his son a snake or a scorpion? Of course not! Christ concluded: "If you then, being evil, know how to give good gifts to your children, how much more shall your heavenly Father give the Holy Spirit to those who ask Him?" (v. 13). What do believers need more than daily food and bread? They need the inner comfort and guidance of the Spirit, though the Holy Spirit had not yet come. While Christ was here, "the Spirit was not yet given, because Jesus was not yet glorified" (John 7:39). But after He departed, the Helper would come, whom Jesus would send from the Father (15:26). Though the doctrine of the Holy Spirit had not been fully developed, these verses make it clear that He was a *person,* that He is a separate personality from the Father and the Son, and that He was omnipresent and would someday abide within the spirit of the child of God. This *coming* of God's Spirit would be fulfilled at Pentecost (Acts 1:5–8; 2:4).

Study Questions

1. The disciple who asked Jesus how to pray is not named. Is he more likely one of the apostles or one of the Seventy? Why?

2. According to Matthew, Jesus taught this prayer in His Sermon on the Mount. Why does Luke give only part of the prayer?

3. Does this prayer teach an imminent return of the Lord Jesus?

4. How does Jesus' instruction, to ask the Father to "forgive us our sins" relate to the Jewish system of atonement through sacrifice?

5. How would the Jews have received such instruction?

6. In Jesus' illustration, 11:5–8, the person being asked is a friend, and the time is night (the worst time to make a request of this type). Compare this request to one being made of God through prayer.

7. What does 11:5–10 teach you about your prayer life?

CHAPTER 19

Growing Rejection by the Jews
Luke 11:14–54

Preview:
The Pharisees stepped up their attack against Jesus and His miraculous powers by saying that He was in league with Satan. Jesus responded in kind, demolishing their arguments as unsound, and He branded them as wicked for demanding signs when they wouldn't believe the miracles He performed every day. He continued, showing the Pharisees for the hypocritical murderers they were.

The Wicked Generation (11:14–36)

"He was casting out a demon, . . . and the multitudes marveled" (11:14). The drama moved forward! When the Lord continued to work His miracles by casting out a demon who had prevented a man from speaking (v. 14), some seeing such a great sign found a pretext to accuse Him of working by the power of "Beelzebul, the ruler of the demons" (v. 15). Others claimed His great works were not from God, and they demanded that He give "a sign from heaven" (v. 16). With seemingly great patience, the Lord gave a long discourse about spiritual good and evil. He first pointed out that a divided kingdom will be laid waste and a divided house will fall (v. 17). Right and wrong, good and evil cannot coexist! Therefore, He said, "If Satan also is divided against himself, how shall his kingdom stand?" (v. 18). Jesus was referring to their use of the word *Beelzebul*. The derivation of this term is still not clear since it is not used in any ancient Jewish writings. The word could mean "Lord of the dwelling." It was thought to be a Philistine name of the god Baal. Jews then picked it up and

147

applied it to Satan. Some scholars believe it is the corruption of *Beelzebub,* meaning "Baal of the flies" or "Baal of the dung." The Pharisees and scribes (Mark 3:22) used this against Jesus as a great slanderous pronouncement.

Jesus reasoned with the Jews: "If I by Beelzebul cast out demons, by whom do your sons cast them out?" (v. 19). He was pointing out their conflicting reasoning, for some of the Jews claimed they could do the same thing. If so, they too must have been doing such a work with the aid of Satan. The Jews apparently could not answer! He then added, "But if I cast out demons by the finger of God, then the kingdom of God has come upon you" (v. 20). Using this argument, He told the Jews that He must be the stronger one because, by His healings, He was spoiling and plundering Satan as one who was valiant over an aggressor (vv. 21–22). Verse 23 seems to be referring to the Jews, the nation of Israel, who are witnesses of His great messianic works: "He who is not with Me is against Me; and he who does not gather with Me, scatters," or brings about destruction upon the people. The Jews by their criticism were negating the blessings He was bringing to the nation.

Matthew records more about this debate. Jesus further said, "Therefore I say to you, any sin and blasphemy shall be forgiven men, but blasphemy against the Spirit shall not be forgiven" (Matt. 12:31). He adds that people may speak against the Son of Man, but whoever "shall speak against the Holy Spirit, it shall not be forgiven him, either in this age, or the age to come" (v. 32).

Can people today, by saying anything against the work of the Holy Spirit, remain eternally unforgiven? Some think so. But the context of this story is important. The Jews were seeing the Lord before their very eyes heal and cast out demons. They were ascribing these clear and objective happenings to the work of Satan rather than to the Holy Spirit, who was working through Christ. Thus, those who saw what was happening and refused to give the Spirit and the Father the glory would be blinded and rejected in a permanent way. This could not happen today, because it had to do with the open work of Jesus and the Spirit of God using Him before the entire nation of the Jews. The apostle Paul recognized that the Jews had rejected all the evidence and had turned against the plain truth. In Acts 28:27 he quoted to the Roman Jewish elders the words of Isaiah 6:10:

> For the heart of this people has become dull,
> And with their ears they scarcely hear,
> And they have closed their eyes,
> Lest they should see with their eyes,
> And hear with their ears,
> And understand with their heart and return,
> And I should heal them.

Luke then records that Christ told another story about the power of an unclean spirit. Being driven out of a man, it desired to go back to this same man and his house (Luke 11:24). Because the man has recovered, he is able to clean his dwelling. The demon "finds it swept and put in order" (v. 25). But the demonic attack continues and the spirit brings back to this man and his house seven more spirits who live there. "The last state of that man becomes worse than the first" (v. 26). In other words, if the Lord was casting out demons and performing miracles and the nation rejected all of this witness, its spiritual and moral state would be disastrous and far more tenuous! In the middle of Jesus' teaching, a woman shouted out, "Blessed is the womb that bore You, and the breasts at which You nursed" (v. 27). The woman was obviously moved by how clear He was explaining things, but she wanted to glorify Jesus' mother Mary and give her credit for His great wisdom. The Lord said, "On the contrary, blessed are those who hear the word of God, and observe it" (v. 28). Humans love symbols, and they love to set up "monuments," in this case, an enthusiastic and emotional praise to the Lord's physical mother. But Christ sidestepped the issue.

Jesus used this emotional interruption of the woman to add, "This generation is a wicked generation; it seeks for a sign, and yet no sign shall be given to it but the sign of Jonah" (v. 29) because Jonah turned out to be a human object of judgment against the nation of the Ninevites (v. 30).

Concerning such a sign, what the people wanted was something profound, awesome, sensational, and certainly a sign *from heaven*. Were they wanting Christ to make the heavenly constellations change places in the zodiac? Were they looking for Him to make the Bull (Taurus) catch up with the Giant Hunter (Orion)? Were they desiring some cosmological event to take place before their very eyes? Maybe they wanted letters of gold to appear emblazoned across the heavens. Their demands were clearly evil, for they felt sure that what they had asked the Lord to do he could not do anyway.

Jesus does not cater to their sinful motives. He starts out by calling these sign seekers "wicked." Matthew adds "adulterous"—unfaithful to Jehovah, Israel's "Husband." (see Isa. 54:5; Jer. 3:8, 20, 21; 31:32; Ezek. 16:35–52; Hos. 2:1; 2 Cor. 11:2).

To say that these men were wicked or evil is not strong enough, because it must be remembered that this request for a sign was made (1) at the very moment when a multiple sign had just been performed; (2) in spite of the fact that all kinds of signs—miracles of healing, demon expulsions, even the raising of the dead—had already occurred; and finally (3) despite Jesus' marvelous discourses—in clear fulfillment of prophecy! It is not surprising then that the Lord Jesus refused to give evil men, the Pharisees and scribes along with their followers, the signs and wonders for which they are asking.

In due time Christ and His Father would give them the correct sign, the sign in which the Lord would be completely victorious over them and over all sin, to their final dismay. The sign of Jonah the prophet was his surviving "three days and three nights" in the stomach of a sea monster. His point is that as Jonah was swallowed up by the sea monster, so Jesus would be swallowed up by the earth. Jonah is a type of the Lord Jesus, for as Jonah in a sense "came back from the dead," Christ was to be raised from the dead, showing His victory over sin and death.

Christ continued by saying that even the pagan Queen of the South, the queen of Sheba journeyed from "the ends of the earth" to hear the wisdom of King Solomon (1 Kings 10:1–13), yet "something greater than Jonah is here" (Luke 11:31). Further, even the men of Nineveh who heard the preaching of Jonah and repented, would someday "stand up with this generation at the judgment and condemn it" (v. 32). Jesus was making the point that even the Gentiles in other lands sought godly wisdom and could be convicted of their sins. But the Jews remained stubborn even when they had the King in their midst and the pronouncement of the kingdom of God!

Winding down His message, the Lord reminded the people that one does not put a light away in a cellar, but instead places it on a lampstand "in order that those who enter may see the light" (v. 33). The lamp of your body is your eye; when the eye is clear, your whole body is full of light (v. 34). "Then," he concluded, "watch out that the light in you may not be darkness. If therefore your whole body is full of light, with no dark part in it, it shall be wholly illumined, as when the lamp illumines you with its rays" (vv. 35–36). Jesus was telling the Jews that if they could see spiritually what He was saying, it would give light to their entire being. But they had become spiritually blind and their whole persons were stumbling about in darkness. They could no longer see clearly.

Rejection by Israel's Leaders (11:37–54)

"A Pharisee asked Him to have lunch with him" (11:37). When the Lord had finished, a Pharisee invited him to eat. While reclining at the table, the man registered surprise that Christ had not "first ceremonially washed before the meal" (v. 38). Though He was a guest, Jesus responded, knowing the evilness of this man and other Pharisees and lawyers who were there. He said, "Now you Pharisees clean the outside of the cup and of the platter; but inside of you, you are full of robbery and wickedness" (v. 39). He followed this up with six woes against those in the room.

1. *Woe* to those who are faithful to give a tenth (a tithe) from the food condiments of mint and rue they raise in their gardens "yet disregard justice and the love of God." They should have tithed on these herbs, but they should not have gone about "neglecting others" (v. 42). The Pharisees were quick to follow the Law but were remiss in caring for people and in worshiping the Lord from their hearts.

2. *Woe* to the Pharisees who love to show piety in the synagogue by sitting on the front seats and crave "respectful greetings in the market place" (v. 43). They love to be seen, honored, and considered religious. Matthew says that Jesus also said, "They tie up heavy loads, and lay them on men's shoulders; . . . they do all their deeds to be noticed" (Matt. 23:4–5).

3. *Woe* to the Pharisees who are like concealed tombs, "and the people who walk over them are unaware of it" (v. 44). The Jews were instructed to avoid the dead. But the people who came in touch with the Pharisees did not know that they were being spiritually defiled. The Pharisees contaminated everyone who came in contact with them. Pharisees and their false holiness were like rotted dead bodies. The whole nation was rendered unclean by the pretended piety and distorted religion of this party. As Jesus was speaking, one of the lawyers said to Him, "Teacher, when You say this, You insult us too" (v. 45). The scribes were equally guilty. This man was only admitting what they all should have recognized. Interestingly, the lawyer calls Jesus a "teacher" (Greek, *didaskalos*), one recognized as knowledgeable in the Law and who communicates wisdom with sharp and clear words. In Greek "insult" is *hubrizō*, meaning "to mistreat, abuse, insult, injure." Jesus was not reluctant to use sharp words to bring about a wounding and then a spiritual conviction.

4. *Woe* to the lawyer as well, the Lord warned. With stinging words, Christ now addressed the temple theologians who "weigh men down with burdens hard to bear, while you yourselves will not even touch the burdens with one of your fingers" (v. 46). As Jesus continued to expose the external religiosity of these men and their crass legalism that violated the intention of the Mosaic code, He used hyperbole to draw a picture of them not even lifting a finger to aid others in their spiritual quest. Instead, these spiritual leaders kept others feeling helpless and bound by the rigors they placed on them.

5. *Woe* to the scribes and Pharisees for giving honor to the prophets by building memorial tombs when "it was your fathers who killed them" (v. 47). Jesus could have in mind the broad and general statement of Nehemiah that recounts how the people of Israel rebelled against God: "[They] cast Thy Law behind their backs and killed Thy

prophets who had admonished them so that they might return to Thee" (Neh. 9:26). Nehemiah added that the Lord actually admonished "them by Thy Spirit through Thy prophets, yet they would not give ear" (v. 30). The generation Jesus was addressing was so guilty of arrogance and sin that in God's wisdom, it is as if He should send to them prophets and apostles that "the blood of all the prophets, shed since the foundation of the world, may be charged against" them (Luke 11:50-51). Adding fuel to the fire of condemnation, He mentioned the shedding of the innocent blood of Abel (Gen. 4:1-15) and the killing by King Joash of the priest and prophet Zechariah, who told the people they had forsaken the Lord (2 Chron. 24:20). As the people stoned him by order of the king, he died crying out, "May the LORD see and avenge!" (v. 22). Again, Christ was probably referring to this event to heap on their heads a mountain of deserved guilt.

6. *Woe* to the lawyers who take away the key to knowledge: "You did not enter in yourselves, and those who were entering in you hindered" (Luke 11:52). The scribes kept from the masses the true intention of the Mosaic Law. The people were kept from understanding what the Law was all about. They also were uninformed about the grace and mercy found in forgiveness. The sacrificial offerings became perfunctory, and the great spiritual lessons inscribed in the sacrifices were covered over and buried. The lawyers themselves were blinded to what the Law was all about. They became the blind leading the blind (6:39).

When the Lord finished speaking, the scribes and Pharisees "began to be very hostile and to question Him closely on many subjects, plotting against Him, to catch Him in something He might say" (vv. 53-54). With the words and the sayings of the Lord Jesus, the religious balance of the nation was turned upside down. Everything that was presupposed about how to come to God, Jesus challenged and contradicted. The leadership was furious, and the people as a whole were mixed in their responses to what He was saying.

Study Questions

1. Satan is referred to in some of these verses as Beelzebul. What is the origin of this name and what does it mean?

2. In 11:19 Jesus queries the Pharisees about the fact that "their sons" cast out demons. Did Jesus mean the literal "sons" of the Pharisees? If not, to whom was He referring?

3. List all of the ways in which Jonah was a type of Christ.

4. Was the ceremonial washing before a meal, spoken of in 11:38, a part of the Law or an addition made by the Pharisees?

5. Why in 11:44 were Jews to be aware of walking over concealed tombs?

6. List some other Old Testament prophets who were killed by Israel and the way they died.

7. Is the prophet, Zechariah, spoken of in 11:51, the same person as the minor prophet named Zechariah?

CHAPTER 20

Great Teaching Ministry of the Son of Man
Luke 12:1–19:27

Preview:

Jesus finished His indictment of the Pharisees and warned His disciples not to follow their example. He then began teaching His disciples not to covet but to depend on their heavenly Father. He continued with a long period of teaching that included readiness for His second coming, repentance, the kingdom of God, true discipleship, and prayer. And all during this time He kept healing those who came to Him. He finished by explaining the difficulty rich persons have giving up their trust in material possessions and trusting in God for salvation but showed, with Zaccheus as an example, that it is not impossible.

The Issue of Hypocrisy (12:1–12)

"Beware of the leaven of the Pharisees, which is hypocrisy" (12:1). Jesus warned the crowds to beware "of the leaven of the Pharisees, which is hypocrisy" (v. 1). Leaven is a germ, the yeast that spreads throughout the dough and makes it rise, ready for baking. It generally is used as an illustration of sin that permeates and ruins all that it touches. What the Pharisees do in the dark (vv. 2–3) will be exposed in the light, and what is whispered in the inner room "shall be proclaimed upon the housetops" (v. 3). Do not fear the Pharisees, but fear the One who "has authority to cast into hell; yes, I tell you, fear Him!" (v. 5).

The word meaning "hell" is *Gehenna. Gehenna* comes from *Ge-Hinnom,* that is, the land of Hinnom, a valley belonging originally to Hinnom and later to his sons (2 Kings 23:10). This valley can still be found just south of Jersualem as the city curves to the west. There is good evidence that in earlier times this was a beautiful valley. However, in time the valley changed. It was in this valley that a high place was built, and it was over time called Topheth (Jer. 7:31–33), meaning, according to some, "place of spitting out" or "abhorrence"; according to others, "place of burning." No matter what meaning, both definitions would fit very well. Many feel that there is proof that on the top of this high place there was a deep hole in which much wood was piled. When the wood was started with a firebrand, it flamed up by a stream of brimstone (see Isa. 30:33). The evil and ungodly kings Ahaz and Manasseh are actually said to have made their children pass through the flames as offerings to the satanic idol Moloch (2 Chron. 28:3; 33:6; cf. Lev. 18:21; 1 Kings 11:7). Others followed the diabolical practices of these heartless monarchs (Jer. 32:35).

Jeremiah made a prediction that the judgment of God Almighty would strike Topheth and that God would visit the terrible wickedness that occurred in Ge-Hinnom. The human carnage was so terrible here with such violent evil, that the valley became known as "the valley of Slaughter" (Jer. 7 :31–34; 19:6; 32:35). The righteous God-fearing king Josiah set about to destroy this idolatrous high place and stopped its abominations (2 Kings 23:10). From that point forward the refuse from the city of Jerusalem's was burned with fire in this place. It is said that the smoke from the burning could be seen by travelers approaching the valley and the city of Jerusalem.

Some think the Lord was referring to the power of Satan to judge men, but that is not what He was talking about. God is the one to whom people must answer. God is sovereign, and He does not forget the smallest sparrow (v. 6). In fact, the very hairs of one's head are numbered by Him. Therefore, "Do not fear; you are of more value than many sparrows" (v. 7).

Christ then added, "And I say to you, everyone who confesses Me before men, the Son of Man shall confess him also before the angels of God; but he who denies Me before men shall be denied before the angels of God (vv. 8–9). It is clear, therefore, that even though Jesus had uttered a similar saying previously (Matt. 10:32–33), he may very well have repeated it here in somewhat altered form. It should be noted that in the Matthew parallel passage, Matthew uses "I": "I will confess." Luke's statement, where the expression "Son of Man" is used, proves that this term is Lord's self-designation. Matthew further reports that Jesus said, "before My Father who is in heaven." Luke reports the Lord saying, "before the angels of God."

Obviously, where the heavenly Father is, there the holy angels are also (see Dan. 7:10; Matt. 16:27; 25:31).

Jesus made a promise that He would acknowledge before the angels of God those who confess Him. This word "confess" or "acknowledge" shows that the message to be brought by the disciples must not be coldly objective, a mere recitation of memorized words. The minds and hearts of these men must be in their message. The preaching of the disciples must be a personal testimony that those hearing give heed to (Ps. 66:16). The Lord then promised that He personally will acknowledge those true witnesses to be His own. He will confess them before His Father and before the angels (Matt. 25:34–36, 40)!

The context of what is happening here is very important. For the most part, the messianic kingdom is in view. The question, especially in Matthew 25, is about the Messiah when He returns to earth to reign. Will God's own people, the Jews, and the Gentiles who expect Jesus' return at the end of the terrible tribulation, be ready for His triumphal arrival to reign on David's throne in Jerusalem? This context must not be forgotten.

Meanwhile, the Lord Jesus while on earth had presented Himself to His own people as the promised King of Israel. Would they at this time accept His works? Would they say His miracles and healings were signs of the Spirit of God working through the King who was in their presence, or would they ascribe these works to Satan? Jesus addressed this issue when He said that a word against the Son of Man would be forgiven, but "he who blasphemes against the Holy Spirit, it shall not be forgiven him" (Luke 12:10). To say that Satan inspired the work of the Messiah would be the ultimate blasphemy.

Finally, after the Lord Jesus had ascended back to His Father, the disciples would find themselves brought before authorities and accused of being His disciples (v. 11), but they need not be anxious about defending themselves, "for the Holy Spirit will teach you in that very hour what you ought to say" (v. 12).

The Problem of Materialism (12:13–34)

"'Teacher, tell my brother to divide the family inheritance with me'" (12:13). The Lord reminded the crowd to avoid every form of greed because life does not consist of possessions (v. 15). He then told the parable about the man who was so wealthy that he needed to tear down his existing storehouses and build bigger barns for his grain (v. 18). To himself the man said, "Soul, you have many goods laid up for many years to come; take your ease, eat, drink and be merry" (v. 19).

The Human Soul

*Soul defines human life: "The first man Adam was made a living soul"
(1 Cor. 15:45).*

*The soul is the seat of human responsibility: "The soul who sins will die"
(Ezek. 18:4).*

It is the soul that finds spiritual rest (Matt. 11:29).

God must be loved with all the heart, soul, and mind (Deut. 6:5; Matt. 22:37).

*The inner conversations within a human being are conscious communications
within the soul (Luke 12:19).*

Both the soul and the body are "required" when one dies (Luke 12:20).

The soul must give an accounting (2 Cor. 1:23).

*Believers are to do the will of God from the heart (**soul**) (Eph. 6:6).*

*At the resurrection of Jesus, both His body and His soul are said to have
come forth from the place of the dead (Acts 2:27, 31).*

Salvation is accomplished for the soul (1 Pet. 1:9).

*Before the saints receive a resurrected body, they are said to be conscious souls
in heaven (Rev. 6:9; 20:4).*

*While humans are multifaceted in the inner being (including heart, mind, and
conscience), Paul refers especially to spirit, soul, and body (1 Thess. 5:23).*

But God answered, "This very night your soul is required of you" (v. 20). It is possible to be rich toward oneself but not rich toward God (v. 21). One must avoid anxiousness for the physical things of life (v. 22) because life "is more than food, and the body than clothing" (v. 23).

The disciples who were poor men might think that they were in no danger of the folly branded in the foregoing parable. They had no barns bursting with plenty, and their concern was how to find food and clothing, not what to do with superfluities. Christ would have them see that the same temper may be in them, though it takes a different shape.[1]

Jesus told his listeners to consider the ravens, for they neither sow nor reap, because God feeds them (v. 24). The lilies do not have to toil for their beauty nor their clothing. In fact, "Solomon in all his glory did not clothe himself like one of these" (v. 27). If God so arrays the grass, and it is gone tomorrow, "how much more will He clothe you, O men of little faith!" (v. 28).

> This verse may also be applied as an assurance of a glorious resurrection. If in each successive spring, after the winter's frost and death, God clothes the flowers of the field with the apparel of such fresh verdure and beautiful colours, will He not much more clothe you with the bright raiment of a glorious body, like to that of the angels (chap. xx. 36), and of Christ (Phil. iii. 21)?[2]

Do not pursue food or drink (v. 29), "for all these things the nations of the world eagerly seek; but your Father knows that you need these things" (v. 30). Jesus then concluded by telling his listeners to: seek "an unfailing treasure in heaven, where no thief comes near, nor moth destroys. For where your treasure is, there will your heart be also" (vv. 33b–34).

The point of these final verses seems to be an exhortation to set the affections on the true treasure (vv. 31–34).

This points out the true way of using outward good so as to secure the higher spiritual riches. Life must have some aim, and the mind must turn to something as supremely good, or better, doing what pleases God the Father. The way to drive out materialism and seeking after that which will soon turn to dust is to fill the heart and its longing for eternal and spiritual good. Christ was prompting the Jews of that generation to seek the kingdom of God.

Believers, whether in Christ's day or now, must be seeking as the chief good what He desires to give them. Christ will not withhold gifts that are needed. If the Jews could trust Him to give them the kingdom, they could surely trust Him to give good gifts that were for their best interest!

Waiting for the Messiah (12:35–48)

"'Be dressed in readiness, and keep your lamps alight'" (12:35). Though the Messiah was in their presence, the Jews had no idea when or how He would secure His rule and begin His earthly kingdom reign. Without repentance that kingdom would not be inaugurated. Without national repentance the Messiah's coming would be delayed. Therefore, the lamp of anticipation should be ready (v. 35), since the Master, the Messiah, could come at any time (v. 36). As good slaves of Him, the Jews should be alert (v. 37), because they do not know at what late watch in the night He may arrive (v. 38). If one knew when the thief would break in, he would have secured the house (v. 39), so "You too, be ready; for the Son of Man is coming at an hour that you do not expect" (v. 40).

As the Lord taught about His coming to establish His earthly reign, Peter became convicted and asked, "Lord, are You addressing this parable to us, or to everyone else as well?" (v. 41). Jesus replied with the story of the sensible steward, or faithful slave, who was put in charge of the master's possessions while he was away. The evil servant who is not anticipating the master's coming home begins to beat the other slaves, both men and women, and eats and drinks and gets drunk (v. 45). Upon his return, the master will beat that slave "and assign him a place with the unbelievers" (v. 46), giving him many lashes with the whip (v. 47). The reason is that "from everyone who has been given much shall much be required; and to whom they entrusted much, of him they will ask all the more" (v. 48). The nation of Israel had all of the revelations of the Old Testament. They had the miracles and teachings of Moses and other prophets. They will be judged severely for rejecting their promised King.

The Problem of Discernment (12:49–59)

"'I have come to cast fire upon the earth; . . .'" (12:49). Jesus said that He came "to cast fire upon the earth" (v. 49). With the rejection of the nation so strong against Him, He came to bring division rather than peace among the people (v. 51). Because of what He says and because of who He is, households would be divided (v. 52), with son and father, daughter and mother, and in-laws turning against each other (v. 53). With biting words, the Lord called the multitudes hypocrites who could tell by the clouds if a shower is coming and whether the day would be hot and dry (vv. 54–55), but they were not able to "analyze this present time" (v. 56). The people had lost their sense of spiritual priorities, their timing of what God was doing, and their moral discernment (v. 57). Again, using illustration and hyperbole, Jesus told the people that their guilt was so great they would be taken to the authorities and cast into prison, and "you shall not get out of there until you have paid the very last cent" (v. 59). The Lord was telling the Jews that they had run out of excuses. The Messiah was in their presence, and they could no longer resist Him. They must make a decision for Him!

The Need for Repentance (13:1–9)

"The Galileans, whose blood Pilate had mingled with their sacrifices" (13:1). While Jesus was speaking ("on the same occasion"), a report came to Him that Pilate had slain some innocent Galileans who had gone to Jerusalem to offer sacrifices. Luke put it this way: "Whose blood Pilate had mingled with

their sacrifices" (v. 1). Neither history nor the Gospels tell us more of this event. Referring to this tragic news, Christ asked, "Do you suppose that these Galileans were greater sinners than all other Galileans, because they suffered this fate?" (v. 2). He answered, "Unless you repent, you will all likewise perish" (v. 3). The entire nation was a sinning people. While the killing of the Galileans by Pilate's troops was tragic, there was a greater spiritual guilt that had to do with spiritual issues and not simply the political. God was speaking to the nation through His Son, who was in their midst. What would the people do with the Lord Jesus?

Christ then described another tragic incident: the tower in Siloam fell, killing eighteen men who were evil renegades and culprits (v. 4). Nehemiah writes about the "wall of the Pool of Shelah at the king's garden" (Neh. 3:15), and Josephus records in his *Wars* (5.4.2) of the walls bending south "above the fountain of Siloam." The age of this structure is probably what brought the tower down. This area was most likely used for criminals, who were worse than all those who lived in Jerusalem. Nevertheless, as bad as this was, the nation was so evil that Jesus said, "Unless you repent, you will all likewise perish" (Luke 13:5). If a man who owns a vineyard of fig trees finds no fruit on one of the trees, he orders his vineyard-keeper, "Cut it down! Why does it even use up the ground?" (v. 7). The vineyard-keeper pleads, give it time "until I dig around it and put in fertilizer" (v. 8), "and if it bears fruit next year, fine; but if not, cut it down" (v. 9). The nation of Israel was in its last hour. If the people did not repent and accept Christ soon, if no fruit appeared, judgment would come upon the people and upon the land!

It seems as if the man suddenly becomes emotional and cannot finish his sentence (v. 9b). Some have observed this in that verse 9 appears to be an incomplete thought. Finally, he utters, "but if not, cut it down." It appears as if on purpose the Lord does not state whether the fig tree of this parable ever bore the appropriate yield. The hearers were left to wonder and guess.

The key to understanding this story is found in verse 3. The nation of Israel was warned, "I tell you, . . . unless you repent, you will all likewise perish." The Jewish people had all of the signs that their King was in their midst. How would they respond to Him? Unfortunately, the verdict would come in with the charge against the people. When the Messiah comes again He will destroy "these vine-growers and will give the vineyard to others" (20:16). The die was cast; the days of vengeance would finally come in A.D. 70 with the fall of Jerusalem (21:20–23). The procrastinators in Israel would die in their sins!

Issues of the Sabbath (13:10–17)

"He was teaching in one of the synagogues on the Sabbath" *(13:10)*. The scene shifts to one of the synagogues in the Galilee area, with Jesus teaching on the Sabbath (v. 10). An evil spirit had held a woman captive for eighteen years so that she could not stand up straight (v. 11). Jesus healed her instantly, and "she was made erect again, and began glorifying God" (v. 13). The chief synagogue elder, the "official," chided the Lord, saying that there were six days to do work. He and the most legalistic Jews saw even a healing as a work. Therefore people should come on the work days for such miracles, "and get healed, and not on the Sabbath day" (v. 14b). Christ replied, "You hypocrites, does not each of you on the Sabbath untie his ox or his donkey from the stall, and lead him away to water him?" (v. 15). He added that this woman was a daughter of Abraham and "should she not have been released from this bond on the Sabbath day?" (v. 16). While the crowd was rejoicing at the "glorious things being done by Him," His opponents were being humiliated (v. 17). The Greek compound word for humiliated is *kataischyno* and means "to put down, to shame." The root idea is to violate in the sense of disfigure. The implication with the imperfect or past tense is that when all those who opposed Him had an argument or debate, they always continually lost over the issue. They could not defeat the arguments of Christ, and therefore they were being seen as losers in front of the people.

On this issue of showing kindness and mercy on the Sabbath, the legalists could never win against the words of Jesus.

Concerning the Kingdom (13:18–35)

"'What is the kingdom of God like, and to what shall I compare it?'" *(13:18)*. The kingdom of God is like a tiny mustard seed that when planted produces a huge shrub upon which the birds sit (v. 19). When the messianic kingdom arrives, it will grow and sprout and its influence will spread far and wide. The tiny mustard seed will yield a giant tree that will become a home for the birds. So the kingdom will spread far and wide and become a haven for those who look for the arrival of the kingdom upon the earth.

The kingdom will be like leaven that will leaven the bread dough and make the entire loaf rise (v. 21). "It was all leavened" is an aorist tense, like the last three aorist tenses used in verse 19. The point is that the kingdom will permeate everything! The aorists give the idea that the kingdom will do what it is intended to do when it arrives. This does not mean that all will embrace it when the King finally comes to earth again to reign. But it does mean that the kingdom will be pervasive and change the entire world. As important as this issue was, not many of the Jews were concerned for their own souls and their personal salvation right then. While traveling from city to city, someone said to Him, "Lord, are there just a few who are being saved?" (v. 23). He answered, "Strive to enter by the narrow door; for many, I tell you, will seek to enter and will not be able" (v. 24). The "narrow door" was the smaller entrance for family, servants, and personal visitors. This was locked and barred at night. The big door to the household compound was wide for the use of animals and wagons. Jesus went on to tell the story of the head of the house who closed His doors and locked the small entrance door. Some will knock, and he will answer, "I tell you, I do not know where you are from; depart from Me all you evildoers" (v. 27). It is probable that only thieves would attempt to come in the smaller door unidentified. When the people of Israel see Abraham, Isaac, Jacob, and all the prophets in the kingdom of God, they will weep and gnash their teeth because they are cast out (v. 28). However, a believing multitude will come from east, west, north, and south into the kingdom, and it will be like at a banquet in which they recline in fellowship and eating (v. 29).

The Pharisees may have used any excuse to stop Jesus' teaching, because right then, "just at that time," they came up and said, "Go away and depart from here, for Herod wants to kill You" (v. 31). Calling Herod Antipas a fox, because of his cunning, Christ tells them to report to him that His exorcisms and healings will be finished when He reaches His goal (Greek, *teleios*) on the third day (v. 32). Here He is probably referring to His coming forth from the grave on the third day after His burial (Matt. 17:23; 27:64; Luke 9:22). But first, in regard to the days coming, He must go to Jerusalem because "it cannot be that a prophet should perish outside of Jerusalem" (v. 33). Most commentators believe that the Lord did not say this in the absolute sense; however, it is true that some of the most well-known prophets died there. The reason this is so is because such deaths would be an indictment against Israel, and it would also be a shame that God's own servants perished at the hands of His people in the capital city itself. The Lord then poured out painful sorrow about the city: "O Jerusalem, Jerusalem, the city that kills the prophets and stones those sent to her! How often I wanted to gather your children together, just as a hen gathers her brood under her wings, and you would not have it!" (v. 34).

With some of His most straightforward language, Jesus warns that "the house," the temple, would be left desolate, and "you shall not see Me until the time comes when you say, 'Blessed is He who comes in the name of the Lord!'" (v. 35). He is quoting from the great messianic paragraph of Psalm 118:22–29.

These verses in this psalm speak of the Anointed One who is "The stone which the builders rejected" and who, when the kingdom arrives, will be "the chief corner stone" (v. 22) by whom God will align and build the kingdom. When that day comes, the Jews will cry out:

> This is the LORD's doing;
> It is marvelous in our eyes.
> This is the day   which the LORD has made;
> Let us rejoice and be glad in it. . . .
> The LORD is God,
> And He has given us light. (vv. 23–24, 27)

Purpose of the Sabbath (14:1–6)

"He went into the house of one of the leaders of the Pharisees on the Sabbath" (14:1). On another day the Lord went into the home of a leading Pharisee to eat. The guests "were watching Him closely" (v. 1). Reclining in front of Him was a man suffering from acute swelling from fluid build-up called the dropsy (v. 2). Knowing the negative thinking of those around Him, and knowing that the issue of "work" on the Sabbath had not gone away, the Lord asked, "Is it lawful to heal on the Sabbath, or not?" (v. 3). While the people kept silent, Jesus suddenly took hold of the man, healed him, and sent him on his way (v. 4). This miracle had to be visually dramatic, because the swelling had to have departed instantly! On this same issue in regard to Sabbath, and using His often repeated answer about mercy, He said to them, "Which one of you shall have a son or an ox fall into a well, and will not immediately pull him out on a Sabbath day?" (v. 5). Again there was silence. "And they could make no reply to this" (v. 6). The issues of both circumcision and the Sabbath seemed to have been "legal" tests of the Jews to verify religious compliance to the Mosaic code. And those who answered correctly and conformed to all of the ceremonial acts were considered pious enough to be accepted.

Lack of Humility (14:7–14)

"He began speaking a parable to the invited guests" (14:7). With this same audience of guests, Jesus noticed that certain ones were given the seats of honor (v. 7). He told them that humility acts in an entirely different way. When you go to a wedding feast, you should, "recline at the last place, so that when the one who has invited you comes, he may say to you, 'Friend, move up higher'; then you will have honor in the sight of all who are at the table

with you" (v. 10). The issue is self-exaltation and self-promotion. God and others may elevate us, but we should not elevate ourselves.

The Lord concluded: "For everyone who exalts himself shall be humbled, and he who humbles himself shall be exalted" (v. 11). It was this worldly pride of the people of Israel, the crass superiority of the Pharisees especially, even their cold spirituality, that made them despise a Messiah who was as humble as Jesus was. In spite of all the pain and torment the Jews have suffered, even to this day, they refuse to consider Jesus as their promised Messiah. A certain legalism and absolute rejection of Him still rules their religious thinking.

The word *exalt* is a present participle from *hupsoō* that means to "raise up, make great." A related word is *hupsōma*, which means "that which towers above," or "a high place" like a mountain. "Humbled" comes from the Greek verb *tapeinoō*, which carries the idea "to humiliate, make low." To paraphrase the verse: "The one who is continually lifting himself up will at some time in the future be brought down and made low." This is a persistent theme in Scripture and can be found in Psalm. 18:27; Proverbs 29:23; Matthew 23:12; Luke 18:14; and James 4:6. Before the Lord, selfishness, pride, and arrogance are the signs of a hypocritical person. With the Lord, only genuine humbleness and repentance can be accepted. God will ultimately and invariably reward, but it may be in the next world.

Jesus concluded this discussion by adding that when you give a reception, you should invite the poor, the crippled, the lame, and the blind, and you will be blessed, not by these who have no means to repay, but "you will be repaid at the resurrection of the righteous" (v. 14). By saying this, the Lord placed before those listening a long-term recognition and reward that would come from God when eternity begins. He was urging the Jews not to be shortsighted, but to consider that things done in time have an eternal consequences.

Making Excuses (14:15–24)

"'Blessed is everyone who shall eat bread in the kingdom of God!'" *(14:15).* While Jesus was reclining and eating, a guest spoke out, saying, "Blessed is everyone who shall eat bread in the kingdom of God!" (v. 15). Jesus' response makes it clear that it is wrong to call this Pharisee's exclamation a mere pious Jewish platitude that anybody could toss out. Christ treated it as a very serious word that was meant to be said in earnest. No doubt the man was responding to Jesus' preceding statement about the kingdom being like a banquet (v. 14). The man may have meant that dining in heaven was a prerogative of the Pharisees, and he may have complacently assumed that he was to be one of the blessed. His response may have sounded like a longing for the heavenly

feast. Hopefully this was the case. Jesus went on to show this man and those in His company at the table how to become righteous in the true and biblical sense and how thus to enter the heavenly banquet.

Knowing that the man thought every Jew would be here on earth for that messianic reign, Jesus responded with a story. He told about a man who gave a big dinner and invited many (v. 16), sending out his slave to tell the guests, "Everything is ready now" (v. 17). Many began to send back excuses. One had to go check on his land (v. 18), another had to try out a new team of oxen (v. 19), while another claimed a new wife and added, "and for that reason I cannot come" (v. 20). Such obvious excuses angered the master, and he instructed his slave to "go out at once into the streets and lanes of the city and bring in here the poor and crippled and blind and lame" (v. 21). After many of these who were not accepted by the wealthy had arrived, the slave brought the news, "And still there is room" (v. 22). The master decided to invite more of those who were usually rejected and looked down upon. He said, "Go out into the highways and along the hedges, and compel them to come in, that my house may be filled. For I tell you, none of those men who were invited shall taste of my dinner" (vv. 23–24). In a like story the Lord added, "For many are called, but few are chosen" (Matt. 22:14). Salvation is a sovereign work of God and comes to those to whom it is often least expected. Arrogance, indifference, and pride keep people from the Lord. And those who are humble and often broken in heart and spirit are beckoned to the table of blessing and are lovingly compelled by the Holy Spirit to come in and receive eternal life (John 6:37, 39, 44).

Carrying One's Own Cross (14:25–35)

"Now great multitudes were going along with Him" (14:25). The Lord Jesus got across to the crowd that discipleship was a costly issue. He warned them of their own personal sacrifice if they decided to align themselves with Him as the promised Messiah. He said that the one coming with Him must "hate" even His own family and, yes, even his own life, or he cannot be His disciple (v. 26). In what context did He use the word "hate" (*miseō*)? This statement has caused much controversy, but what is most startling is the object—one's own family! In a most powerful sense, and at the other end of the spectrum of love, the word *hate* can be used to imply rejection. The overall context is the fact that almost the entire nation of the Jews was turning against Jesus' claim to be the Anointed One of God. All the evidence was there, but the people and the leadership were hardening spiritually. They wanted to continue on in their sin. While they were spiritually miserable and poor, their religious works gave

them a sense of satisfaction that kept them in their comfort zone. Loyalty to the Messiah meant that His disciples had to turn their backs even on their families who were repudiating Him. But more, they had to carry their own cross as if going to the place of crucifixion (v. 27). The people were familiar with the horrible Roman practice of executing criminals in this public manner. They would have gotten His point!

The Lord then told of the man who wanted to build a tower but could not finish it because he had not calculated the cost (v. 28). With only the foundation finished, his neighbors ridiculed him (v. 29). Jesus went on and told the story of a king facing an enemy army of twenty thousand—would he not sit down and take counsel whether his ten thousand troops could defeat such a force? (v. 31). While the enemy army was still far away, the intelligent thing would be to send a delegation and ask for peace terms (v. 32). In other words, Jesus was cautioning his hearers to count the cost of following Him. He concluded, "So therefore, no one of you can be My disciple who does not give up all his own possessions" (v. 33). These stories seem to have two points: the issues for the builder and the king (1) had to do with considering the implications of Him being the promised King, (2) but also of subduing stubborn pride. Jesus closed this portion of His teaching by saying that salt that has lost its taste is good for nothing: "It is useless either for the soil or for the manure pile; it is thrown out. He who has ears to hear, let him hear" (vv. 34–35). Israel was "good for nothing" without witnessing to Christ and was in jeopardy of losing its place of importance and being rejected by the Lord.

Finding What Is Lost (15:1–10)

"The tax-gatherers and the sinners were coming near Him to listen to Him" (15:1). Suddenly it seemed Jesus was surrounded with crooked tax-gatherers, unsavory sinners, hypocritical Pharisees, and legalistic scribes, all grumbling, "This man receives sinners and eats with them" (vv. 1–2).

> This is an old charge (Luke 5:30) and a much more serious breach from the standpoint of the Pharisees. The implication is that Jesus prefers these outcasts to the respectable classes (the Pharisees and the scribes) because he is like them in character and tastes, even with the harlots. There was a sting in the charge that he was the "friend" (*philos*) of publicans and sinners (Luke 7:34).[3]

In a parable the Lord told of the hundred sheep with one missing. What shepherd would not go out to find this lost sheep? (v. 4). When found, he places the sheep on his shoulders, returns rejoicing, and says to his neighbors and friends, "Rejoice with me, for I have found my sheep which was lost!" (v. 6). Jesus concluded: "I tell you that in the same way, there will be more joy in heaven over one sinner who repents, than over ninety-nine righteous persons who need no repentance" (v. 7). In a similar parable, a woman lights a lamp to find one of her ten silver coins that is missing. When it too is found, her friends and neighbors join her in rejoicing (v. 9). The Lord added, "In the same way, I tell you, there is joy in the presence of the angels of God over one sinner who repents" (v. 10). The Jewish leaders showed their blindness and spiritual insensitivity to the lost. They had isolated themselves from religious reality and had forgotten God's mercy toward those who were far from Him!

The Rebellious Son (15:11–32)

"And He said, 'A certain man had two sons . . .'" (15:11). Often called the parable of the prodigal son, this story carries many lessons:
- *The demanding attitude of the son to receive his inheritance (v. 12)*
- *The greed of the son who took and squandered his inheritance (v. 13)*
- *The wanton and sinful lifestyle the son engaged in (v. 13)*
- *The physical and spiritual depths to which the son fell (v. 16)*
- *The humility to which the son descended (v. 17)*
- *The confession of the son as to his sins before heaven and before his father (v. 18)*
- *The compassion of the father to accept his son back home (vv. 20–24)*
- *The jealousy and anger of the elder brother over the return of his younger brother (vv. 28–31)*

The parable shows the younger son asking for his part of his father's estate and then leaving, because the older son was expected to keep the land and the homestead and to carry on the family business. The Lord built His story on this ancient custom of inheritance. The younger son, therefore, prepares to leave home. In doing so he has not thought out all of the ramifications of his decisions. Those decisions are mainly based on greed and self-will. Inexperience, dislike of restraint, and the glamour of being independent all come together in this story. The *heart* of the son was no longer with his father. "Father," he says in making his demand. What a different tone and meaning the same word has in verse 21, where he cries out, "Father, I have sinned against heaven and in your sight." Here in verse 12 he speaks only to be rid of his father and his father's care, guidance, and control.

In Jewish law the oldest son received two-thirds of the inheritance; the remainder was divided among the rest of the children. Thus a third would go to this younger son (Deut. 21:17). In the story Jesus told, the father gives in to the younger son's demand and makes the division, giving each his part. Younger sons had no right to do this; nor did older ones. No child had a right to divide the parental inheritance until after the parent's death.

This well-known story is full of emotional language. Going to the "distant country," the young man "squandered" (*diaskorpizō,* "thoroughly scattered") the estate his father had given to him (v. 13). He spent his time in "loose" living. "Loose" is *asōtōs,* implying a "wasteful, prodigal" existence. When a severe famine struck the land, "he went and attached himself to one of the citizens of that country, and he was then sent into his fields to feed swine" (v. 15). This would have been offensive to Jews who were instructed from the Law about the filthiness of pigs (Lev. 11:7; Deut. 14:8). Soon the young man was eating vegetable pods that were being fed to the swine (Luke 15:16).

Finally, he "came to his senses" (Greek, *phēmi*), that is, "he became enlightened," or "began to see the light"! He reasoned that his father's hired hands had enough bread to eat, "but I am dying here with hunger!" (v. 17). With emotional reasoning, he decided to go home and say, "Father, I have sinned against heaven, and in your sight" (v. 18). He recognized that he had sinned first against the heavenly Father, then his earthly father! Being so humbled by the experience, he wanted to tell his father, "I am no longer worthy to be called your son; make me as one of your hired men" (v. 19). But regardless of what the young man had done, the mercy of his father was beyond measure. When the father saw his son coming down the road toward home, (1) from a distant he spotted him, as if he looked each day for him to come back, and (2) he felt compassion for his son, (3) ran to him, (4) embraced him, and (5) kissed him (v. 20). The son told his father exactly what he vowed to say: "I have sinned against heaven and in your sight; I am no longer worthy to be called your son" (v. 21).

> The depth of the son's repentance is matched only by the depth of the father's love. His actions touch the heart. The father saw the young man while he was still a long way off. This suggests the father longed and looked for his son's return one day. Then, he had pity on his son by running to meet him. This indicates that the father took the initiative in being reconciled to his son.[4]

Without responding to the young man's confession, the father ordered his son clothed in the best robe, with a ring placed on his hand and sandals put on his feet (v. 22). Furthermore, he commanded that a banquet be prepared (v. 23). Movingly the father said, "This son of mine was dead, and has come to life again; he was lost, and has been found" (v. 24). This statement is used over and over again to show the merciful love God the Father has for the wayward. Sometimes the story is applied to His love for the lost, but in reality the story is really about confession of sin, recovery, and restoration in a relationship. However the story is applied, the depth and breadth of grace are deep and wide. It does not hold grudges but gives complete forgiveness.

Coming in from the field and hearing the music and dancing (v. 25), the older brother inquired as to what was going on (v. 26). When he heard that his brother had returned safely, and that the fattened calf had been killed, "he became angry, and was not willing to go in" (v. 28a). To his father he complained that he had always been loyal, continually doing what he was asked, but his father had never thrown a banquet for him (v. 29). With bitterness he accused, "But when this son of yours came, who has devoured your wealth with harlots, you killed the fattened calf for him" (v. 30). With calmness, affection, and patience, the father called this elder brother *teknon*, implying "my little boy." The father continued: "You have always been with me, and all that is mine is yours. But we had to be merry and rejoice, for this brother of yours was dead and has begun to live, and was lost and has been found" (vv. 31b–32).

Loyalty and Trust (16:1–31)

The unfaithful servant (vv. 1–13). When the Lord finished teaching the Jewish leadership about mercy, He turned to His disciples and began discussing the issue of faithfulness. He told the story of a steward squandering the wealth of a rich man (v. 1). As the steward is about to be fired by the master, he says to himself, "What shall I do . . . ? I am not strong enough to dig [in the ground]; I am ashamed to beg" (v. 3). He then figures he can go and stay in the homes of his master's debtors (v. 4) and bargain with them just before he is let go. With one debtor he reduces the debt of a hundred measures (or ladles) of oil to fifty (vv. 5–6), and for the man who owes a hundred measures of wheat, he reduces it to eighty (v. 7). When the master discovers the steward had "acted shrewdly" (used his mind) and gotten back at least a portion of what was owed him, he commends the man. However, the commendation is sort of a sideways compliment. He said that even "the sons of this age are more shrewd in relation to their own kind than the sons of light" (v. 8). The Lord then spoke of "the mammon of unrighteousness" (v. 9). *Mammon* is a Syriac word meaning "riches." He admonished, "Make friends for yourselves by means of the mammon of unrighteousness; that when it fails, they may receive you into the eternal dwellings." There are two views on

this. perhaps the Lord was simply bantering with humor to make the opposite point: "Do not make friends through unrighteous wealth." The second
view is like the first but leaves out the idea that Jesus was using humor.

Faithfulness in small things leads to faithfulness in large things. Likewise,
unrighteousness in a very little thing is "unrighteous[ness] also in much" (v.
10). If one has been unfaithful with what belongs to someone else, "who will
give you that which is your own?" (v. 12). No one can serve two masters, for
either one will hate the one and love the other, or "else he will hold to one,
and despise the other" (v. 13). You cannot serve God and riches!

Loving money (vv. 14–17). The Pharisees who loved money heard Jesus
and "were scoffing at Him" (v. 14). Hitting them head-on, Jesus responded that
they were like those who justify themselves in the sight of men, "but God knows
your hearts" (v. 15a). What men esteem, God detests (v. 15b). He then added
that since the coming of John the Baptist, everyone was trying to force his way
into the kingdom of God (v. 16), "but it is easier for heaven and earth to pass
away than for one stoke of a letter of the Law to fail" (v. 17). Many of the Jews
wanted the benefits of the kingdom proclaimed by John and the Lord Jesus, but
the rigors of the Law and its conviction about the nature of sin were being
ignored. God was examining hearts, and the judgment of the Law was standing.

The unfaithful relationship (v. 18). No subject is more heated than that of
divorce, but R. C. H. Lenski well points out that this passage is not exactly and
specifically an exposition on marriage and divorce.[5] The Pharisees had
accused Jesus of being involved with "sinners," more than likely meaning
adulterers (15:2). But it was the Pharisees who were breaking the sixth commandment, "You shall not commit adultery" (Ex. 20:14). In Luke 16:18 the
Lord is not talking technically about divorce (as the word is translated in the
NASB), but about "release, dismissal" (Greek, *apoluō*) so that they could then
marry someone else. The one noun ("Everyone") with the two present par-
ticiples that follow could read this way: "Everyone who is dismissing his wife
and then is marrying another . . . " That there is a sexual *tryst* going on seems
to be clear from the last part of the verse. There, Lenski says the English translation "commits adultery" (Greek, *moicheuō*) is inadequate and really has the
force of "to ruin [a] marriage"[6] The Pharisees regarded marriage as imperma-
nent. It could be dissolved at will; they could discard their wives as they
wished. Jesus was attacking these Pharisaic violators. The issue of dismissal
practiced by the Pharisees was not divorce for sexual sins as defined in the Law
(Deut. 24:1–3). Rather, many of the Jews in Christ's day were "trading partners." While there are many views on this subject, Lenski seems to have a fair
and honest balance. On this passage he writes, "A discarded innocent wife
(Mark says also husband) may marry again even as Paul so plainly declares in

1 Cor. 7:15; and the man who marries her as he should honors marriage as it was made permanent by God, condemns the man's action in breaking his own and her marriage, and commits no sin."[7]

The issuing of the certificate of divorce in Deuteronomy 24:1–4 seems to be part of the backdrop of the Luke passage. While the meaning of Luke 16:18 may never be fully settled in everyone's mind, a statement by the historian Josephus, a Pharisee who was contemporary with the apostles, may explain Deuteronomy 24 as seen in that period of history. He writes, "He that desires to be divorced from his wife for any cause whatsoever (and many such causes happen among men), let him in writing give assurance that he will never use her as wife any more, for by this means she may be at liberty to marry another husband."[8]

The cruel rich man (vv. 19–31). Jesus then told tells another story, this one about a rich man living in splendor (v. 19) who had a poor, sore-ridden beggar named Lazarus laid out before his gate (v. 20). The beggar existed in abject poverty, eating the crumbs that fell from the rich man's table, and dogs came up and licked his sores (v. 21). This poor man was a righteous believer who, when he died, was carried lovingly by the angels to Abraham's bosom (v. 22a). Since Abraham was the father of the Jewish people, this was a comforting illustration of going home and being in the company of the first patriarch of the Jewish nation. Leaning on Abraham's bosom, or chest, is a sign of being accepted and having arrived among the Jewish family in glory.

But when the rich man died and was buried (v. 22b), he went to Hades, the word that is used as the broad expression to describe the place of the dead. Jesus went into Hades, but because of His deity and holiness, His soul was not left there (Acts 2:27–31). Jesus indicated here in Luke 16 that Hades, which seems to have been a place of waiting until the atonement was finished at the cross, had two compartments. The beggar was being comforted while the rich man was in torment (v. 23a). Somehow this man could see Abraham "far away, and Lazarus in his bosom" (v. 23b). He cried out, "Father Abraham, have mercy on me, and send Lazarus, that he may dip the tip of his finger in water and cool off my tongue; for I am in agony in this flame" (v. 24). Jesus was using anthropomorphic hyperbole (human forms and symbols used in exaggeration to explain something that has real meaning and truth) to convey the horrors of this place of torment. Nevertheless, the rich man and Lazarus are real figures. The consciousness, regret, suffering, and pain are real as well. Abraham reminded the wealthy man that during his life he received good things, while Lazarus experienced bad things; "but now he is being comforted here, and you are in agony" (v. 25). Abraham added, "Beside all this, between us and you there is a great chasm fixed, in order that those who wish to come over from here to you may not be able, and that none may cross over from there to us" (v. 26). The dialogue continued with the rich man begging, "Father, . . . send [Lazarus] to my father's house" (v. 27), and warn my other brothers "lest they also come to this place of torment" (v. 28). "If someone goes to them from the dead, they will repent!" (v. 30). Abraham answered back that the living have Moses and the Prophets, "let them hear them" (v. 29). However, "If they do not listen to Moses and the Prophets, neither will they be persuaded if someone rises from the dead" (v. 31).

This drama, with the characters of the rich man and Lazarus, provides many important lessons. (1) There is consciousness after death, (2) there is bliss for the righteous and torment for the wicked, (3) there is regret for what is done in life, (4) great spiritual consequences follow after death, (5) the die is cast in this life, with no "second chance" in view, and (6) the witness of the prophets (and later the writings of the apostles) is sufficient so that one can know the truth. However, the hardness of the hearts of the lost is so great that even the witness of one coming forth from the dead will not persuade those who are spiritually resisting.

Most scholars believe that the death of the Lord Jesus atoned for the sins of all the righteous who lived before the crucifixion and had a saving trust in God. This belief comes from Romans 3:25. Jesus as a propitiation, a place of satisfaction with God concerning sin, demonstrated "His righteousness, because in the forbearance of God He passed over the sins previously committed." On this side of the death of Christ, when a believer dies, he or she goes directly into the presence of God. As the apostle Paul writes, "I . . . prefer rather to be absent from the body and to be at home with the Lord" (2 Cor. 5:8).

Learning to Forgive (17:1–6)

"'It is inevitable that stumbling blocks should come, but woe to him through whom they come!'" (17:1). Continuing to instruct His disciples, the Lord shifts His teaching to the issue of responsibility of what one says and does to others. In this account in Matthew 18:1–6, the Lord calls a child to Himself (v. 2) and warns against being a stumbling block (Luke 17:1). If one causes "one of these little ones to stumble," it would be better for the one causing this that a millstone be tied around his neck, "and [that] he were thrown into the sea" (v. 2).

The millstone of which Jesus speaks is the top stone of the two between which the grain is crushed. The reference is not to the handmill but to the much heavier stone drawn by a donkey. In the middle of the topstone there is a hole through which grain can be fed so as to be crushed between the two stones. The presence of this hole explains the phrase "a millstone hung around his neck." With such a stone around the neck to have been hurled into the sea makes drowning doubly sure.[9]

Do not hold grudges, but "Be on your guard!" (v. 3a), "If your brother sins, rebuke him; and if he repents, forgive him" (v. 3b). Even if he sins seven times, and then truly repents, "forgive him" (v. 4).

> How often should believers forgive other believers who sin against them? Jesus gave a hypothetical situation that provides the answer to that question: "If a brother sins against you seven times in one day and seven times says to you, 'I repent,' then you are to forgive him." In other words, Christians are to forgive each other indefinitely, without limit. After all, does not God do the same for us (cf. 11:4)?[10]

Acceptance and forgiveness should always be available. To withhold mercy is wrong. To restore a relationship quickly should be the desire of every child of God. The apostles must have seen themselves in what Christ said, because they cried out, "Increase our faith!" (v. 5). This must have been said in the context of possessing enough trust to treat other people in a right, loving manner. The Lord answered that if they had faith like a mustard seed, they would say to a nearby mulberry tree, "'Be uprooted and be planted in the sea'; and it would obey you" (v. 6). By exaggeration Christ made a profound point. The smallest amount of trust can bring about incredible positive results in human relationships. Jesus was expanding the idea of "faith" to encompass the walk of believers, who will learn to watch what they say to the smallest of helpless creatures, such as a little child, and they will be quick to forgive repenting sinners.

The Duty of Serving (17:7–10)

"'Which of you, having a slave . . . will say . . . when he has come in from the field, 'Come immediately and sit down to eat'?" (17:7). A faithful servant is faithful until the very end. Christ asked, Would a master say to his hardworking servant who came in from the fields, "Come immediately and sit down to eat"? (v. 7). Of course not! He would instruct his servant to dress properly and to fix him something to eat (v. 8). The servant is not thanked, because he is simply doing what he is commanded (v. 9). Jesus then came to the point: "So you too, when you do all the things which are commanded you, say, 'We are unworthy slaves; we have done only that which we ought to have done'" (v. 10). In this illustration, Christ was using His usual method of employing extremes to communicate a message. On one hand, we have what seems to be the insensitive master, but on the other, we see the servant whom the Lord calls "unworthy." No matter what the circumstances, the servant must do what he has been hired to do. Faithfulness to what is required, to one's duty, cannot demand a compliment. The Jews constantly sought reward and recognition, but the Lord set forth the higher calling of honor and faithfulness.

Expressing Gratitude (17:11–19)

"He was passing between Samaria and Galilee" (17:11). Abraham Lincoln once said that ingratitude was one of the greatest sins. That truth was amply illustrated when Jesus healed the ten lepers. They cried out when they saw him from a distance, "Jesus, Master, have mercy on us!" (v. 13). The Lord instructed them to go to the priests and show themselves, according to Leviticus 14:1–32. On the way, their healings were accomplished, and "they were cleansed" (Luke 17:14). In both the Old and New Testaments, leprosy was seen as the great scourge of the people. Through Moses, God have an elaborate ritual for the healing and cleansing of lepers. Jesus followed the Mosaic Law in order to be faithful to it but also for a witness to the crowds that God had performed a miracle in the lives of these ten men.

One of the men who was healed turned back toward Jesus and began "glorifying God with a loud voice" (v. 15). Though he was a Samaritan, an outsider, a dog in the eyes of most of the Jews, he fell down at Christ's feet and gave thanks to Him (v. 16). Jesus then asked a question of those within hearing: "Were there not ten cleansed? But the nine—where are they?" (v. 17). "Was no one found who turned back to give glory to God, except this foreigner?" (v. 18).

> The nine others were already healed and hastening to the priest, that they might be restored to the society of men and their life in the world; but the first thoughts of the Samaritan are turned to his Deliverer. He had forgotten all [because of] God's mercy and . . . His own unworthiness.[11]

Jesus made no further comment to the crowd—the conclusion was obvious. The nine were not truly grateful; they went on their way without acknowledging the mercy of God, and they did not give thanks to Jesus. To the one man who returned, the Lord said, "Rise, and go your way; your faith has made you well" (v. 19). This command does not imply the others were not cured; it simply recognizes this man's trust in Jesus as the Messiah who can heal.

> This was not yet soteriological faith, justifying faith that saves the soul. It was to lead to this type of faith. The power that saved from leprosy is divine, and he who has it must be able to save also the soul with the power of grace.[12]

The Suddenness of the Arrival of the Kingdom (17:20–37)

"'The kingdom of God is not coming with signs to be observed; . . .'" (17:20). The
backdrop to the Gospels is the presentation of the kingdom of God. Because
the King was in their presence, the messianic kingdom had come near and
was waiting for the repentance of the Jews. As the events of the Gospels
unfold, it is clear that this contrition, from the nation as a whole, would not
come. The nation would reject its Anointed One! Because of more questions
about the kingdom of God by the Pharisees, the Lord answered, "The kingdom of God is not coming with signs to be observed; nor will they say, 'Look,
here it is!' or, 'There it is!' For behold the kingdom of God is in your midst"
(v. 21). In every reference to the arrival, or the coming, of the kingdom in the
Gospels, the verb is in the perfect tense. In Luke the NASB translates 10:9, 11
correctly: "The kingdom of God has come near to you." It has arrived but it
has not been inaugurated. "It has been on its way, and it has arrived, but it
has in no way begun!"

In 17:21 Jesus continued this thought and told the Pharisees, "It is existing in your midst, but it certainly has not started!" When kingdom of God
(and kingdom of heaven) is mentioned, it is accompanied by a perfect tense,
meaning the kingdom has come up to the moment but it has not been inaugurated. The kingdom itself will not come with signs (Greek, *sēmeion*) to be
observed. However, before it arrives there will be a terrible period of tribulation. "The powers of the heavens will be shaken, and then the sign of the Son
of Man will appear in the sky, and then all the tribes of the earth will mourn,
and they will see the Son of Man coming on the clouds of the sky with power
and great glory" (Matt. 24:29b–30). "To be observed" (Luke 17:20) is the verb
paratērēsis, meaning "in a way that can be observed [by external signs]," with
"critical observation."[13] Jesus described His coming: "Just as the lightning,
when it flashes out of one part of the sky, shines to the other part of the sky,
so will the Son of Man be in His day" (v. 24).

The doctrine of the postponement of the kingdom is clear in verse 25: "But
first He must suffer many things and be rejected by this generation." When the
Messiah comes to reign, it will be like the judgment days of Noah and of
Sodom. People were quickly destroyed by water (Gen. 7), and Sodom was
rained upon by brimstone from heaven (Gen. 19). Concerning the Tribulation,
Jesus warns some future generation of Jews to leave all of one's household
goods and flee (Luke 17:31), because "then there will be a great tribulation,
such as has not occurred since the beginning of the world until now, nor ever
shall. And unless those days had been cut short, no life would have been saved"
(Matt. 24:21–22). But when He arrives to reign and to judge, "there will be two

men in one bed; one will be taken, and the other will be left. There will be two women grinding at the same place; one will be taken, and the other will be left" (Luke 17:34–35). The disciples asked, "Where, Lord?" (v. 37a), and He answered them, "Where the body is, there also will the vultures be gathered" (v. 37b). In other words, they are consigned to death! This is obviously not the rapture of the Church at which the saints on earth are caught up to heaven and given new bodies; and the dead in Christ are raised (1 Thess. 4:13–18). Here in Luke and in the parallel reading in Matthew 24–25, Jesus is talking about His coming as Israel's King. The one taken is the "evil slave" who did not have faith in Jesus' messianic reign (Matt. 24:48). He is taken before the Master for judgment because he did not stay alert (v. 43), "for the Son of Man is coming at an hour when you do not think He will" (v. 44). The end is terrible, for he shall be cut in pieces and be assigned "a place with the hypocrites; weeping shall be there and the gnashing of teeth" (v. 51).

The Issue of Prayer and the Coming Kingdom (18:1–8)

"He was telling [the disciples] a parable to show that at all times they ought to pray and not to lose heart" (18:1). No matter what the circumstances, "at all times" believers are to pray and not lose heart (v. 1). "Lose heart" is actually the one Greek word *egkakeō*, which means "to respond badly, become tired." While there is a universal principle here for all believers, the context is actually about the coming of the Son of Man. To illustrate, Jesus gave a parable about a poor widow seeking protection who came before a judge "who did not fear God, and did not respect man" (v. 2). By her "continually coming" and pleading (v. 4), she wore the judge down (v. 5). Jesus asked, if an unrighteous judge finally does what is right, "shall not God bring about justice for His elect, who cry to Him day and night" (v. 7). Will Jesus, as the Messiah, delay His coming? Jesus concluded, "He will bring about justice for them speedily" (v. 8a). "Speedily" is the Greek word *tachus*, meaning "in a hasty manner, with rapidity of speed." Especially for the righteous suffering in the Tribulation, when the Lord begins redemption, it will tumble into place quickly, with no delay. When the terrible things of the Tribulation begin, with the "powers of the heavens . . . shaken" (21:26), then, Jesus urged, "straighten up and lift up your heads, because your redemption is drawing near" (v. 28).

What It Means to be Justified (18:9–14)

"He also told this parable to certain ones who trusted in themselves" (18:9). The Lord told a parable to some in the crowd who "trusted in themselves." The

parable was about a self-righteous Pharisee and a crooked tax-gatherer who went up to the temple to pray (vv. 9–10). The Pharisee stood (positioned himself) before the temple and prayed "to himself," thanking God that he was not like other people: swindlers, unjust, adulterers, or even "like this tax-gatherer" (v. 11). To make himself look better, he reminded the Lord, that "I fast twice a week; I pay tithes of all that I get" (v. 12). But the broken tax-gatherer, "standing some distance away," would not even lift his eyes to heaven, but beat his breast, saying, "God, be merciful to me, the sinner!" (v. 13). "Be merciful" is the Greek verb *hilaskomai*, which is used as a noun in Hebrews 9:5 to mean the mercy seat. The thought behind the word is "propitiation, atonement." The unworthy tax-gatherer was claiming the mercy seat, the place of satisfaction, where the Lord, by the blood sprinkled upon it, forgave the sins of the people of Israel. This of course was a picture of what Christ would do at the cross as the ultimate sacrifice for sins. The apostle Paul says that Christ was displayed publicly "as a propitiation in His blood through faith" (Rom. 3:25). All that was done in the ceremonial system of the temple was but a "picture" of what Christ would come and do.

Jesus concluded: "I tell you, this man went down to his house justified rather than the other; for everyone who exalts himself shall be humbled, but he who humbles himself shall be exalted" (Luke18:14; 14:11). "Justification" (Greek, *dikaioō*) means "to legally acquit, make righteous." Paul again says that God "justified as a gift by His grace through the redemption which is in Christ Jesus" (Rom. 3:24). Now in the church age, this happens by direct trust in Jesus, the object of faith, because of His finished work at the cross. Paul says that we receive "the righteousness of God through faith in Jesus Christ [meant] for all those who believe" (Rom. 3:22).

Faith and the Kingdom of God (18:15–30)

"They were bringing even their babies to Him so that He might touch them" (18:15). Parents were bringing their little children to Jesus to bless, but the disciples rebuked them (v. 15). Jesus responded by saying that the children should be permitted to come to Him, "for the kingdom of God belongs to such as these" (v. 16). With tenderness, the Lord "took them in His arms and began blessing them, laying His hands upon them" (Mark 10:16). Jesus used these children to make His point about the simplicity of faith: "Truly I say to you, whoever does not receive the kingdom of God like a child shall not enter it at all" (Luke 18:17). A ruler, probably a leader in a local synagogue, did not get the Lord's message about simple, childlike faith. He asked, "Good Teacher, what shall I do to inherit eternal life?" (v. 18).

In Matthew's gospel the stranger introduced in this passage is called a "young man" (19:20), by Luke a "ruler" (here in Luke 18:18), and is by all three of the Synoptic writers described as a property owner who was extremely rich (Matt. 19:22; Mark 10:22; Luke 18:23). With these three accounts a full picture of this wealthy young man is presented. Some have surmised that, because of his wealth, he was also probably an official overseer in charge of the synagogue nearby.

In the Gospel of Mark, the most vivid description of this ruler's actions is recorded. The way Mark tells it, not only did this young man run up to Jesus, but he also fell on his knees in front of Him. Luke simply says that a particular ruler asked a question of Christ. Because the man was so emotional, and because he appears to have dropped so quickly on his knees, one can imagine him gasping and crying out the address: "Good Teacher." Just what the emotional young man meant by "everlasting life" might be up for conjecture. To answer it is important to look at what the scribes and the Pharisees taught. But it is also important to see what is said in the Old Testament. Daniel 12:2 reads, "And many of those who sleep in the dust of the ground will awake, these to everlasting life, but the others to disgrace and everlasting contempt (or rejection)." The apocryphal literature of 2 Maccabees 7:9 says, "The King of the world shall raise us up . . . unto an everlasting renewal of life." Therefore it would be more than likely that for those who were well acquainted with Jewish religious literature, the term "life everlasting" was referring to the resurrection when the messianic kingdom begins. The rich young ruler's question can therefore perhaps be paraphrased, "What must I do to become a partaker of salvation at the close of the age?" This motivation for asking was undoubtedly a desire to gain assurance that he was headed in the right direction toward that ultimate destiny of the resurrection to eternal life and peace with God. It appears that at the moment that he was willing to do almost anything necessary to reach this goal.

Jesus said to Him, "Why do you call me good? No one is good except God alone." What did Jesus mean? Was He denying His deity? Was He disclaiming both His divinity and His goodness? Did he mean, "You should not have called me *good*, for God alone is good. I am not God; therefore I am not good"?

Jesus knew that the rich young ruler, in addressing him as "Good Teacher," was being very superficial. Thus the Lord's first response was, "No one is good except God alone" (v. 19). Some have used that statement to argue that Christ Himself was saying that He was not God! In truth He was forcing the man to think twice about what he had said. Lenski well writes:

So far is this from denying the Godhead of Jesus that it actually asserts it for him. "Good," Jesus intends to say, if you mean that in the common sense, it is too cheap to apply to me! It is quite another thing to use good in its real meaning as it applies only to God! The man is thus led to look at Jesus in a new way, to consider that Jesus may, indeed, be God, essentially one with God as his Son.[14]

Jesus then quoted some of the Ten Commandments to him from Exodus 20:12–16: "Do not commit adultery, do not murder, do not steal, do not bear false witness, honor your father and mother." Is it possible that the Lord only mentioned these because they were the commandments the man most often broke? Without flinching, the ruler answered, "All these things I have kept from my youth" (v. 21). Because no one can truthfully say that, this man was bearing false witness against himself! Instead of correcting him, Jesus came in the back door and told the man to sell all his possessions, distribute them to the poor, and he would have treasures in heaven. Then he should follow Him! (v. 22). The man became very sad because of his great wealth (v. 23). Actually, "very sad" comes from *perilupos*, meaning something like "everything fell around him." Speaking directly to the man, the Lord added, "For it is easier for a camel to go through the eye of a needle, than for a rich man to enter the kingdom of God" (v. 25). Lenski points out that there has been some misunderstanding on this verse because of a fifth-century change of the word "camel" (Greek, *kamēlos*) to a "heavy rope" (Greek, *kamilos*).[15] But the illustration and the humorous picture the Lord drew actually stands. "The impossibility that is thus illustrated is without a single exception" by all reputable Bible scholars.[16]

Those who heard Jesus said, "Then who can be saved?" (v. 26). That the Jews were wrapped up in works-salvation is evident. "Doing something" for salvation had been engrained in them by the distorted teachings of the priests about the Law and by the false piety of the Pharisees. The Lord responded to their question by answering, "The things impossible with men are possible with God" (v. 27). When Peter responded that the disciples had left their homes to follow Him (v. 28), Jesus complimented him by saying that no one who had left family "for the sake of the kingdom of God" would go without. That person would receive "many times as much at this time and in the age to come, eternal life" (v. 30). Jesus was not calling for family abandonment, but He was speaking about leaving family "for the sake of the kingdom of God" if some in the family were rejecting the Messiah (v. 29). "Eternal life" is not a reward for forsaking family relations. To stand for the kingdom is to accept by faith the person of the Anointed One.

Prediction of His Death (18:31–34)

"'Behold, we are going up to Jerusalem'" (18:31). Jesus began His journey to Jerusalem for His final earthly trials and death on the cross. He told His twelve disciples, "All things which are written through the prophets about the Son of Man will be accomplished" (v. 31b). This would include (1) the major events that took place around the cross (Ps. 22), (2) His death as a sacrificial lamb for sin (Isa. 53), and His triumphant resurrection from the grave (Ps. 16). Giving some description to His disciples, He told them He would be delivered to the Gentiles to be mocked, mistreated, spat upon, scourged, and killed (Luke 18:32–33a). Peter remembered the Lord's words when he remarked that Pontius Pilate and the Gentiles (Acts 4:27), were gathered "to do whatever [God's] hand and . . . purpose predestined to occur" (v. 28). However, the disciples "understood none of these things, and this saying was hidden from them, and they did not comprehend the things that were said" (Luke 18:34). Their lack of a grasp on this subject was brought about by a divine "blinding," because it would have overwhelmed them. Yet, from the human standpoint, it would still be impossible for mortal, limited human beings to fully comprehend the resurrection, though that doctrine was always a part of Jewish belief.

The Confirmation of Jesus as the Promised Messiah (18:35–43)

"As He was approaching Jericho, a certain blind man was sitting by the road, begging" (18:35). Jesus and His party came from the north, down the Jordan Valley, to the city of Jericho. There they would turn west to go up 1,200 feet to Jerusalem. While approaching Jericho a blind man was told that Jesus of Nazareth was passing by. Though he was sternly rebuked, he called out twice, "Son of David, have mercy on me!" (vv. 38–39). Willcock writes:

> The blind man saw Jesus with the eye of faith, and prayed to Him as his Saviour; while the world, who could see His person, saw Him not. And yet the blind world, which did not see Jesus, rebuked the blind man, who saw and worshipped Him; but he was nothing daunted by the rebuke, but cried to Him the more earnestly. Thus the blind recovered sight, and they who saw [remained] blind.[17]

It was common knowledge that the Messiah would be the son of David, as made clear in what is called the Davidic covenant prophesied by Nathan the prophet (2 Sam. 7:12–29). The Old Testament kings of Israel were said to sit on David's throne (Jer. 13:13). And the Branch of David would "spring forth; and He shall execute justice and righteousness on the earth" (33:15).

Mary the mother of Jesus was reminded of things before His birth: "The Lord God will give Him the throne of His father David" (Luke 1:32). The blind man was well aware of all of these prophecies. When the Lord asked him what he wanted, he said, "Lord, I want to regain my sight!" (v. 41).

Throughout the Gospels the Lord Jesus shows Himself to be not only very able to do as He pleases, but also very merciful. The heart of Christ was continually going out to those who were hurting. So also as He approached the cross, He stood still and ordered the people to bring the blind man to Him. With great tenderness Jesus asked him what he wanted. Was he simply asking for alms? As the Son of God, Jesus knew what the blind man both needed and wanted, but He wanted it to come from him so that his faith could be seen by all. While it is true that the Father in heaven is certainly acquainted with the needs of all His children, He still instructs them, "Open your mouth wide" (Ps. 81:10), so that the Lord will fill it. Jesus' desire is to cure the blind man but also to enter into fellowship with him. While almost all of the Jews had no idea that Christ was going to the cross to die for their sins, to acknowledge Him as the promised Messiah was tantamount to salvation. We must remember that Christ came under the dispensation of the Law. In the Old Testament, salvation was brought about by sincerely trusting in God. In the Gospels, the issue is the messiahship of Jesus.

Jesus responded to the man's plea, "Your faith has made you well" (18:42). When the man was healed, he determined to follow Jesus. He began glorifying the Lord, with all the people as well giving praise to God (v. 43). With no vision, and limited in movement and travel, this blind man had heard and then absorbed into his very soul great prophetic truths. He knew of the power and authority of the Messiah, and he appropriated these promises for himself!

The Great Faith of Zaccheus (19:1–10)

"He entered and was passing through Jericho" (19:1). Every child in Sunday school knows the song about the little man Zaccheus climbing the sycamore tree to see Jesus coming by. But there is more to the story of this man. He was a "chief" tax-gatherer, and he was rich (v. 2). "Chief" means that he was responsible for all the tax collection in Jericho. More than likely he became rich by cheating the people out of their money. Only Jesus, the Son of God, would know that Zaccheus had more than common curiosity.

Since Zaccheus was short and probably small, he was unable to catch a view of Jesus passing by. Yet his interest was so strong in the Master that he was willing to do almost anything to get a glimpse of Him. Thinking ahead as to where Jesus was going, he quickly sped ahead of the pushing and shoving crowd and then, though he was a respected man of the community, clamored up into a sycamore tree that had been planted by the side of the road. A "sycamore fig tree" is highly prized for the shade it gives in hot weather. Also, since many of its branches extend from the trunk down close to the ground, even a small man like Zaccheus could easily climb it.

Zacchaeus apparently had a genuine spiritual thirst. When the Lord told him to come down out of the tree and informed him that He was going to his house that day, Zaccheus "hurried and came down, and received Him gladly" (v. 6). As often happened, many of the people complained, saying, Jesus "has gone to be the guest of a man who is a sinner" (v. 7). Zaccheus must have heard these words, because Luke records that he stopped suddenly and said to Christ, "Behold, Lord, half of my possessions I will give to the poor, and if I have defrauded anyone of anything, I will give back four times as much" (v. 8). At first this sounds like "works salvation," but it is not. It is a proof that great spiritual change had taken place in his soul. Conviction replaced self-ishness. He realized he was a sinner, and without hesitation his heart was cleansed and the demonstration of this was a complete change of priorities. The Lord Jesus confirmed this when He said, "Today salvation has come to this house, because he, too, is a son of Abraham" (v. 9). And no matter what one's social, physical, or religious appearance, "the Son of Man has come to seek and to save that which was lost" (v. 10).

Being Faithful to the End (19:11–27)

"[The disciples] supposed that the kingdom of God was going to appear immediately" (19:11). When Jesus and the disciples were getting close to Jerusalem, they "supposed that the kingdom of God was going to appear immediately" (v. 11). The Lord then told a parable of a nobleman who went to a distant country to receive a kingdom and then return (v. 12). Before he left he entrusted his ten slaves with funds and said, "Do business with this until I come back" (v. 13). He gave each of them ten "minas," worth one hundred denarii. A mina was worth about fifty shekels, and a denarii was valued at about a day's wage for the average worker. In the middle of his story, the Lord inserted a side note about the people who saw this nobleman coming to take over his kingdom. They said, "We do not want this man to reign over us" (v. 14). This statement would play a part at the end of the narration.

When the man returned after receiving his kingdom, he called his slaves together to see how they fared with his money. One slave had doubled his minas, and another added five minas. They had invested the nobleman's for-tune. This was important, because in a wealthy man's estate, he fed, housed, and clothed many servants besides their wives and children. It was important that these funds produce income. These servants who invested and multiplied the funds were rewarded with responsibility over ten and five cities respectively (vv. 16–19).

But the next slave hid the minas, saying, "I was afraid of you, because you are an exacting man; you take up what you did not lay down, and reap what you did not sow" (v. 21). "If you knew that," the nobleman replied, "why did you not put the money in the bank to draw interest?" The mina was taken from the slave and given to the one who had ten minas already (v. 25). The nobleman concluded, "I tell you, that to everyone who has shall more be given, but from the one who does not have, even what he does have shall be taken away" (v. 26). The nobleman's final words are a response to the disgruntled citizens of his new kingdom in verse 14. "But these enemies of mine, who did not want me to reign over them, bring them here and slay them in my presence" (v. 27).

Two stories are intertwined in this parable. If the minas that are hidden represent the fact that the Jews buried the prophecy about the coming messianic kingdom, this becomes a sign of the most heinous of evils. And the citizens who said they did not want the new nobleman king "to reign over us" (v. 14), represent the soon coming final rejection of the Jews of their promised Sovereign! "The destruction of Jerusalem with its streams of Jewish blood is the preliminary reality that is back of these words."[18]

Study Questions

1. What does 12:5–30 tell us about the sovereignty of God?

2. What did Jesus mean in 13:30 when He said, "And behold, some are last who will be first and some are first who will be last?"

3. What is 13:35 telling the Jews about the kingdom they were anticipating to begin?

4. What application can we take for today from Jesus' statement, "Whoever does not carry his own cross and come after Me cannot be My disciple?"

5. Relate 16:19–31 to the concept of divine election.

6. Give reasons why 17:34–36 is not referring to the rapture of the Church.

7. What great truth can be found by comparing the story of the rich young ruler (18:18–27) with the conversion of Zaccheus (19:1–10)?

SECTION V

Final Days of the Ministry of the Son of Man

Luke 19:28 – 23:56

The Lord Jesus now moved toward His rejection and death at the hands of His countrymen in Jerusalem. Luke 19:28 took place on Sunday, the first day of the Jewish week. On each day, up to His crucifixion on Friday, dramatic events took place that amplified the nation's guilt. Each day would be a confrontation with the Pharisees and the authorities, but also a teaching time for the Lord's disciples. The Lord would have His final time with His apostles during the Passover meal. He would then go to pray at Gethsemane, be tried, crucified, and buried. This section of Luke is the climax of the ultimate rejection by the nation of Israel.

CHAPTER 21

Authority of the Son of Man Revealed
Luke 19:28–21:4

Preview:
Jesus arrived at Jerusalem for His last visit and Passover before being crucified. He was welcomed by the crowds as a conquering hero because of their expectation that He would establish His kingdom. After cleansing the temple of the merchants, Jesus was once again challenged by the Pharisees, Sadducees, and scribes on a number of topics. In correcting them on their beliefs and practices, Jesus continued to incite their wrath against Him because of their greed, hypocrisy, and lust for power.

Sunday and Monday (19:28–44)

"He was going on ahead, ascending to Jerusalem" (19:28). The Lord Jesus was on the way to the cross.

The words "After saying these things Jesus kept proceeding ahead, going up to Jerusalem" connect with the parables of the . . . rejected king and the nobleman who traveled to a distant land, thereby clarifying the purpose of Jesus' journey to Jerusalem. To avoid any misunderstanding about Jesus' ascent to Jerusalem, Luke intends that the preceding parables guard against the expectation that Jesus was about to set up his physical kingdom when He arrived there. He first had to suffer and die, go to heaven, and then, and only then, return from the "distant country" before setting up the kingdom of God in Jerusalem.[1]

Jesus also showed the crowds that He was the earthly Messiah of Israel's dreams, the One who would wage war to establish David's throne on earth (though that kingdom would be postponed because Israel would not repent of their sins). Spiritually at this time He also came to bring and establish "the things which make for peace" (Luke 19:42), that is, lasting peace: reconciliation between God and man and between persons. Therefore, the Lord Jesus entered Jerusalem mounted on a colt, the foal of a donkey, an animal associated not with the rigors of war but with the pursuits of peace, for He is the Prince of Peace (Isa. 9:6). While many understood who He was, the vast throng of people did not fully understand. In hailing Him as the messianic King, the people were right; the Pharisees, chief priests, and scribes (Matt. 21:15–16; Luke 19:39–40) were wrong because they simply saw Him as an imposter. The "righteous" crowd was correct in expecting this Messiah to reveal Himself as a political, earthly potentate, the expected and prophesied King of the Jews. Those shouting, "Glory to God!" (Hosanna!) were correct, though the kingdom would not be set up at this time because of the rejection of Jesus by the masses. It is not surprising therefore that Luke pictures a weeping King in the midst of a shouting multitude (19:39–44). Later the rejecting crowd would shout with the urging of their leaders, "Crucify (Him)!"

It is clear from verse 28 that Jesus was taking the lead in proceeding with his little band of disciples from Jericho to Jerusalem (cf. Mark 10:32).

Before entering Jerusalem, more than likely the Lord spent the previous days and weeks in Perea and Judea. Some days before Passover, He came to the outer suburb of Jerusalem (John 11:55), to the city of Bethany (12:1). This period is known as Passion Week. On the evening of the Sabbath, the Lord was anointed by Mary, the sister of Lazarus, at the house of Simon the leper (Matt. 26:6–13; Mark 14:3–9; John 12:1–8). On the following day, a crowd came to the town to see Jesus (John 12:9–11).

Before arriving at Bethany, the Lord sent two disciples to go find a colt, tied, and bring it to Him (Luke 19:30). How did Jesus know that the two disciples would find everything as he had predicted? The answer is quite simple. Jesus is very God and very Man, the God-Man, and He knows everything in an infallible way just as the heavenly Father does. As God, the Lord Jesus has supernatural knowledge and understanding. Note also that verse 33 must be interpreted as meaning that there had been no previous communication with respect to this incident between Jesus and the owners of the colt. Jesus often received information in "natural" ways, but that He had prescience beyond human comprehension is clear from such passages as Matthew 17:27; John 1:48; 2:4, 25 (see also Mark 10:33–34).

If the disciples were asked why they were taking the colt, they were to say, "The Lord has need of it" (v. 31). This may indicate that the news about Jesus had spread far and wide and probably even down to the teeming thousands in Jerusalem who had come for Passover. Matthew 21:5 pointed out that this fulfilled Zechariah 9:9, which predicts the first coming of the Messiah:

> Rejoice greatly, O daughter of Zion!
> Shout in triumph, O daughter of Jerusalem!
> Behold, your king is coming to you;
> He is just and endowed with salvation,
> Humble, and mounted on a donkey,
> Even on a colt, the foal of a donkey.

Zechariah in the next verse predicts His universal reign, which is yet to take place when the kingdom is established: "His dominion will be from sea to sea" (v. 10).

When the disciples returned with the colt, they placed their garments on its back and then sat Jesus on it (Luke 19:35). Many threw their garments on the road as with honoring the arrival of a sovereign king (v. 36). It must not be forgotten that many thousands of people believed all the evidence that Jesus was the Christ. Luke calls them "the whole multitude of the disciples" (v. 37), who fully realized that He was the promised Anointed One! They started singing Psalm 118:26 and "began to praise God joyfully with a loud voice for all the miracles which they had seen," saying, "Blessed is the King who comes in the name of the Lord; peace in heaven and glory in the highest!" (v. 38). When the Pharisees saw this display of emotion, they told Jesus, "Teacher, rebuke Your disciples" (v. 39), to which Jesus replied, quoting Habakkuk 2:11, "I tell you, if these become silent, the stones will cry out!" (Luke 19:40). As He looked upon the city of Jerusalem, He began weeping and saying, "If you had known in this day, even you, the things which make for peace!" (v. 42). While many Jews were believing in Jesus, the vast majority did not have a clue as to what He was really all about. This peace Jesus spoke about would have been twofold: personal peace with God and international peace because the prophesied King of the people of Israel was there!

He then spoke of the terrible things coming on that generation because of its rejection of Him. Enemies would soon surround them (v. 43), the city and the population would be leveled to the ground, and "they will not leave in you one stone upon another, because you did not recognize the time of your visitation" (v. 44). "Visitation" is the Greek word *episkopē* and means "to look upon, investigate." The nation was under investigation as to its reception of the Son of God, as clearly prophesied by the prophets of Israel. Would the Jewish people believe God or not? Unfortunately, they would not. The visitation would be the judgment that would fall on Israel in A.D. 70. The Romans, under General Titus, would come against Jerusalem and destroy it and the great temple that supposedly was the symbol of God's blessing and revelation.

Tuesday (19:45–48)

"He entered the temple and began to cast out those who were selling" (19:45). On Monday evening Jesus returned to stay overnight in Bethany (Mark 11:11). On Tuesday morning He returned to Jerusalem (v. 12). As the Son of God who represents His Father among the Jews, the Lord entered the temple and began casting out those who were selling sacrificial animals in the upper courtyard (Luke 19:45). The money changers had traditionally been confined to small booths on the west side, near the outer temple wall. The temple authorities had allowed these merchants to move closer to the entrance of the complex itself, which was considered holier. More than likely the authorities were receiving a portion of the funds taken in. The merchants were giving change for monies that were dropped into the temple coffers, but they also sold some of the animals that were used for sacrifices. The Lord Jesus, driving these men from their stalls back to the places where they were supposed to stay, quoted Isaiah 56:7: "And My house shall be a house of prayer." He then added, "But you have made it a robbers' den" (Luke 19:46). This act, along with the fact of His daily teaching in the temple, provoked the chief priests, scribes, and leading men among the people even further to try to destroy Him (v. 47). They were jealous that the people "were hanging upon His words," but "they could not find anything that they might do" to immediately kill Him (v. 48).

Wednesday (20:1–22:6)

"The chief priests and the scribes with the elders confronted Him" (20:1). While there is some confusion concerning the events of the next few days, Harold Hoehner places those events on Wednesday rather than on Tuesday.[2] This seems to make the most sense chronologically. On the way back to Jerusalem after again staying overnight in Bethany, the disciples passed the withered fig tree that the Lord had earlier cursed (Matt. 21:20–22; Mark 11:20–26). The cursed fig tree was a sign of what would happen to the Jewish people in A.D. 70. At that time the Romans will exact vengeance on Israel for their rejection

of their Savior and Lord! At the temple He again engaged the religious leaders about His authority. They goaded Him by repeating the question, "By what
permission does He do the things He is doing?" (Luke 20:2). As a master
teacher, the Lord answered a question with a question: "I shall also ask you a
question, and you tell Me: 'Was the baptism of John from heaven or from
men?'" (vv. 3b–4). The leaders realized they were trapped. If they answered
that John's abilities came from God, Jesus would then ask them why they did
not believe John as a prophet (v. 5). If they answered that John's authority was
from men, the people would stone them to death, because they were convinced the Baptist was a prophet (v. 6). Avoiding the question, they answered
that they did not know (v. 7). Jesus responded, "Neither will I tell you by what
authority I do these things" (v. 8). The hatred of the Jewish religious authorities was so great that His trapping them in their own lack of spiritual logic
only inflamed them more!

Jesus then turned to the people standing around and told them a parable
about an owner of a vineyard. Jesus would describe what was about to happen to Him but also what would then be the fate of the nation of Israel. The
vineyard owner sends his slave out to his vineyard to collect some of the harvest produce (v. 10). Three times the vine-growers turn away the slaves sent
out to gather in the master's crops. One slave is beaten (v. 10b), another is
beaten and treated worse (v. 11), and finally, the third is wounded (v. 12).

Next, the owner sends his son, who is killed by the evil vine-growers
(v. 15). What is the master to do? "He will come and destroy these vine-growers and will give the vineyard to others" (v. 16a). The people shouted, "May it
never be!" (v. 16b). With their emotional answer, the Lord puts it back on
them and asks by quoting Psalm 118:22, "What then is this that is written,
'The stone which the builders rejected, this became the chief corner stone'?"
(v. 17). This great messianic prophecy points to Him and to His rejection by
the Jewish nation. In ancient days, the foundation and walls of a building
were plumbed from a perfectly cut triangular stone. Though Jesus was about
to die at the cross, He would ultimately be the one through whom all future
blessings for the nation of Israel would take place. He was the chief corner
stone! With sober warning He added, "Everyone who falls on that stone will
be broken to pieces; but on whomever it falls, it will scatter him like dust"
(v. 18). These chilling words would take away in a whirlwind the Jewish people in A.D. 70!

Knowing that Jesus' words were aimed at them, the Jewish leaders tried to
capture Him that very hour (v. 19). They even sent spies who acted pious and
religious around Him to catch Him in some statement on which they could
deliver Him up to the authorities (v. 20). They flattered Jesus and said,

"Teacher, we know that You speak and teach correctly, and You are not partial to any, but teach the way of God in truth. 'Is it lawful for us to pay taxes to Caesar, or not?'" (vv. 21–22). Another trap was laid. If He answered that it was not lawful by Jewish custom to pay Roman taxes, the Romans would arrest Him, but if He said openly it was lawful, then the strict legal party would say that He was not honoring the Mosaic Law and that He was placing Gentile authority over Jewish religious duties. Their either/or question would have incensed the Jews who held contrary convictions! Knowing their trickery (v. 23), the Lord called for a coin with the inscription of Caesar (v. 24). When asked whose face was on the coin, the Jews had to answer "Caesar's." "Then," He replied, "render to Caesar the things that are Caesar's, and to God the things that are God's" (v. 25). The people marveled at His answer, but His enemies were unable to catch Him, and "they became silent" (v. 26b).

The liberal Sadducees stepped forward to try their hand at tricking the Lord (v. 27). The Sadducees did not believe in the doctrines of resurrection, angels, or miracles. They asked a foolish Gordian knot legal question about a childless woman whose husband has died (v. 28).

Before continuing, we must answer, Who were these Sadducees? The way this party originated in many decades past is not fully known. The Sadducees relished tracing their name and origin back to Zadok, the man who during David's reign shared the high priestly office with Abiathar (2 Sam. 8:17; 15:24; 1 Kings 1:34). Abiathar was made the only officiating high priest by Solomon (1 Kings 2:35). It is not positive that the Sadducees were right in so claiming this beginning. While it cannot be proved, they may well have been correct. That there was indeed, even during the days of Christ's sojourn on earth, a close relationship between priesthood, temple, and Sadducees is not open to doubt. This is made evident in Acts 4:1; 5:17.

As to their doctrinal beliefs, the Sadducees accepted only the written Word while the Pharisees also embraced the oral traditions. Much of this is spelled out in Josephus (*Antiquities* 13.297). But the Sadducees had many heretical beliefs. For example, they denied the soul's immortality. As they taught, the soul perishes forever along with the physical body (*Antiquities* 18.16, 17). The famous statement of the Sadducees was, "There is no resurrection, nor an angel, nor a spirit" (Acts 23:6–8). They also discarded and rejected the eternal divine decree, calling it but "fate." The Sadducees also promoted the freedom of the human will over God's sovereignty in the affairs of humanity (*Antiquities* 13.171–73).

Coming up to Christ, the Sadducees probably intended to strike a double blow. They began with a two-pronged attack. First they exposed to ridicule the Lord's teaching about a bodily resurrection. They hoped also to triumph over the Pharisees who likewise accepted the doctrine and teaching about life after death. In their arguments with Jesus they perhaps were already gloating over the prospect of "killing two birds with one stone," that is, of ridiculing both Jesus and the Pharisees.

From Deuteronomy 25:5–10 and what is called the levirate law (from the Latin word meaning "husband's brother"), one of the brothers of the dead man could marry her to produce offspring for his name's sake. As his *seven* brothers come forward and take her in marriage, each dies without producing children! The question: "Which one's wife will she be?" (Luke 20:33). This situation was monstrous and ludicrous and was intended to make the Lord a laughingstock before the crowds and before the Pharisees who believed in the resurrection.

Jesus, however exposed the folly of the Sadducees. While He confirmed the doctrine of the resurrection, He also pointed out that marriage is an earthly institution that is a part of this age (v. 34) and will not be a part of the new dynamics of the future age following the resurrection (v. 35a). He answered that those who are worthy of that future age (Greek, *eon*) "neither marry, nor are given in marriage; for neither can they die anymore, for they are like angels, and are sons of God, being sons of the resurrection" (vv. 35b–36). Jesus was saying that the biological relationship people have in marriage here on earth is not applicable to eternity. The assumption also is that in heaven the worship of God takes the place of relationships that are considered necessary and blessed here on earth.

Jesus pointed out that resurrection is clearly implied in Exodus 3:6. When Moses encountered the Lord in the burning bush, he called Him "the God of Abraham, and the God of Isaac, and the God of Jacob" (v. 37). The point is that the patriarchs are now in heaven enjoying a relationship with God, and they will be again on earth in their resurrected bodies. Jesus added, "He is not the God of the dead, but of the living; for all live to Him" (v. 38). What the Lord said must have brought great spiritual conviction to some of the scribes who responded: "Teacher, You have spoken well" (v. 39). But His opponents did not have the courage to question Him any longer (v. 40).

Jesus then used the moment of verbal sparing to raise another question: "How is it that they say the Christ [the Anointed One] is David's son?" (v. 41). He then quoted Psalm 110:1: "The Lord said to My Lord, sit at My right hand, until I make Thine enemies a footstool for Thy feet" (v. 42–43). In the Hebrew text of the verse, the first "Lord" is Yahweh ("the ever-existing One"), and the second "Lord" is Adonai ("the Master"). The scene that David is prophesying in Psalm 110:1 is that God the Father is speaking to the Messiah in the glory of the heavenly throne room. Using this puzzling passage as a counterquestion, Jesus then asked, if "David therefore calls Him 'Lord,' . . . how is He his son?" (v. 44). Psalm 110:1 is clearly hinting at the fact of the deity of the Messiah; therefore, how could David be His far-off earthly father? Again, as Matthew records, no one dared ask Jesus another question from that day forward (Matt. 22:46).

The Lord took this opportunity to strike at the religious hypocrisy of the falsely pious leadership. He made two additional important points. He warned the disciples to beware of the scribes who liked to walk around in long robes, loved respectful greetings, and wanted to sit in the chief seats in the synagogues and in the places of honor at banquets (Luke 20:46). These same ones "devour widows' houses, and for appearance's sake offer long prayers; these will receive greater condemnation" (v. 47). He then attacked the rich people who gave gifts into the temple treasury expecting some kind of social recognition (21:1).

Christ also saw a poor widow drop into the temple collection box two very small coins. The original says "two lepta." As best as it can be determined today, it took two lepta to make one quadrant (Mark 12:42); four quadrants or eight lepta to equal one as or assarion; and sixteen of the latter to reach the value of one denarius. The denarius was the daily wage for an average worker (Matt. 20:9–10). By this calculation the widow's contribution was about one-quarter of a penny in today's terms.

However, this calculation is not exactly accurate, because it is impossible to figure the actual buying power of this money. Without doubt, what the woman put into the collection box was small. All that can be safely said is that, by any human economic standard, what the widow gave did not seem to be very much. What is more important, then, was the value Jesus Himself placed on her gift. "Thus I say to you, this poverty burdened widow dropped in much more than all the others." By human calculation what this widow gave was insignificant. Measured by the divine standard, however, her contribution was priceless.

According to Mark 12:43, on another occasion, Jesus called attention to a similar incident and made His disciples look closely at the motive of the woman. In the Gospels this calling of the disciples around Him had happened before, and it meant that this was a very important occasion. In line with this is the fact that the Master introduced his teaching by saying, "Truly I say to you" (Luke 21:3a) shows that what He was about to say was of great significance and should be taken to heart by them.

"This poor widow put in more than all of them" (v. 3b) said Jesus, indicating how precious He considered her offering. In his estimation the two copper coins were as bright and shining as pure gold. One might even say they resembled talents, which over a period of time doubled in value (Matt. 25:20, 22)—yes, doubled and redoubled, for her gift would inspire countless numbers of people to follow her selfless example.

Because the temple plays such a key role in this story, and because of what is coming next in Luke's narration, it is important to look at a brief description of the temple and its history.

The Holy Spirit put in the heart of David to conceive and build a temple for the Lord. But because David was a man of war, the Lord said in 1 Chronicles 28:3 that David's son Solomon would be given the privilege to build it. He started construction in the fourth year of his reign, around 969 B.C. (see 1 Kings 6:1). It was finished seven years later (v. 38). Cedar and cypress wood from Lebanon, and white limestone were used in its building. Because the mountain the temple was to be built on (Moriah) was limited in space, the area had to be built up and the foundation had to be laid very deep and filled in. (For an account of the temple dedication see 1 Kings 6–8.) Over many centuries the temple was neglected, restored, and often desecrated (1 Kings 14:26; 15:18; 2 Kings 14:14; 15:35; 16:17–18; 23:4). Its treasures were carried to Babylon (2 Kings 24:13), and it was finally destroyed, along with the city of Jerusalem, in the year 586 B.C. The Chaldean army, led by Nebuchadnezzar, destroyed Jerusalem, including Solomon's beautiful temple.

Some fifty years later, at the return of a remnant from the Babylonian captivity, an altar for a new temple was constructed (Ezra 3:3). What was completed was nothing like the glory of the Solomonic structure. The older people, who had known that first building, wept (Ezra 3:12–13). It was this temple that was desecrated and plundered by Antiochus Epiphanes in 168 B.C. Approximately three years later it was cleansed and rededicated by Judas Maccabaeus. The Roman general Pompey captured the temple but did not destroy it. However, Crassus took away the temple treasures in 54–53 B.C.

Next came Herod the Great who renovated and enlarged the temple and extended the area. Herod beautified it to such an extent that the result could be called a new temple. However, devout and pious Jews refused to consider it such. Herod told the Jews that he wanted to make a thankful return, after the most pious manner, to God for the blessings he received from Him who had given him the kingdom. He desired to do this, he said, by making his temple as complete as he was able. He started the construction work around 19 B.C. But many years following his death it had not yet been entirely completed (see John 2:20). The great beauty of the Herodian temple was well along by the time of Christ (Luke 4:9; 21:5, 6; Matt. 4:5; 24:1–2; Mark 13:1–2; see also Matt. 4:5; Luke 4:9). It is an important note to both history and to prophecy that this great and elaborate structure was not finished until a few years before it was destroyed by the Romans in A.D. 70.

The temple described above is but the backdrop to the story of the poor widow. In God's sight a poor widow who put in two small copper coins actually put in more than all of them (Luke 21:3). The reason is that the rich gave "out of their surplus," but "she out of her poverty put in all that she had to live on" (v. 4).

As in other teachings, the Lord was not driving home a legalistic principle of salvation by giving nor by human effort and religious works! He was touching on the issue of religious motives. The widow was wholly giving herself to the Lord as shown in her offering, while the hearts of the wealthy were revealed by what they did not give. This passage has to be analyzed carefully lest it be misunderstood, because the Jews for the most part were making claim to their faith simply by their outward works, and Christ was aiming at this problem in a harsh and direct manner. He was also striking hard at what He knew of their hearts, minds, and souls. Many of the Jewish people at this time were almost totally external in their religious expression, rather than serving God out of personal love and devotion.

Study Questions

1. Why did Jesus choose to enter Jerusalem, on this visit, riding a colt?

2. Compare Luke 19:38 with Matthew 21:9; Mark 11:10; and John 12:13, and give a complete picture of what the people were announcing about Jesus.

3. Luke 19:45–46 tells of Jesus driving the traders out of the temple. What application can the Church take from this event for today? Cite supporting evidence from the Epistles for your application.

4. Why had the religious leaders of Israel rejected the ministry of John the Baptist?

5. In 20:16 (the parable of the vine-growers), the Greek word for "others" means "another of a different kind." What new information did this give Jesus' disciples concerning His coming kingdom?

6. What types of people made up the sect known as the Sadducees, and why did they not believe in a resurrection?

7. Luke 20:37 speaks of Moses' belief in a resurrection. What evidence do we have that Abraham also believed in a resurrection?

CHAPTER 22

Final Discourse about Coming Judgment
Luke 21:5–38

Preview:

As the time of Jesus' death drew closer, He shared the prophetic future with His disciples to strengthen their faith after He was gone. He gave prophecies concerning the coming destruction of Jerusalem and the temple in A.D. 70 by the Romans, as well as a vision of the end times, when He will return to redeem Israel. Jesus finished with a parable telling His disciples of the future generation that will see His return, and warning them to stay alert.

Questions about End-Time Events (21:5–7)

"While some were talking about the temple . . ." *(21:5)*. This section in Luke is called the Olivet Discourse. As Jesus was leaving the temple area, His disciples began showing Him the beautiful stones and the votive gifts that embellished this great religious edifice (v. 5). The temple was a vast complex with more than fifty steps leading up to the main sanctuary. Some of the stones were over sixty-seven feet in length, seven feet in height, and six feet in breadth. The sanctuary was buttressed by very high and formidable substructures. The entire height of the sanctuary itself was over a hundred feet. The entire temple, with the exception of the outer porch, was covered with a gabled roof of cedar wood. From its summit protruded sharp golden spikes to prevent birds

from settling upon and polluting the roof. The temple was also covered with great plates of gold that shined with awesome brilliance in the hot sun.

To pilgrims coming from afar, the temple had the appearance of a snow-covered mountain. What was not covered with gold was encased in pure white marble. History records that the rabbis who did not favor Herod had to admit that he who had not seen Jerusalem in her splendor had never in his life seen a desirable city. The temple in all its glory was meant to instill worship in the minds of the Jews (1 Kings 8:13, 31–61; 9:3). Even Jesus as a child called it "My Father's house" (Luke 2:49).

The adulation of the Jews, and here of the disciples, about the glory of the temple form the backdrop to this discourse, which is also recorded in Matthew 24:1—25:46 and Mark 13:1–37. The issues Jesus covered are more than the glory of the temple. They are: (1) the coming days of vengeance on the nation, (2) the terrors of the seven-year tribulation, including (3) an account of the persecution of the Antichrist, and as well (4) the horrors of terrible cosmic events. They also include (5) the revelation of the coming of the Son of Man to earth to reign on the throne of David and (6) His judgment of the Jewish people and of the Gentiles who survive the Tribulation.

The Olivet Discourse is a central passage of prophetic events for the future. It is a hub for the scenario of the end times. To avoid confusion about what it is setting forth, the student of Scripture must go to the Old Testament for the chronology of what will happen. Here is a broad outline:

1. Israel will be scattered "among all peoples, from one end of the earth to the other end of the earth," and "among those nations you shall find no rest" (Deut. 28:64–65). The beginning of this worldwide scattering began with the destruction of Jerusalem in A.D. 70.

2. Among the nations the Jews "shall have no assurance of [their] life" (Deut. 28:66).

3. Someday God will gather the Jewish people "from all the peoples where the LORD your God has scattered you" (30:3). They will then turn to the Lord their God with all their heart and soul (v. 10).

4. As that return is developing, there will come a time of "terror, of dread, with no peace. . . . Alas! for that day is great, there is none like it; and it is the time of Jacob's distress" (Jer. 30:5–7). This terrible period will also include cataclysmic events such as a scattering of the earth's inhabitants (Isa. 24:1), people on earth burned with few people left (v. 6), and the earth broken, split apart, and shaken violently with earthquakes (v. 19).

5. A remnant of God's people will be saved, and they will be gathered from the remote parts of the earth (Jer. 31:7–8). "He who scattered

Israel will gather him, and keep him as a shepherd keeps his flock" (v. 10).

6. God will take the Jews from the nations, gather them from all the lands, and bring them into their own land (Ezek. 36:24). He will put a new spirit within them, remove their hearts of stone, and give them hearts of flesh (v. 26).

7. The Messiah will rescue His people, and they will look upon Him "whom they have pierced; and they will mourn for Him" (Zech. 12:10).

8. All the nations will be gathered against Jerusalem to battle, and the Lord will go forth and fight against those nations. Then the Messiah's feet will stand on the Mount of Olives, and it will split in two (Zech. 14:2–4). The Son of Man, the Word of God, will come with His armies from heaven. With a sword from His mouth, He will smite the nations. "He will rule them with a rod of iron; and He [will] tread the wine press of the fierce wrath of God, the Almighty" (Rev. 19:13–15). The faithful Jewish elect will be gathered "from the four winds, from one end of the sky to the other," and will reside in peace in the land (Matt. 24:31).

9. The Antichrist, the lawless one, "the Lord will slay with the breath of His mouth and bring to an end by the appearance of His coming" (2 Thess. 2:8).

10. The Messiah, the "righteous Branch of David" will spring forth, and "execute justice and righteousness on the earth" (Jer. 33:15).

With these prophecies in view, the Olivet Discourse makes sense. While the disciples were bragging about the beauty of the temple, the Lord said, "The days will come in which there will not be left one stone upon another which will not be torn down" (Luke 21:6). With His disciples, Jesus then went out of the temple area and sat down on the Mount of Olives (Matt. 24:3a). Peter, James, John, and Andrew (Mark 13:3) then asked Him in secret, "Teacher, when therefore will these things be? And what will be the sign when these things are about to take place?" (Luke 21:7), and "What will be the sign of Your coming, and of the end of the age?" (Matt. 24:3b). The Lord's followers had in mind the day when He would reveal Himself as the Son of Man, when He would establish His kingdom, and when He would end the "age" of the Roman occupation. But they were also shocked at His statement about the destruction of the temple and the fact that this great edifice would be torn down stone by stone!

The Lord Answers (21:8–11)

"Many will come in My name, saying, 'I am He'" *(21:8).* Most of the answers the Lord gave extended beyond the time of the disciples. By examining the contexts of the Olivet Discourse as recorded in the Gospel writers, it seems clear that when Jesus said "you," He was using a "generic you" that was inclusive of the nation of Israel and for the most part was not referring to the disciples standing before Him. Jesus was speaking to a far-off generation of Jews, and context determines when His words are aimed at some Jews who would witness the destruction of Jerusalem and the temple in A.D. 70 or beyond. Almost all of the disciples had been martyred before that period. Only John survived into his nineties and lived to about A.D. 90–95.

Sometime in the future false messiahs will come in the name of Jesus and mislead many, saying, "I am He" (Luke 21:8). Do not go after them! There will be the sound of "wars and disturbances." "Do not be terrified; for these things must take place first, but the end does not follow immediately" (v. 9). Nations and kingdoms will rise up against each other (v. 10), and "in various places there will be famines and earthquakes" (Matt. 24:7) and "terrors and great signs from heaven" (Luke 21:11). Jesus was speaking not about "normal" earthquakes but worse, as described in Isaiah 24—concentrated and sudden quakes like nothing the earth has ever experienced!

Near Prophetic Events (21:12–24)

"'But before all these things . . .'" *(21:12).* Here in Luke 21:12–24, Jesus answered the question of the disciples about the stones being "torn down" and the destruction of the temple (v. 6). "Before all these things" refers to what will transpire before that terrible tribulation period of cosmic signs. How many years separate these things, Jesus does not address. "Before all these things" refers to A.D. 70! Jews who read the words of Christ and believe Him would be persecuted, thrown in prison, and be brought "before kings and governors for [Christ's] name's sake" (v. 12). This would happen also to some of the Lord's disciples who were hearing His words. They would have an opportunity to testify for Christ (v. 13) and would not have to prepare in advance what to say (v. 14), for they would be given wisdom to answer and refute their enemies (v. 15). They would be hated for Christ's name (v. 17) but for a period would be protected so that "not a hair of [their] head[s] will perish" (v. 18).

The prophecy of stones being torn down would come to pass when later disciples saw Jerusalem surrounded by armies; this would signal that "her desolation is at hand" (v. 20). Those seeing this and believing Jesus' words are to depart from the city, flee Judea to the mountains, and not return to it (v. 21), "because these are days of vengeance, in order that all things which are written may be fulfilled" (v. 22). The Greek word for "vengeance" or "punishment" (*ekdikasis*) is related to the verb *dikaioō*, generally translated "justify, do justice, vindicate." With the preposition *ek*, the idea is of justice coming forth as retribution in response to a particular crime. The word is translated "vengeance" fourteen times in the New Testament.

Events Leading Up to the Fall of Jerusalem

1. Roman procurator Florus steals gold from the temple treasury, A.D. 64.

2. A riot begins.

3. Jewish resistance groups, the Sicarii and the Zealots, vow to kill all supporters of Rome.

4. Civil unrest and riots break out and last for three years.

5. Roman general Vespasian gains back control over Galilee, A.D. 67.

6. Vespasian marches south to besiege Jerusalem, A.D. 68.

7. Roman emperor Nero commits suicide; Vespasian is declared emperor and returns to Rome.

8. General Titus replaces Vespasian and encircles Jerusalem. His troops storm the city and burn the temple down on the ninth of Av, the anniversary of the fall of the first temple in 586 B.C.

9. One hundred thousand Jewish men and women are captured and sent to the salt mines of Egypt.

10. The temple vessels and the menorah (the temple candelabra) were taken to Rome, where an arch was later constructed to commemorate the fall of Jerusalem.

When this vengeance came in A.D. 70, the Lord was executing judgment because of the Jewish rejection of Christ. The disciples suffered great persecution and martyrdom. A mountain of wrath had been built and had come down on the heads of the people, as brought about by the Romans. The Jewish people were not at war with Christians, but they were at war with the Lord, because this was "His vengeance." Some see this Lukan passage about Jerusalem being surrounded and destroyed coming from Hosea 9. The prophet writes, "The days of punishment have come, the days of retribution have come; . . . because of the grossness of your iniquity, and because your hostility is so great" (v. 7). With dispersion in mind, as happened in A.D. 70, Hosea cries, "My God will cast them away because they have not listened to Him; and they will be wanderers among the nations" (v. 17). This is exactly what happened when the city was destroyed and thousands were led into captivity. Barnes writes: "Judgment had been threatened by almost all the prophets against [Jerusalem]. They had spoken of its crimes and threatened its ruin. Once God had destroyed Jerusalem and carried the people to Babylon; but their crimes had been repeated when they returned, and God had again threatened their ruin."[1]

R. C. H. Lenski adds that vengeance has the thought of "the handing out of justice."[2] It is the vindication or retribution for the sin of unbelief and for Jerusalem's crimes against the gospel and for "her complete and final rejection by God."[3]

Jesus warned a future generation of the time of the fall of Jerusalem. He said, "Woe to those who are with child . . . for there will be great distress upon the land, and wrath to this people" (Luke 21:23). The Jews, He said, will fall by the edge of the sword "and will be led captive into all the nations; and Jerusalem will be trampled underfoot by the Gentiles until the times of the Gentiles be fulfilled" (v. 24).

The Coming of the Son of Man (21:25–38)

"'There will be signs in sun and moon and stars, . . .'" (21:25). Jesus then picked back up where He left off in verse 11. He continued describing the far-off seven-year tribulation that is yet to take place. There will be signs in sun, moon, and stars, "and upon the earth dismay among nations, in perplexity at the roaring of the sea and the waves" (v. 25). Men will die, fainting (Greek, *apopsuchō*, "breath-departing") because of what is coming upon the world, "for the powers of the heavens will be shaken" (v. 26). Then Jesus the Messiah will Himself come in the clouds as the Son of Man, "with power and great glory" (v. 27). This will fulfill what Daniel said: "And behold, with the clouds of heaven One like a Son of Man was coming" (7:13). Those Jews in the Tribulation who believe Christ's words are to lift up their heads because their redemption is drawing near (Luke 21:28). As fig trees put forth the leaves for summer (vv. 29, 30), so the Jews are to know, "When you see these things happening, recognize that the kingdom of God is near" (v. 31).

Verse 32 is controversial. "Truly I say to you, this generation will not pass away until all things take place." Some try to claim that "this generation" has to do with those Jesus is speaking to. Some commentators say this is A.D. 70, but that was about forty years away. And besides, most of the disciples (except John) and others standing around would be dead. "This generation" (Greek, *hē genea autē*) has to do with those seeing the beginning of the seven-year Tribulation. If they survive the horrors, they will see the end of it! The Lord then confirmed what He had just announced by adding, "Heaven and earth will pass away, but My words [specifically, what I am presently discussing] will not pass away" (v. 33). In other words, it will be fulfilled!

No matter which event the Jews find themselves in, the near destruction of the temple in A.D. 70, or the yet-to-come Tribulation known as "the time of Jacob's distress" (Jer. 30:7), all are to be on guard (Luke 21:34). These things will come suddenly like a trap, and "it will come upon all those who dwell on the face of all the earth" (v. 35). They need to keep alert and have the strength to escape "all these things that are about to take place, and to stand before the Son of Man" (v. 36).

During Jesus' final week, He taught in the temple during the day but went out to the Mount of Olives to sleep (v. 37). Many of the people were fascinated with what He had to say and would rise up early in the morning to hear Him speak in the temple (v. 38).

Study Questions

1. Compare and contrast Herod's temple with the two previous temples built in Israel.

2. What additional question was asked by the disciples and recorded by Matthew? How does that question add to our understanding of the Olivet Discourse?

3. Preterists say that all of this prophecy was accomplished with the destruction of Jerusalem in A.D. 70. How do they reinterpret Scripture to support their viewpoint?

4. What is "the time of the Gentiles"? When did it start, and when will it end?

5. Luke 21:27 contains a reference from the book of Daniel. What details does Daniel give us concerning this future period of which Jesus is speaking?

6. The term "Son of Man" is used many times in the Old Testament referring to different people. How does the meaning differ when used in reference to Jesus Christ?

7. Luke 21:37 tells us that Jesus would teach in the temple during the day and leave Jerusalem at night. How many actual trips did Jesus make into Jerusalem during this, His last visit, leading up to His death?

CHAPTER 23

Final Hours with the Disciples
Luke 22:1-46

Preview:
Judas, empowered by Satan, plotted with the chief priests and scribes to betray Jesus. Jesus sent Peter and John to prepare the place of their last Passover together before His death. At dinner, Jesus instituted the remembrance we call the Lord's Supper and announced the introduction of the new covenant. In the midst of all of this, the disciples still quarreled over which of them was greatest. Finally, Jesus and the disciples returned to the Mount of Olives where He prayed to the Father concerning His upcoming sacrifice.

The Feast of Unleavened Bread (22:1–6)

"The Feast of Unleavened Bread . . . was approaching" (22:1). The first part of this chapter completes the events of Wednesday of Passion Week. The Feast of the Passover is also called Unleavened Bread (Ex. 23:15; Deut. 16:16), because only unleavened bread was consumed for seven days after the Passover period (Ex. 12:15–20; 13:6–8; Deut. 16:3–8). Unleavened bread commemorated the fact that the Jews did not have time to put leaven, or yeast, in their bread before their quick departure from Egypt. This feast was also related to the barley harvest (Lev. 23:4–14).

As Passover approached, the chief priests and scribes began to conspire about how to put Jesus to death, though they were afraid of what the crowds might do (Luke 22:2). At this time, Satan entered the disciple Judas Iscariot (from the tribe of Issachar) (v. 3), who then went to the chief priests and officers with a plan to betray Him (v. 4).

The Career of Judas
1. He was of the tribe of Issachar (Matt. 10:4).
2. He was counted among the disciples (Acts 1:17).
3. He had his portion in the ministry of the disciples (Acts 1:17).
4. Early on he was planning to betray Christ (John 12:4).
5. He was a thief, with the money meant for the disciples (John 12:6).
6. He pilfered from the money box he was responsible for (John 12:6).
7. At the Passover meal, he denied that he was planning to betray the Lord (Matt. 26:25).
8. His betrayal was prophesied by David (Ps. 41:9).
9. The devil put into his heart to betray the Lord (John 13:2).
10. Satan entered into him to carry out the betrayal (John 13:27)
11. After the Passover meal, he left hurriedly into the night to betray the Lord (John 13:30).
12. He betrayed the Lord to the chief priests (Mark 14:10).
13. He betrayed the Lord for thirty pieces of silver (Matt. 26:15).
14. On the Mount of Olives, Judas kissed Jesus to reveal Him to the officers (Luke 22:47).
15. Jesus addressed Judas as the one who betrayed Him with a kiss (Luke 22:48).
16. When Judas saw the Lord condemned, he tried to return the thirty pieces of silver to the Jewish leaders (Matt. 27:3).
17. With the thirty pieces of silver, a burial place was purchased in the Potter's field (Matt. 27:6–10) in fulfillment of Zechariah 11:12, 13.
18. Judas hanged himself and fell from a cliff to his death (Acts 1:18).
19. Judas's home was made desolate as predicted (Acts 1:20; Ps. 69:25).
20. Matthias would take Judas's place as a disciple, as predicted (Acts 1:20–26; Ps. 109:8).

The chief priests were delighted to give Judas the thirty pieces of silver for betraying the Lord. "And he consented, and began seeking a good opportunity to betray Him to them apart from the multitude" (v. 6).

Thursday, and Passover (22:7–38)

"Then came the first day of Unleavened Bread on which the Passover lamb had to be sacrificed" (22:7). It is estimated that one million Jewish pilgrims came to Jerusalem for Passover from around the Mediterranean area. This day was also called Unleavened Bread (Ex. 12:1–28; Lev. 23:5–6). On this special day the Passover lamb had to be sacrificed. This was a memorial of the first Passover when the blood of lambs brought release for the Jews from Egypt. The blood of perfect lambs spread on the doorposts of the Jewish slaves protected them from "the destroyer" (the death angel?) who passed over their homes (Ex. 12:23). Moses said: "It is a Passover sacrifice to the LORD who passed over the houses of the sons of Israel in Egypt when He smote the Egyptians, but spared our homes" (v. 27). By His sacrifice on the cross, the Lord Jesus would be "our Passover" sacrificed for our sins (1 Cor. 5:7).

Moses emphasized the importance of the Feast of Unleavened Bread (cf. 12:15–20) as a perpetual ordinance stressing holy separation of the redeemed. The ritual of this feast was to be followed by a perpetual ordinance in connection with the celebration of the Passover. The unleavened bread, as noted in connection with Passover, typifies holiness and separation of life. The redeemed are to be a holy people.[1]

The Ceremony of Passover

Passover was one of three annual festivals required of the Jews.

It reminded the Jews of their redemption from Egypt (Ex. 12).

It commemorated the final plague on Egypt.

It was to be celebrated on the evening of the fourteenth day of the first month of Nisan (around April) (Lev. 23:5).

A spotless sacrificial animal was to be selected on the tenth of the month (Ex. 12:3).

Passover was also called the feast of Unleavened Bread, which followed immediately the next day (Ex. 12:15–20).

The Jewish Passover points to Christ who "has been sacrificed" (1 Cor. 5:7).

Jewish tradition prescribed that each family celebrate Passover together with an extended and elaborate meal. Since the disciples had no specific home in Jerusalem, they had to find a place to celebrate this occasion. The

Lord commanded Peter and John to make preparation, probably by going into the animal market and buying a lamb (v. 8). But they asked, "Where do You want us to prepare it?" (v. 9). Jesus told them to look for a man carrying a pitcher of water, "and to follow him into the house that he enters" (v. 10). They were to tell the owner that the Teacher asks, "Where is the guest room in which I may eat the Passover with My disciples?" (v. 11). Following the Lord's instructions, the upper room was found and preparation began for the meal that would take place that evening (vv. 12–13).

When the meal began and the disciples were reclining with Jesus at the table, He told them that He would suffer (v. 15) and that He would not eat this meal again until "it is fulfilled in the kingdom of God" (v. 16). For these Jewish disciples of the Lord, Passover was a very distinct spiritual event. The wine of the ceremony was blessed and shared (v. 17). And for the second time, Jesus told them that He would not again partake of the Passover "until the kingdom of God comes" (v. 18). The Lord will someday in the future share this rite with His disciples when He returns to earth to reign.

In the middle of the Passover meal, Christ made a prophetic proclamation that, when He went to the cross, He would ratify by His sacrifice a new covenant that would replace the covenant of the Law, i.e., the Mosaic covenant. The broken bread passed around pictured the coming sacrifice of His body: "This is My body which is given for you; do this in remembrance of Me" (v. 19). The cup of wine represented the soon shedding of His blood: "This cup which is poured out for you is the new covenant in My blood" (v. 20).

In Old English the New Testament refers to the new covenant. The word *covenant* means "an agreement, contract." The Hebrew word is *bᵉrît*, and the Greek word is *diathēkē*. Jeremiah speaks of the new covenant that is first predicted as a blessing for "the house of Israel (the northern kingdom) and with the house of Judah (the southern kingdom)" (Jer. 31:31). This covenant contrasts the Mosaic covenant that God made when He brought His people out of the land of Egypt (v. 32). It would replace the Mosaic code, whereby the Law would no longer simply be a set of commands written on stone or parchment, but it would be recorded in the hearts of the people (v. 33). All would have a personal knowledge of the Lord. And, "I will forgive their iniquity, and their sin I will remember no more" (v. 34b). Besides (1) a permanent forgiveness of sins, (2) the Holy Spirit is the dynamic of the new covenant. "I will put My Spirit within you and cause you to walk in My statutes" (Ezek. 36:27).

The new covenant was ratified by the death of Christ, was inaugurated at Pentecost with the outpouring of the Holy Spirit (Acts 2:1–13), and now benefits the Church age. Since the nation of Israel had rejected Christ, they rejected the blessings of the new covenant. Presently, the body of Christ, made up of both Jews and Gentiles, enjoys this covenant, but someday it will be fulfilled with the believing nation of Israel. Merrill F. Unger writes:

I "shall put my Spirit in you" denotes regeneration by the Spirit (John 3:3–4; Joel 2:28–29). Israel in that glad day will enjoy every ministry of the Spirit operative in this church period, except for the baptism of the Spirit, which of necessity is confined to this age of the outcalling of the Body of Christ (1 Cor. 12:13).[2]

The New Covenant

The new covenant is an extension of the **blessing** of the Abrahamic covenant that would bring blessings to "all the families of the earth" (Gen. 12:3).

It was prophesied in Jeremiah 31:31–34.

It was first promised to the descendants of both the house of Israel and the house of Judah (Jer. 31:31).

It would replace the Mosaic covenant (Jer. 31:32).

It would bring about a permanent forgiveness of sins (Jer. 31:34).

The Holy Spirit would be given to dwell within (Ezek. 36:27).

For the Jewish people, the new covenant has its ultimate fruition in the kingdom (Ezek. 37:14).

The blood of Christ, symbolized by the wine of Passover, would ratify the new covenant (Luke 22:20).

Presently the Church benefits from the new covenant (2 Cor. 3:1–8).

Believers in Christ are now "the servants" of the new covenant (1 Cor. 3:6).

It is called a "better" covenant (Heb. 8:6).

It replaces the old and obsolete Mosaic covenant (Heb. 8:13).

The Lord again mentioned the coming betrayal of Judas (v. 21) and pronounced the judgment "as it has been determined" because of his role in the evil he was about to commit (v. 22). Hearing these words, the other disciples started arguing among themselves and asking who Jesus was speaking about (v. 23), but in their argument, they soon forgot about this subject and launched into their possible positions in the kingdom and "as to which one of them was regarded to be the greatest" (v. 24). Listening to their heated debate, Christ interjected, "Let him who is the greatest among you become as the youngest, and the leader as the servant" (v. 26). The apostles here fell into what is natural to the carnal mind. Ambition, power, and recognition all came to the surface. They completely forgot about the Lord and what their mission was as His followers. Jesus then prodded them with questions: "Who is greater, the one who reclines at the table, or the one who serves?" Is it not the one who reclines at the table? (v. 27). In the realm of the spiritual, everything is opposite of how the flesh would respond. In the natural world, the competitive spirit dominates, and those who push themselves forward, desiring a prominent place in society, are the ones who receive earthly honor.

The Lord then added, that those who have remained with Him through trials (v. 28) and shared His table (v. 30a), will be the ones granted a place with Him (v. 29) and "will sit on thrones judging the twelve tribes of Israel" (v. 30b). The disciples would have to maintain a close relationship with Him, motivated by the heart, in order to be elevated to spiritual leadership in the future kingdom. Possibly Simon Peter led in this argument about rank in the kingdom. Jesus turned to him and said, "Simon, Simon, behold, Satan has demanded permission to sift you like wheat; but I have prayed for you, that your faith may not fail; and you when once you have turned again, strengthen your brothers" (vv. 31–32). Harvested wheat was piled into a mound on a flat threshing floor and tossed into the air to separate the eatable grain from the chaff. In other words, "it was torn apart." In like manner, Satan wished to tear Peter apart and ruin his leadership among his fellow disciples. On the other side of the cross, and following the resurrection of the Lord, Peter would be the front-and-center apostle who would be fearless in strengthening and leading the others.

With his normal bravado, Peter spoke out: "Lord, with You I am ready to go both to prison and to death!" (v. 33). Peter may have thought that Christ would have to suffer some minor political harassment or trial of inconvenience. He did not understand the great tragedy unfolding that very hour! Jesus then made a fateful pronouncement about Peter's denial. "I say to you, Peter, the cock will not crow today until you have denied three times that you know Me" (v. 34). While Peter seems to have gone quiet, the Lord then turned to the other disciples and reminded them that earlier in their ministry they were sent out traveling light, without purse or sandals (v. 35), but soon they would go forth to do "spiritual" battle. He said, "Let him who has no sword sell his robe and buy one" (v. 36). What did Jesus mean by this? "The precise meaning is unclear."[3] With these words, the Lord may have smiled, using hyperbole or tongue-in-cheek! This idea is reinforced by the fact that the men around him shouted, "Lord, look, here are two swords" (v. 38a). Christ then said, "It is enough," probably meaning, "No, no, we're not going out to use force with those who hate us!" Later that night, when the crowds came to arrest Jesus on the Mount of Olives, it was impetuous Peter who grabbed a sword and cut off the ear of the high priest's slave (v. 50; John 18:10). Mercifully, Jesus restored the ear and healed the man while the arresting mob looked on (v. 51).

The Lord made it clear that He was going to die for the sins of the Jewish people and fulfill the prophecy of Isaiah 53:12 about the substitution of the Suffering Servant: "He will be numbered with transgressors." Though the Lord Jesus was the sinless God-man, He would voluntarily relate to humanity. He would represent people at the cross where God the Father poured forth His wrath in order to provide redemption for all people. Isaiah continued his pronouncement about the Messiah's work for sinners:

> My servant will justify the many,
> As He will bear their iniquities. . . .
> He [will] pour out Himself to death, . . .
> Yet He Himself [will bear] the sin of many,
> And [will] intercede for the transgressors (vv. 11–12).

After these words, the Lord and His disciples went out into the night.

The Garden of Gethsemane (22:39–46)

"He came out and proceeded as was His custom to the Mount of Olives" (22:39). Luke tells us that, "as was His custom," the Lord went out with His disciples to the Mount of Olives (v. 39). This is where the Lord would go to sleep during the Passover night, probably as on many occasions before. Because of the heavy Passover meal, the gentle evening breeze, and fear of the future, the disciples were tempted to slumber. Jesus said to them, "Pray that you may not enter into temptation" (v. 40). With their usual insensitivity, His followers failed to notice the emotional pain that was coming upon Him. Going a short distance, Jesus kneeled and began to pray (v. 41), saying, "Father, if Thou art willing, remove this cup from Me; yet not My will, but Thine be done" (v. 42). Though Jesus is the Son of God and could easily escape the coming ordeal, He would be faithful to His Father—faithful unto death (Rev. 2:10)—to save sinners. As a human being, yet sinless, He would dread the torture of dying on a cross. He could have summoned the angelic hosts to save Him, but that was not the eternal plan of redemption set forth by God the Father.

Because of Jesus' heaviness of heart, an angel from heaven appeared to strengthen Him (v. 43). And while suffering such agony of spirit and praying "very fervently," the Lord began sweating drops of blood (v. 44). Arising from prayer, He found the disciples asleep "from sorrow" (v. 45). The word *sorrow*

(Greek, *lupē*) means "to be pained, to be sad." While the disciples on the one hand appeared to be oblivious to what was happening, on the other hand they surely must have had an uneasy feeling that something was wrong. Abruptly, Jesus told them, "Rise and pray that you may not enter into temptation" (v. 46). The Greek word *peirasmos* is an unusual word and could be translated "to be challenged." Few commentators give an explanation about how the disciples would "be tempted." However, one short verse in Mark 14 may give a clue: "They all left Him and fled" (v. 50). These followers of Christ were about to cross over a great divide whereby their lives would never be the same again.

Study Questions

1. Luke 22:3 tells us that Satan entered into Judas Iscariot. How many times was Judas possessed by Satan? (Consult the other Gospels.)

2. What was unusual about the instructions Jesus gave to Peter and John on how to find the upper room for the Passover (i.e., something that would make it easy for them to locate)?

3. Some groups believe that in 22:19 Jesus is actually turning the bread into His body and that we are to believe the bread is actually Jesus' body today when we share communion. Why is their interpretation in error?

4. What does 22:31 tell us about the extent of Satan's power?

5. Regarding the "cock crowing" incident (22:34), both Luke and Matthew (26:33–35) just mention the cock crowing in general, but Mark (14:29–31) says, "before the cock crows twice." Is there an error in the recording of this statement between the three Gospels?

6. What may 22:36 be telling the Jews (and us today) about self-defense? How does this statement square with Matthew 5:38–39, where the Jews are told not to resist an evil person and to turn the other cheek?

7. Some ancient Greek texts do not include 22:43–44. Why do Bible scholars believe these verses were removed?

CHAPTER 24

Arrest and Trials of the Son of Man
Luke 22:47–23:25

Preview:
During the night and into the early morning of Passover, the Lord would be falsely tried before the high priest, the Sanhedrin, Pilate (twice) and Herod the king. These trials were illegal and certainly meant to be kept from the general public. They were carried out quickly to rid the nation of Jesus the troublemaker!

The Arrest (22:47–53)

"The one called Judas, . . . approached Jesus to kiss Him" *(22:47)*. The drama intensified when suddenly Judas arrived leading in the darkness a multitude of rabble and soldiers to take Jesus captive (v. 47). Judas used the kiss as a sign to identify Jesus, "Judas, are you betraying the Son of Man with a kiss?" Jesus asked (v. 48). "Son of Man" was the messianic designation well-known by the entire nation of Israel, and His kingship was clearly prophesied in Daniel 7:13–14. Quickly Peter and some of the other disciples realized what was happening and said, "Lord, shall we strike with the sword?" (v. 49). Remember that they were carrying at least two swords with them (v. 38), though Jesus had said, "It is enough," or "No, do not even think that way!" Without waiting for an answer, Peter stepped forward and with a violent motion cut off the ear of Malchus, the servant of the high priest (v. 50; John 18:10). Christ shouted out, "Stop! No more of this," and miraculously replaced the ear and healed the wound (v. 51).

With stinging words, Jesus laid heavy guilt on the chief priests, officers of the temple, and elders: "Have you come out with swords and clubs as against a robber? While I was with you daily in the temple, you did not lay hands on Me" (vv. 52–53a). "But now you are acting cowardly by coming in the night," He implied. "This hour and the power of darkness are yours" (v. 53b).

> By addressing the crowds in this manner Jesus was in reality doing them a favor. He was exposing their guilt. Is it not true that it takes confession of guilt to bring about salvation? Though it is a fact that the great majority of those who heard Jesus speak these words hardened themselves in sin, we have no right to conclude that the message, together with other messages that followed . . . was completely ineffective.[1]

By arresting Jesus this way, the leadership proved how greatly they feared the masses.

Peter's Denial (22:54–62)

"Peter was following at a distance" (22:54). Jesus was quickly swept away to the dwelling place of the high priest. The palace of the high priest probably had an open courtyard with a gate and gatekeeper. Jesus could have been "tried" here or in a gallery and court area. Caiaphas was high priest that year (Matt. 26:57–58), and Annas, his father-in-law, was high priest emeritus, who probably lived in the same spacious mansion (John 18:13–15, 24). Annas before, and now Caiaphas, played a political game with both the Romans and the people. They ruled by fleshly power and not by spiritual might. While they acted "religious," God's will and His revelation about the prophesied coming of the Messiah were far from their thoughts.

We read that when the officers took Jesus to this residence, Peter "was following at a distance" (v. 54). Sitting around a fire kindled in the middle of the courtyard (v. 55), Peter was recognized by a servant-girl who exclaimed, "This man was with Him too" (v. 56). In quick order, Peter would deny the Lord three times. This incident must have been a traumatic, for it is recorded in all four Gospels.

Peter answered the girl's accusation, saying, "Woman, I do not know Him" (v. 57). When another person standing by said that Peter was one of the Lord's followers, Peter snapped back, "Man, I am not!" (v. 58). An hour later, when another man accused him of being a Galilean follower of Christ, Peter shouted back, "Man, I do not know what you are talking about" (v. 60a). Luke records that immediately, while Peter was still speaking, a cock crowed, as predicted by Jesus. Jesus must have been held in confinement nearby, because Luke says that when Jesus turned around and looked at Peter, the disciple remembered what the Lord had said about denying Him three times before the cock crowed (v. 34). Peter was crushed with conviction, "and he went out and wept bitterly" (v. 62). Though Peter denied his Lord, the other disciples had fled and were hiding out. On the other side of the resurrection and ascension of Christ, Peter, along with John, would become the most outspoken of the disciples.

The Lord was now illegally condemned by the Jewish leaders, the scribes and the elders, at the home of the high priest, though Luke does not mention this in his account (Matt. 26:57–66; Mark 14:53–64). In fact, the entire Sanhedrin was present (Matt. 26:59). Before these "venerable" men, a false witness was brought forward who testified that Jesus proclaimed He would destroy the temple and rebuild it in three days (v. 61). He was of course referring to His soon death and resurrection (Mark 14:58). The high priest stood up, pressing Him to answer against this foolish charge, but Jesus kept quiet (Matt. 26:63a). The high priest pressed forward with his attack: "I adjure You by the living God, that You tell us whether You are the Christ, the Son of God" (v. 63b). Christ answered: "You have said it yourself; nevertheless I tell you, hereafter you shall see the Son of Man sitting at the right hand of power, and coming on the clouds of heaven" (v. 64). The Jewish religious authorities knew well that the expressions "Christ" ("the Anointed," Ps. 2:2), "Son of God" (v. 7), and "Son of Man" (Dan. 7:13) were the most prominent messianic expressions. They knew also that this meant that the Messiah somehow had a mysterious divine relationship with God. This is why the high priest tore his robe and cried, "He has blasphemed!" (Matt. 26:65). The Jews knew that Jesus was related to deity!

The Cruelty of the High Priest (22:63–65)

"[They] were mocking Him, and beating Him" (22:63). For His so-called blasphemy, the Lord was ordered beaten by the authorities. The temple guard held Jesus, mocked Him, and beat Him while blindfolded, saying "Prophesy, who is the one who hit You?" (vv. 63–64). The men then began blaspheming, saying many other things against Him (v. 65). Many commentators believe this picture was so horrible to Luke that he refused to record the details. What was happening was taking place with the full authority of the civil and spiritual leadership of the Jewish nation. No wonder vindication would fall upon the land and in A.D. 70 sweep hundreds of thousands into Roman exile!

The Sanhedrin (22:66–71)

"The Council of elders of the people assembled" (22:66). Now the Lord was taken before some of the same men that were with the high priest. Many of the same questions were asked in light of what He had said at the house of Caiaphas. "If

You are the Christ, tell us" (v. 67). Jesus pointed out that their questioning was but a charade, for they refused to accept the right answers. Jesus said, "If I tell you, you will not believe; and if I ask a question, you will not answer. But from now on the Son of Man will be seated at the right hand of the power of God" (vv. 68–69). Still not satisfied with His answer, they asked, "Are You the Son of God, then?" And He answered, "Yes, I am" (v. 70). The theology of these leaders about the Messiah was correct. They understood the Old Testament prophetic passages perfectly well, yet they refused to believe that Jesus was the One! These leaders had all they needed to get rid of Christ. They said, "What further need do we have of testimony? For we have heard it ourselves from His own mouth" (v. 71).

Pontius Pilate the Governor (Procurator)

1. In 1961, a stone inscription with his name was found in Caesarea.

2. Pilate was the fifth Roman governor assigned to the holy land.

3. He inflamed the Jews by bringing pagan Roman military standards into Jerusalem.

4. His official residence was the palace of Herod.

5. He had about 3,000 men under his authority, with a scattering of cohorts (about 500 men each) throughout the country.

6. Pilate was commissioned to crush all Jewish resistance to Roman rule.

7. He ruled in the Holy Land for ten years.

8. He was ruthless with the Jews yet often conciliatory.

9. Before Jesus came before Pilate, his wife had warned him of a dream she had about Jesus (Matt. 27:19).

10. The church fathers Justin and Tertullian say Pilate made a report about Jesus to the Roman emperor Tiberius.

11. The apostle Paul wrote that Jesus suffered under his evil (1 Tim. 6:13).

12. Because of Pilate's cruelty against the Samaritans, the Syrian governor Vitellius removed him from power and ordered him to go to Rome.

13. Supposedly, after the time of Paul, a document entitled **The Acts of Pilate** *was circulated.*

14. According to the Coptic Church of North Africa, Pilate died a believer and was labeled a saint and a martyr, but the facts of this are doubtful.

Before Pilate (23:1-5)

"The whole body of them arose and brought Him before Pilate" (23:1). The entire body—the high priests, scribes, and elders—then brought Jesus before Pilate, who was the procurator or governor of Samaria and Judea. Pilate had to do a balancing act to keep the "peace of Rome" and at the same time prevent the Jews from rebelling against Roman authority. The Holy Land was the land bridge between Europe and Africa and was a strategic geopolitical region that had to be held by the Roman Empire at all costs.

Agrippa I, writing to Caligula, said that Pilate was merciless and obstinate in inflicting punishment and was very inflexible in character. Agrippa added that he had unmercifully punished offenders without a trial or hearing. He did all of this, of course, to keep the population in constant fear of his rule. Though attempting to hold the Jews in check, he still carried out acts that poured fuel on the fire. He used the temple treasury to pay for an aqueduct, brought pagan Roman standards into Jerusalem, and defamed the temple with golden shields inscribed with the images of Roman gods. Earlier it was recorded that he slew a large number of Galileans and mixed their blood with sacrificial animal blood (13:1-2). Pilate was utterly devoid of human sympathy. The Gospels portray him as proud (John 19:10), cruel (Luke 13:1), and along with his wife, probably extremely superstitious (Matt. 27:19).

> By combining the Gospel accounts one gains the impression that from start almost to finish Pilate did everything in his power to get rid of the case respecting Jesus. He had no love for the Jews. He hated to please them and to grant their request. Yet, on the other hand, deep down in his heart he was afraid of them and of the possibility that they might use their influence to hurt him. Up to a point he was willing to do what justice demanded, but only up to a point. When his *position* was threatened, he surrendered.[2]

The leaders knew how to get to Pilate. They accused Jesus, saying, "We found this man misleading our nation and forbidding to pay taxes to Caesar, and saying that He Himself is Christ, a King" (v. 2). The Jews brought this charge knowing that blasphemy would not be enough to condemn Him before the Romans. Pilate then asked, "Are You the King of the Jews?" The Lord answered, "It is as you say" (v. 3). This answer was clearly in the affirmative (Matt. 26:25; John 18:36-37). John 18:33-38 records that the Lord explained to Pilate that the source of His kingdom was not of this world: "My kingdom is not of this realm" (v. 36). When the messianic kingdom arrives, it will not compete with other nations. It will overwhelm the entire globe. The time for this to happen is yet future. Pilate seemed to be quite satisfied and believed the controversy surrounding Jesus had to do with Jewish religious infighting. He said to the chief priests and the crowd, "I find no guilt in this man" (Luke 23:4). But the leaders kept insisting, "He stirs up the people, teaching all over Judea, starting from Galilee, even as far as this place" (v. 5).

Before Herod Antipas I (23:6–12)

"Pilate . . . asked whether the man was a Galilean" (23:6). Hearing that Jesus was from Galilee (v. 6), Pilate sent Christ to Herod, who had jurisdiction over Galilee and was in Jerusalem at the time, probably to attend the Passover festivities (v. 7). When Jesus came before him, Herod admitted that he had wanted to meet Him, hoping that He would perform some sign before him (v. 8). Jesus would not answer any of the questions put to Him by Herod, probably because the king was not serious and considered the entire affair a joke (v. 9). But the leaders, with much emotion, kept accusing Christ before Herod (v. 10). Finally, Herod gave up and began to treat Jesus with contempt, even dressing Him in a "gorgeous robe" and sending Him back to Pilate (v. 11). "It was by the interchange of these civilities that [Herod and Pilate] were made friends. It would seem that Pilate sent him to Herod as a token of civility and respect, and with a design, perhaps, of putting an end to their quarrel. Herod returned the civility, and it resulted in their reconciliation."[3] Because Herod and Pilate appeared to be working together on this issue, and because they were common enemies of the Jews, they became friends that very day, "for before they had been at enmity with each other" (v. 12).

Before Pilate Again (23:13–25)

"Pilate summoned [again] the chief priests and the rulers and the people" (23:13). As Pilate began his second interrogation, he called not only the chief priests and the rulers, but also the people before him (v. 13). By opening the hearing to the mob, he believed he would be justified and the people would not rebel at an unjust sentence that they may have heard about by rumor. Turning to the leaders, he accused them of bringing Christ before him because supposedly He was inciting the people to rebellion. But, he added, "I have found no guilt in this man regarding the charges which you make against Him. No, nor has Herod, for he sent Him back to us; and behold, nothing deserving death has been done by Him. I will therefore punish Him and release Him" (vv. 14b–16). Even someone found innocent was beaten to discourage any thought of carrying out a crime.

Now a tradition had been created that, on a feast day such as the Passover, an act of mercy would be shown to a condemned prisoner. An insurrectionist and a murderer by the name of Barabbas was scheduled for death. "Release him," the mob cried (v. 18), and "Crucify, crucify" this Jesus (v. 21). Pilate tried to reason with the crowd, but it was no use (v. 20). He asked why he should crucify Jesus. "What evil has this man done? I have found in Him no guilt demanding death; I will therefore punish Him and release Him" (v. 22). Insisting that Christ be crucified, "their voices began to prevail" (v. 23). Pilate may have realized that the situation was dangerous and that he must give in to restore order. He went ahead and pronounced the death sentence "that their demand should be granted" (v. 24). He released Barabbas, "but he delivered Jesus to their will" (v. 25).

While on the surface the death of the Lord looks like "an accident," it was not. In God's mysterious providence, a plan was put in place. This included using even the evil and wicked deeds of many actors on the stage at the time of Christ's crucifixion. Peter says concerning these events that took place in Jerusalem: "For truly in this city there were gathered together against Thy holy servant Jesus, whom Thou didst anoint, both Herod and Pontius Pilate, along with the Gentiles and the peoples of Israel, to do whatever Thy hand and Thy purpose predestined to occur" (Acts 4:27–28). "Pilate, anxious to get rid of the case regarding Jesus, immediately saw an opportunity to reach his goal. He already knew that it was because of envy that the chief priests had delivered Jesus to him, envy aroused by the Nazarene's popularity."[4]

Study Questions

1. Jesus' arrest took place at night. What was wrong with that procedure?

2. In 22:52 we learn that one of the groups that arrested Jesus were the "officers of the temple." Who were these "officers"?

3. Comparing all of the Gospels, how many trials did Jesus face?

4. Why did the Jewish council have to take Jesus before the Romans after they had accused Him of blasphemy?

5. Why did Jesus speak to Pilate but refuse to speak to Herod?

6. In 23:12 we are told that Herod and Pilate became friends over this event. Why did this event make them friends?

7. Why did Pilate eventually give in to the wishes of the Jews calling for Jesus' crucifixion? Neither he nor Herod had found any fault in Jesus. Why did he bow to the pressure?

CHAPTER 25

Crucifixion and Burial of the Son of Man
Luke 23:26–56

Preview:
Simon carried Jesus' cross, and they made their way to Calvary. Jesus gave the women following Him a prophecy and made a prophetic promise to a thief as they both hung on crosses. Jesus was nailed to a cross to die a horrible death for our sins. He freely gave up His own life and was taken away for burial by Joseph of Arimathea, a member of the Sanhedrin who was brave enough to admit his belief in Jesus Christ as Messiah by claiming Jesus' body and giving Jesus his tomb.

The Jewish leaders were hoping to move the events of the death of Christ to a speedy conclusion. They certainly wanted Him dead and buried before Passover officially began in the evening. The Jews were going to have their way, and they hoped the pious and innocent people among the great numbers who were in Jerusalem would not cause problems.

Death of Christ (23:26–49)

"They laid hold of one Simon of Cyrene, . . . and placed on him the cross to carry behind Jesus" (23:26). As the Lord was led away to the cross, a man by the name of Simon from Cyrene was just arriving in the city. Maybe because Jesus was stumbling, the Roman soldiers made Simon carry the cross behind Him (v. 26). A large crowd followed with women mourning and lamenting (v. 27).

221

To console them, Christ turned and said, "Daughters of Jerusalem, stop weeping for Me, but weep for yourselves and your children. For behold, the days are coming when they will say, 'Blessed are the barren, and the wombs that never bore, and the breasts that never nursed'" (vv. 28–29). Jesus was repeating the warning of the coming distress, wrath, and vengeance that would come upon the nation with the destruction of the city of Jerusalem by Titus in A.D. 70 (21:22–23). In these same verses He had said, "Woe to those who are with child and to those who nurse babes in those days" (v. 23a). The Lord added that many will cry to the mountains, "Fall on us," and to the hills, "Cover us" (23:30).

Christ then quoted a common proverb about consuming fires that burn up the trees. "For if they do these things in the green tree, what will happen in the dry?" (v. 31). The Lord was saying something like, "If the fiery judgment is so terrible to burn up a green tree, imagine what will happen to a dry one." The lamenting women did not know of the truly awful judgment of God that was hanging over the entire nation!

Two criminals were to die with Jesus, one on either side of Him (23:33). Isaiah had prophesied that Christ would be "numbered with the transgressors" (Isa. 53:12), yet He was the only perfect man on the face of the earth! Coming to the Place of the Skull (Aramaic, Golgotha), the soldiers offered Jesus a sedative of wine and myrrh, but He refused it (Mark 15:23). Pilate had a sign placed on the cross that read, "JESUS THE NAZARENE, THE KING OF THE JEWS" (John 19:19). The Jewish leaders protested, "Do no write, 'The King of the Jews'; but that He said, 'I am King of the Jews'"(v. 21). Pilate responded: "What I have written I have written" (v. 22).

The crowds hurled insults, saying, "If You are the Son of God, come down from the cross" (Matt. 27:40), and "He saved others; He cannot save Himself. He is the King of Israel; let Him now come down from the cross, and we shall believe in Him" (v. 42; Luke 23:35). While all of the insults were shouted at Him, one of the robbers crucified with Him also spat abuses in His face (Matt. 27:44). He shouted, "Are you not the Christ? Save Yourself and us!" (Luke 23:39). But the other, under conviction for his crimes, rebuked the other thief and said, "Do you not even fear God, since you are under the same sentence of condemnation?" (v. 40). He confessed, "We are receiving what we deserve for our deeds; but this man has done nothing wrong" (v. 41). Turning to the Lord, he uttered, "Jesus, remember me when You come in Your kingdom!" (v. 42). Although he may not have fully understood what he said, he must have realized that Jesus was the promised messianic Son of David who would someday sit on the throne of Israel! Jesus answered, "Truly I say to you, today you shall be with Me in Paradise" (v. 43).

Paradise is an old Persian word meaning "enclosure" or "parklike place of peace." It was used to describe King Artaxerxes' forest (Neh. 2:8) and orchards (Eccl. 2:6). In the Septuagint the word is used to translate the Hebrew word "garden," as in Garden of Eden (Gen. 2–3). In time the word came to be synonymous with heaven in Jewish theology. Paul wrote about being "caught up to the third heaven" (2 Cor. 12:2) and then added, that a man (likely Paul himself) "was caught up into Paradise" (v. 4). John the apostle in Revelation 2:7 quotes the Spirit as saying that the overcomer in the church of Ephesus will be granted to "eat of the tree of life, which is in the Paradise of God." This "tree of life" is in the eternal and heavenly holy city of Jerusalem that comes down from glory (22:14, 19).

The Lord God sent forth an omen in nature that brought frightening attention to the fact that His Son was dying on the cross. By noon, the sixth hour of the day, a great darkness covered the whole land, and it lasted until about three o'clock in the afternoon, the ninth hour (v. 44). The sun was obscured, and the great veil of the temple was torn in two just before Christ gave up His spirit (v. 45). This veil was actually the temple curtain that was said to be four inches thick and about two stories in height. When it was no longer used, teams of horses had to be used to tear it apart. Matthew adds that there was also a great earthquake and the tombs were opened with many saints coming forth from the dead! (Matt. 27:52–53).

The Lord cried out with a loud voice, "Father into Thy hands I commit My spirit" (v. 46). And then He breathed His last. In a distinct technical sense, Christ was not killed, nor did anyone take His life from Him. He voluntarily gave it up for the sake of sinful human beings. The apostle Paul writes that "God was in Christ reconciling the world to Himself" (2 Cor. 5:19), and God "made Him who knew no sin to be sin on our behalf, that we might become the righteousness of God in Him" (v. 21). By the sacrifice of Jesus, we can be reconciled to God, and by His death, we can be given the absolute righteousness of God through Him. Now when we die, we go into the very presence of God the Father, because we do not enter heaven on our own goodness or perfection, but on that which is imputed to us through Christ! Paul adds that when we were helpless as the ungodly, Christ died for us (Rom. 5:6), and we now have been justified by the shedding of His blood and are escaping the divine wrath which we were due (v. 9). The apostle concludes, "For if while we were enemies, we were reconciled to God through the death of His Son, much more, having been reconciled, we shall be saved by His life" (v. 10). By this Paul means that Christ, as the Son of God, lived a perfect and holy life, and therefore He could die under the wrath of God on our behalf. God's righteousness was satisfied, and our sins were purged and punished at the cross!

It seems quite evident that one of the soldiers became a believer while watching the horrors of the crucifixion. "He began praising God, saying, 'Certainly this man was innocent'" (Luke 23:47). He also said, "Truly this man was the Son of God!" (Mark 15:39). Others also seeing what was happening began leaving the place of crucifixion, "beating their breasts" in anguish (Luke 23:48). The extended family of Jesus, His acquaintances, and "the women who accompanied Him from Galilee, . . . standing at a distance, seeing these things," all seem to have given up in despair (v. 49). Their world had coming crashing down. The messianic hopes of the reign of the Son of David had vanished! His followers had no idea that God was working the greatest miracle in human history that would bring redemption to sinful human beings!

The skeptical world tries to argue that Jesus simply fainted or swooned while on the cross. But no amount of doubt can shake the fact that the Lord truly died that day. His death was real! However, as the Holy One of God, He did not die for His own sins, but for those of humanity.

The Jews wanted the bodies on the crosses quickly removed because of the "special" Sabbath of Passover (John 19:31). The Roman soldiers were ordered by Pilate to break the legs of those who were hanging to keep them from pushing up on the nails in their feet for air. This way, criminals would die quickly. But coming to Jesus, the soldiers discovered that He had already expired. This fulfilled the instructions concerning the sacrifice of the Passover lambs—the bones of the animals were not to be broken (Ex. 12:46; Num. 9:12), and it fulfilled the prophecy that no bones of the Messiah were to be broken in His sacrifice for sinners (Ps. 34:20).

Burial of Christ (23:50–56)

"Behold, a man named Joseph, . . . a member of the Council, a good and righteous man" (23:50). One of the good, prominent, and righteous men of the Sanhedrin, a man by the name of Joseph from Arimathea, a village just north of Lydda, came forward to remove the body of Christ from the cross (v. 50). Joseph had not agreed to the evil schemes of the religious leaders and the other members of the council, because he was among many who were waiting for the Messiah to establish His earthly reign on the throne of David (v. 51). Boldly, he had approached Pilate earlier and asked for the body of Jesus (v. 52). Accompanying Joseph was Nicodemus, another member of the Sanhedrin, who was now a firm believer in Christ. He is the same one who had come to Jesus by night with questions about the kingdom (John 3:1–6). To keep the body from smelling, Nicodemus had brought seventy-five pounds of a mixture of sweet-smelling myrrh and aloes (19:39). As was the custom of

the Jews, the body of Jesus was wrapped tightly with the spices in strips of linen, in mummy fashion, though it was not sealed over with wax.

A wealthy man, Joseph wanted to be buried in the holy city of Jerusalem. He had purchased a large rock cavelike tomb, fixed with a large rock to cover the entrance (Matt. 27:60). The tomb was brand-new and had never been used (Luke 23:53). The body was placed in the tomb just in time, because "it was the preparation day, and the Sabbath was about to begin" (v. 54). By hurrying up this process, it was supposed that the holy day would not be desecrated. A group of women from Galilee followed after the man to see where the Lord's body had been placed (v. 55). They returned home to prepare more spices, and they planned to come back to the tomb after the Sabbath rest (v. 56).

Study Questions

1. Luke 23:26 introduces us to Simon of Cyrene. Where was Cyrene? How far had he traveled?

2. Which culture invented crucifixion?

3. Considering the answer for question 2, explain Isaiah 53:5 and Zechariah 12:10.

4. In Jesus' prayer (23:34), which group(s) constitutes the "them" for whom He is asking forgiveness?

5. In 23:43 Jesus tells one of the criminals, "Today you shall be with Me in Paradise." What is Paradise and where is it?

6. What was the significance of darkness falling over the whole land from the sixth hour (noon) to the ninth hour (3:00 P.M.)?

7. What is the significance of the temple veil being torn in two?

SECTION VI

Resurrection and Ascension of the Son of Man

Luke 24:1–53

The greatest miracle of all of history was about to take place. No human being had ever returned to this world with a brand-new eternal body that was impervious to disease and the ravages of time. But Jesus Christ, the God-Man would arise out of the dark realm of death. He would make appearances to His followers and display to the world the miracle of miracles! Because of the resurrection, many doubters would simply argue that He had not died but was only in an unconscious state. Others would argue that His resurrection is simply a fabricated story created by the apostles. Others believe that Jesus had a spiritlike body that was not truly flesh and blood. But the resurrection story, with all of its many evidences, stands as the corner stone of truth encompassing both the Old and New Testaments!

CHAPTER 26

Triumph over Death by the Son of Man Luke 24:1-12

Preview:

The miraculous resurrection! The women went to the tomb to finish the embalming but found it open and empty. Two angels told them that Jesus had risen. The women hurried back to report this to Jesus' disciples. Although the disciples exhibited disbelief, Luke tells us that Peter ran to the tomb to confirm the information.

Mary Magdalene, the leader of the group of women; Joanna; Mary the mother of James; and other women (24:10) came to the tomb on Sunday, the first day of the week, bringing the spices they had prepared (v. 1). Finding the stone rolled away from the entrance (v. 2), they entered and found the body of Jesus missing (v. 3). The Pharisees had earlier gone to Pilate and asked that the opening be secured because, they said, the disciples were going to steal the body of Jesus and tell the people that He had risen from the dead (Matt. 27:62–64). Pilate then ordered the tomb secured with a guard posted (v. 65).

What the Women Found (24:1-10)

"On the first day of the week, . . . they came to the tomb, bringing . . . spices" (24:1). Some have questioned the time of Christ's resurrection. In Matthew

28:1 the text actually reads, "after the Sabbath, as it began to dawn." But the order of facts seem to run this way: (1) Mary Magdalene and the other Mary, the mother of James, watched the burial just before the Sabbath began on the evening of the day of the crucifixion. (2) They stayed at home during the twenty-four hours of the Sabbath. (3) On the evening of that day (the Sabbath rest being over) they brought spices for the embalmment. (4) And finally, at earliest dawn, around 4:00 A.M, they set out to make their way to the sepulcher. Because sunrise in the spring in the Holy Land is a protracted event, there is no contradiction between Matthew (who says, "it began to dawn") and Mark (who writes, "very early on the first day of the week"; 16:2). Luke simply says, "at early dawn" (Luke 24:1). A great earthquake announced the event of Christ's impending resurrection (Matt. 28:2), and the angel of the Lord rolled back the stone that was sealing the entrance (v. 2b). The women found the tomb doorway open (Luke 24:2), and after entering it, they found the body of the Lord Jesus gone (v. 3). With all of the Gospel accounts, the issue seems to be settled: the Lord rose from the grave on the first day of the week.

While confused and perplexed, the women were suddenly confronted with "two men" who stood before them in "dazzling apparel" (Luke 24:4b). These standing in front of them were angelic beings who had taken on the appearance of humans in order to communicate with them. The women fell on their faces terrified and heard, "Why do you seek the living One among the dead? He is not here, but He has risen. Remember how He spoke to you while He was still in Galilee, saying that the Son of Man must be delivered into the hands of sinful men, and be crucified, and the third day rise again" (vv. 5b–7). Probably accompanied by joy, fright, and hope, the women then remembered the Lord's words and left to go and tell the eleven disciples (vv. 8–9).

In verse 10 Luke wants to leave a permanent remembrance of who these women were. Mary Magdalene had been healed of the seven demons who controlled her (8:2). Joanna was the wife of Chuza, Herod's steward, and Susanna may have been one of the other women (v. 3). R. C. H. Lenski comments:

> The second Mary in Luke's record is identified by a reference to her husband Clopas or to her sons James and Joses, Luke uses only James for this purpose. She was the Virgin's sister or half-sister (John 19:25). When Luke writes, "and the rest with them kept telling," etc., he uses brevity by telling us about the presence of these other women and how they joined with the ones who are named in a repeated telling of these things. The news was so astounding, the things they had seen and heard so mighty and true, that they would of their own accord go over the story again and again; but

they were surely also questioned most closely and thus had to relate the occurrences again and again.[1]

Response of Peter and John (24:11–12)

"And these words appeared to [the disciples] as nonsense, and they would not believe them" (24:11). When the women reported what had happened to the disciples, "these words appeared to them as nonsense, and they would not believe them" (v. 11). Actually, it was Mary Magdalene who spoke to Peter first. She said, "They have taken away the Lord out of the tomb, and we do not know where they have laid Him" (John 20:2). Both Peter and John took off in a sprint, with John outrunning Peter and arriving first at the tomb (v. 4). Though John arrived first, he seems to have been hesitant to enter. Peter, "stooping and looking in, . . . saw the linen wrappings only; and he went away to his home, marveling at that which had happened" (Luke 24:12). What he observed shocked him! He saw the linen wrappings lying by themselves and the face cloth folded and lying by itself (John 20:5–7).

The disciples cannot be painted as wide-eyed mystics or conniving and diabolical liars. While they had heard the words of Jesus, "they did not understand the Scripture, that He must rise again from the dead" (John 20:9). David, acting as a prophet, voiced the words of His son the Messiah:

> My flesh also will dwell securely.
> For Thou wilt not abandon my soul to Sheol;
> Neither wilt Thou allow Thy Holy One to undergo decay.
> (Ps. 16:9b–10)

Zechariah writes that the Messiah would someday return to Jerusalem. "They will look on Me whom they have pierced" (12:10), and "His feet will stand on the Mount of Olives" (14:4). Peter quotes Psalm 16 to the Jews and adds that Jesus is now in glory seated with His Father.

> The Lord said to my lord,
> "Sit at My right hand,
> Until I make Thine enemies a footstool for Thy feet." (Acts 2:34)

Before he was stoned to death, Stephen "saw the glory of God, and Jesus standing at the right hand of God; and he said, 'Behold, I see the heavens opened up and the Son of Man standing at the right hand of God'" (Acts 7:55–56).

The disciples were reluctant to believe what their eyes were seeing. That Jesus would come forth from the grave was too much for them at this time.

Study Questions

1. Describe the Jewish burial process and the role of the spices.

2. What were the obstacles to rolling away the stone from in front of Jesus' tomb?

3. Was the stone rolled away for Jesus to get out or for the people to get in?

4. Luke 24:3 tells us that the disciples did not find Jesus' body in the tomb. What do the other Gospels tell us they did find?

5. Considering the answers to questions 1 and 3, how did Jesus apparently arise?

6. What do 24:4 and other scriptural passages concerning angels tell us in relation to their having "wings"?

7. Some who doubt the Bible say that the apostles came and stole Jesus' body from the tomb. Gather all the details on the tomb and the resurrection from the four Gospels and discuss the feasibility of this view.

CHAPTER 27

Appearances to the Disciples and the Ascension of the Son of Man Luke 24:13–53

Preview:

Jesus appeared to the disciples on the Emmaus Road and corrected their knowledge concerning Himself and the purpose of the crucifixion. Jesus then appeared to His disciples in the upper room, where He exhibited His glorified body by letting them touch Him and by eating food, proving that He was not a ghost. After this, Jesus took them out to Bethany, where they witnessed His bodily ascension into heaven.

The Disciples on the Emmaus Road (24:13–35)

"Two [disciples] were going that very day to a village named Emmaus" (24:13). Thousands of people were still straggling out of Jerusalem and heading home after the Passover celebration. Two of Jesus' followers were journeying on the road to a village named Emmaus, "which was about seven miles from Jerusalem" (v. 13). One was Cleopas and the other may have been his wife, Mary (cf. John 19:25). They were in deep conversation about all that had taken place (Luke 24:14) when suddenly Jesus came alongside and began traveling with them (v. 15). By divine intervention, however, "their eyes were prevented from recognizing Him" (v. 16). To pull out of them their thoughts, Jesus asked, "What are these words that you are exchanging with one another

233

as you are walking?" His question hit like a hammer, for Luke says, "They stood still, looking sad" (v. 17). With these few words can be seen the terrible confusion and grief they must have felt. Finally Cleopas asked, "Are You the only one visiting Jerusalem and unaware of the things which have happened here in these days?" (v. 18). On one hand, the reader can sense the impatience of Cleopas with this "stranger" who did not know what happened at the cross! But his question also suggests that the witness of the death of Christ was talked about among the city's residents and as well among possibly one million Jews and proselyte Gentiles to Judaism who may have been on pilgrimage for Passover! To prod their thinking, Jesus asked, "What things?" (v. 19a). Cleopas then gave a detailed review (vv. 19b–24).

Cleopas told how Jesus of Nazareth was a prophet mighty in deed and word in the sight of God and all the people. He described the intrigue of the rulers who sentenced Him to death. Many had hoped He was the Savior who would redeem Israel. On the third day after His crucifixion, some women went to the tomb and found it empty. Angels told them Jesus was alive, and several disciples found the tomb empty just exactly as the women had said.

Christ interrupted Cleopas, saying, "O foolish men and slow of heart to believe in all that the prophets have spoken!" (v. 25). He then asked, "Was it not necessary for the Christ to suffer these things and to enter into His glory?" (v. 26). He then began with the writings of Moses and all the prophets and "explained to them the things concerning Himself in all the Scriptures" (v. 27).

Arriving at Emmaus, the Lord stayed with the pair in their home by their invitation (vv. 28–29). While He was reclining at the table and blessing and breaking bread with them (v. 30), "their eyes were opened and they recognized Him" (v. 31a). That "their eyes were opened" implies that they were temporarily kept from knowing that they were speaking with Jesus. This ties together with verse 16, which says that "their eyes were prevented from recognizing Him." All that the Lord said before "prepared them for this awaking of the inner sense."[1] The word "recognize" is *epiginōskō* and means here to have "an exclusive and exact discovering" of the resurrected Lord. The idea further means an intellectual, deep revelation based on fact. The question is, why did He suddenly show Himself to them this way? The best answer is that "the granting to the disciples [of] the recognition of Jesus was a divine act."[2] These two people "acknowledged the truth of the reports about Jesus' resurrection, for they had recognized Him themselves. The disciples who were meeting together now had at least three reports of the Resurrection: the women, Peter, and Cleopas and his companion [or wife]."[3]

Jesus then suddenly "vanished from their sight" (v. 31b). The two then said to one another, "Were not our hearts burning within us while He was speaking to us on the road, while He was explaining the Scriptures to us?" (v. 32). This may best answer why Christ withheld His identity from them. He tied together the Old Testament revelations about Himself, and about all that had happened to Him. "Our hearts burned within us"

> is an expression denoting the deep interest and pleasure which they had felt in his discourse before they knew who he was. They now recalled his instruction; they remembered how his words reached the *heart* as he spoke to them; how convincingly he had showed them that the Messiah ought to suffer, and how, while he talked to them of the Christ that they so much loved, their hearts glowed with intense love.[4]

The next day, these followers of Jesus returned to Jerusalem, found the eleven disciples, and reported to them all that happened (v. 33), saying, "The Lord has really risen, and has appeared to Simon" (v. 34). By mentioning Peter, they are confirming, "His appearance to Peter was genuine. We too have seen Jesus alive!" The two disciples began relating their experiences on the road and "how He was recognized by them in the breaking of the bread" (v. 35). This appearance to Peter alone is not recorded in the Gospels. However, the apostle Paul seems to allude to it in 1 Corinthians 15:5.

An Appearance before All the Disciples (24:36–43)

"[Jesus] Himself stood in their midst" (24:36). As the disciples were discussing these things, the Lord suddenly appeared in their midst (Luke 24:36), startling and frightening them. They thought that they were seeing a spirit! (v. 37). Though the truthfulness of His resurrection was dawning on them and sinking into their minds, they were still "spooked" by His quick and dramatic appearance. Jesus was trying to help them connect fact with emotion. "Why are you troubled, and why do doubts arise in your hearts?" (v. 38), He asked. The word "hearts" (Greek, *kardia*) is probably here a reference to their emotions and mental state.

Christ then returned to the facts! "See My hands and My feet, that it is I Myself; touch Me and see, for a spirit does not have flesh and bones as you see that I have" (v. 39). But they still could not fathom what they were seeing. Their emotional "joy" and "marveling" were getting in the way (v. 41)! They must have been vacillating between happiness and shock; they could not think straight! Thomas was absent from this appearance, but a week later, when the Lord returned to this same room while the doors were shut (John 20:26), he cried out some of the most well-known words in the Gospels, "My Lord and my God!" (v. 28). These words later greatly impacted the church to further examine the nature of the Trinity and the deity of Christ.

To further confirm the fact that He was not a ghost, Jesus asked the disciples if they had anything to eat (Luke 24:41b). Possibly stunned with curiosity, the disciples "gave Him a piece of a broiled fish; and He took it and ate it before them" (vv. 42–43). Jesus was not a figment of the disciples' imagination; nor was He some kind of spirit being without a physical body. He was the resurrected Son of Man now existing in an eternal body that had certain functions as before, such as eating. In the apostle John's first epistle, he tells us that we do not fully comprehend what we will be like in our "changed" and resurrected bodies (1 John 3:2). However, he adds, "We know that, when He appears, we shall be like Him, because we shall see Him just as He is" (v. 2b). Every believer in Christ who has a future resurrection "hope fixed on Him purifies himself, just as He is pure" (v. 3). Looking forward to Christ's coming for His church is a kind of sanctification that fosters a life of purity.

Another Examination of the Old Testament (24:44–48)

"All things which are written about Me . . . must be fulfilled" (24:44). Jesus reviewed again the Old Testament prophecies about Himself. He reviewed with them the Torah, the Law of Moses, the prophetic books, and the Psalms, and showed verses that were fulfilled concerning Him. "He opened their minds to understand the Scriptures" (v. 45) and concluded, "Thus it is written, that the Christ should suffer and rise again from the dead the third day; and that repentance for forgiveness of sins should be proclaimed in His name to all the nations, beginning from Jerusalem" (vv. 46–47). Isaiah predicted that the Messiah would be "greatly exalted" (52:13), and that He would "sprinkle many nations" (v. 15a). His suffering is graphically prophesied in Psalm 22.

> All my bones are out of joint;
> My heart is like wax;
> It is melted within me.
> My strength is dried up like a potsherd,
> And my tongue cleaves to my jaws;
> And Thou does lay me in the dust of death. . . .
> They divide my garments among them,
> And for my clothing they cast lots. (vv. 14–15, 18)

Jesus also took the disciples to the great resurrection passage of the Messiah: "For Thou wilt not abandon my soul to Sheol; neither wilt Thou allow Thy Holy One to undergo decay" (Ps. 16:10). His death was to bring about salvation for sinners. "He was pierced through for our transgressions,

He was crushed for our iniquities" (Isa. 53:5a). And, "He was cut off out of the land of the living, for the transgression of my people to whom the stroke was due" (v. 8b).

Promise of the Holy Spirit (24:49)

"I am sending forth the promise of My Father upon you" (24:49). This clear salvation message was to be proclaimed "to all the nations, beginning from Jerusalem" (Luke 24:47b), and delivered initially by the disciples who would be "witnesses of these things" (v. 48).

> How solemn was their office—to *testify* these things to the world, and, in the face of suffering and death, to go and proclaim them to all nations! In like manner, *all* Christians are witnesses for Christ. They are the *evidences* of his mercy and his love, and they should so live that others may be brought to see and love the Saviour.[5]

But first, the apostles would receive the promise from the Father of the Holy Spirit (v. 49), as Jesus had told them during the Passover meal in the upper room. "But the Helper, the Holy Spirit, whom the Father will send in My name, He will teach you all things, and bring to your remembrance all that I said to you" (John 14:26). The King and kingdom were rejected by the Jewish people. The kingdom would be postponed until some far-off future time. Meanwhile, a new dispensation, the Church, would begin at the feast of Pentecost, some fifty days from the time of Passover (Acts 2). The disciples would then be sent forth, "clothed with power from on high" (Luke 24:49).

Departure into Glory (24:50–53)

"He lifted up His hands and blessed them" (24:50). The Lord Jesus remained on earth some forty days before ascending to His Father (Acts 1:3). Toward the end of that time, He met the disciples by the Sea of Galilee (John 21:1–23). Then, back in Jerusalem, they gathered and asked Him, "Lord, is it at this time You are restoring the kingdom to Israel?" (Acts 1:6). He made it clear that the times and epochs "the Father has fixed by His own authority" (v. 7). He then apparently led them out near the Mount of Olives going toward Bethany. Suddenly, He lifted up His hands and blessed them, then quickly and dramatically "parted from them" (Luke 24:51). He was received "out of their sight" (Acts 1:9b). Instantly, two men, angelic beings, stood beside them and said, "Men of Galilee, why do you stand looking into the sky? This Jesus, who has been taken up from you into heaven, will come in just the same way as you have watched Him go into heaven" (vv. 10–11).

Returning to Jerusalem, they were filled with joy (v. 52) "and were continually in the temple, praising God" (v. 53). They waited in the upper room for the coming of the Holy Spirit. Luke continues this story in his "second volume," the book of the Acts of the Apostles. R. C. H. Lenski aptly writes:

> No Sanhedrin frightened them; they went regularly and in public to the Temple—all men could see them. But they only worshipped, they did not preach—they waited. "Praising God" is Luke's last word. It is fitting, indeed, as the final note. Close the book and also praise God![6]

Summary of the Book of Luke

It is important to read Luke's Gospel before reading his account of the acts of the apostles. Some have even suggested that the two volumes are simply two parts of the same book of the continuing drama.

Luke's gospel is a brilliant and detailed compilation of testimonies of many who observed all that the Lord Jesus said and did. Luke interviewed many of these followers and then weaved a tapestry of compelling evidence that Jesus was the Messiah promised in the Old Testament. To demonstrate this, Luke used the messianic title "Son of Man" twenty-five times in his gospel. This means that Christ is related to humanity. He died for the human race and entered the throne room of God as the Son of Man to receive all dominion and power from God the Father (Dan. 7:9–28).

With great emotional detail, Luke shows how so many of the Jewish people resisted the evidence that Jesus was the promised King. Toward the end, Christ told a parable about the evil vine-dressers who would not give respect to the "beloved son" of the owner of the vineyard (20:13). They reasoned, "This is the heir; let us kill him that the inheritance may be ours" (v. 14). This parable is the capstone of how the nation of Israel rejected God's Messiah, the Deliverer, the predicted Chief Corner Stone, promised as a Savior long ago (vv. 17–18). In His final words to the people, Jesus said, "Everyone who falls on that stone will be broken; but on whomever it falls, it will scatter him like dust." The fate of the nation of Israel was sealed!

There are a thousand personal spiritual lessons on the pages of this gospel. Those lessons are harvested by all who study its pages in depth. However, one cannot escape the overriding message that Jesus was rejected as King over the Jewish nation. It is impossible to conclude anything else than the fact that the earthly kingdom of Israel has been postponed until the Church age and the Tribulation period are completed. Because this fact seems so obvious, some call the Church age the "parenthesis" or period of the postponement. John Walvoord writes: "The ultimate proof of the teaching that the present age is a parenthesis is in the positive revelation concerning the church as the body of Christ. . . . The kingdom predictions of the Old Testament do not conform to the pattern of this present age."[7] And "the present age is a parenthesis or a time period not predicted by the Old Testament, and therefore, not fulfilling or advancing the program of events revealed in the Old Testament foreview" concerning the earthly messianic reign.[8]

Luke records in Acts 3 how Peter relates the postponement theme to the Jewish people. He reminds them that the prophets had written "that [the things] Christ should suffer, He has thus fulfilled" (v. 18). And following His death and resurrection, the nation should "repent" (v. 19) "in order that times of refreshing may come from the presence of the Lord; and that he may send Jesus, the Christ [Messiah] appointed for you, whom heaven must receive until the period of restoration of all things about which God spoke by the mouth of His holy prophets from ancient time" (vv. 19–21).

Note carefully the phrases Luke uses: "Christ should suffer," or "the suffering was certain"; Peter speaks of "you," that is, the Jewish people, and of a future plan "for them" in contrast to the Church age and the salvation of the Gentiles. Peter speaks of the kingdom as "times of refreshing" and "the period of restoration of all things." Finally, Luke records in Acts how Peter reminds the Jews that in the future God will send "Jesus the Christ appointed for you," which can refer only to His kingship, as so clearly set forth in the ministry of the Lord, by Luke in his Gospel![9]

Study Questions

1. Luke 24:16 tells us that the eyes of the disciples going to Emmaus were prevented from recognizing Jesus. What do you think prevented them?

2. Cleopas comments that their mysterious companion must be the only one visiting Jerusalem who was not aware of Jesus, His claims, and His proofs. What does this say about the culpability of the nation of Israel in Jesus' death?

3. What does 24:27 tell us of the importance of the Old Testament to Christians of today?

4. What can we learn about Jesus' glorified body from His appearances before His ascension?

5. How many prophecies are there in the Old Testament regarding the Messiah?

6. What was the promise made by the Father of which Jesus speaks in 24:49?

7. When writing of Jesus' ascension, Luke leaves an important event out of his gospel that he includes in the book of Acts. What is this event, and why is it important?

Bibliography

Alford, Henry. *The Greek Testament*, 4 Vols. Chicago: Moody, 1958.

Balz, Korst & Schneider, Gerhard. Exegetical Dictionary of the New Testament, 3 Vols. Grand Rapids: Eerdmans, 1990.

Barnes, Albert. *Notes on the New Testament*, 14 Vols. Grand Rapids: Baker, 1981.

Couch, Mal. "Inerrancy and the Gospels," Mal Couch, ed. The Conservative Theological Journal, Vol. 4, No. 11, March 2000, Ft. Worth, TX.

Gaebelein, Frank E. *The Expositor's Bible Commentary*, 12 Vols. Grand Rapids: Zondervan, 1984.

Gilbert, Martin, ed. *The Illustrated Atlas of Jewish Civilization*. New York: MacMillan Publishing Company, 1990.

Godet, Frederick. *A Commentary on the Gospel of St. Luke*. New York: I. K. Funk, 1881.

Hendrickson, William. *The Gospel of Luke*. Grand Rapids: Baker, 1981.

Lenski, R. C. H. *The Interpretation of St. Luke's Gospel*. Minneapolis, MN: Augsburg, 1946.

Marshall, Howard I. *Commentary on Luke*. Grand Rapids: Eerdmans, 1995.

Nicoll, Robertson W. *The Expositor's Greek Testament*, 5 Vols. Grand Rapids: Eerdmans, 1988.

Pate, C. Marvin. Luke. Chicago: Moody, 1995.

Robertson, A. T. *Word Pictures in the New Testament*, 6 Vols. Nashville, TN: Broadman, 1930.

Vincent, R. Marvin. *Word Studies in the New Testament*, 4 Vols. Peabody, MA: Hendrickson Publishers, 1886.

Walvoord, John F., Roy Zuck, eds. *The Bible Knowledge Commentary*. Wheaton, IL: Victor Books, 1978.

Wilcox, J. *The Preacher's Complete Homiletic Commentary*, 31 Vols. Grand Rapids: Baker, n.d.

Notes

Introduction

1. Everett F. Harrison, *Introduction to the New Testament* (Grand Rapids: Eerdmans, 1974), 195.
2. Mal Couch, gen. ed., *A Bible Handbook to the Acts of the Apostles* (Grand Rapids: Kregel, 1999), 13.
3. Ibid.
4. Marvin R. Vincent, *Word Studies in the New Testament*, 4 vols. (Peabody, MA: Hendrickson, 1886), 1:240.
5. R. C. H. Lenski, *The Interpretation of St. Luke's Gospel* (Minneapolis: Augsburg, 1946), 33.
6. Cited by: C. Marvin Pate, *The Canon of Scripture* (Downers Grove, IL; InterVarsity Press, 1988), 159.
7. Lenski, *Luke*, 17–18.
8. C. Marvin Pate, *Luke* (Chicago: Moody Press, 1995), 11–12.
9. John F. Walvoord and Roy Zuck, gen. eds., *The Bible Knowledge Commentary, New Testament* (Wheaton, IL: Victor Books, 1983), 30.

Section I—Title Page

1. Fredric Godet, *Commentary on St. Luke's Gospel* (New York: I. K. Funk, 1881), 33.

Chapter 1—Greetings to Theophilus

1. Mal Couch, "Inerrancy and the Gospels," Mal Couch, ed. *The Conservative Theological Journal* 4, no. 11 (March 2000).
2. W. Robertson Nicoll, *The Expositor's Greek Testament*, 5 vols. (Grand Rapids: Eerdmans, 1988), 1:460.

Chapter 2—Announcement of the Coming of John the Baptist

1. Martin Gilbert, ed., *The Illustrated Atlas of Jewish Civilization* (New York: Macmillan, 1990), 43
2. Henry W. Soltau, *The Holy Vessels and Furniture of the Tabernacle* (Grand Rapids: Kregel, 1851), 94.
3. Albert Barnes, *Notes on the New Testament*, 14 vols. (Grand Rapids: Baker, 1981), 9:5.
4. *The Preacher's Homiletic Commentary*, 31 vols. (Grand Rapids: Baker, n.d.), 23:24.

Chapter 3—Announcement of the Birth of the Son of Man

1. Merrill F. Unger, *Unger's Commentary on the Old Testament* (Chattanooga, TN: AMG Publishers, 2002), 1173–74.
2. Frank E. Gaebelein, gen. ed., *The Expositor's Bible Commentary*, 12 vols. (Grand Rapids: Zondervan, 1984), 8:832.
3. Marvin R. Vincent, *Word Studies in the New Testament*, 4 vols. (Peabody, MA: Hendrickson, 1886), 1:262.

4. Ibid., 71.
5. John F. Walvoord and Roy Zuck, gen. eds., *The Bible Knowledge Commentary, New Testament* (Wheaton: Victor Books, 1983), 206.

Chapter 4—Birth of John the Baptist
1. Howard Marshall, *Commentary on Luke* (Grand Rapids: Eerdmans, 1995), 86.

Chapter 5—Birth of the Son of Man
1. Harold Hoehner, *Chronological Aspects of the Life of Christ* (Grand Rapids: Zondervan, 1977), 15.
2. Ibid., 22.
3. I explored such a cave just on the edge of Bethlehem that archaeologically proved to be several thousands of years old. The ceiling was blackened from the fires of shepherds during cold weather. In the corner, carved out of the stone wall, was an inset with hay for feeding the animals.
4. A. T. Robertson, *Word Pictures in the New Testament*, 6 vols. (Nashville: Broadman, 1930), 2:23.
5. Frank E. Gaebelein, gen. ed., *The Epositor's Bible Commentary*, 12 vols. (Grand Rapids: Zondervan, 1984), 8:846.
6. Albert Barnes, *Notes on the New Testament*, 14 vols. (Grand Rapids: Baker, 1981), 9:20.
7. Robertson, *Word Pictures*, 2:25.

Chapter 7—Early Years of Jesus
1. A. T. Robertson, *Word Pictures in the New Testament*, 6 vols. (Nashville: Broadman, 1930), 2:31.

Chapter 8—Baptism and Beginning Ministry of the Son of Man
1. R. C. H. Lenski, *The Interpretation of St. Luke's Gospel* (Minneapolis: Augsburg, 1961), 195.
2. Ibid., 216.

Chapter 9—Genealogy of the Son of Man
1. R. C. H. Lenski, *The Interpretation of St. Luke's Gospel* (Minneapolis: Augsburg, 1961), 221.

Chapter 10—Temptations of the Son of Man
1. I. Howard Marshall, *Commentary on Luke* (Grand Rapids: Eerdmans, 1995), 165–66.
2. R. C. H. Lenski, *The Interpretation of St. Luke's Gospel* (Minneapolis: Augsburg, 1961), 240.
3. Frank E. Gaebelein, gen. ed., *The Expositor's Bible Commentary*, 12 vols. (Grand Rapids: Zondervan, 1984), 8:864.

Chapter 11—Teaching in the Synagogues
1. Marvin R. Vincent, *Word Studies in the New Testament*, 4 vols. (Peabody, MA: Hendrickson, 1886), 1:290.
2. Albert Barnes, *Notes on the New Testament*, 14 vols. (Grand Rapids: Baker, 1981), 9:37.

Chapter 12—Healing Miracles of the Son of Man
1. R. C. H. Lenski, *The Interpretation of St. Luke's Gospel* (Minneapolis: Augsburg, 1961), 268.
2. William Hendriksen, *The Gospel of Luke* (Grand Rapids: Baker, 1981), 277.
3. Mal Couch, gen. ed., *An Introduction to Classical Evangelical Hermeneutics* (Grand Rapids: Kregel, 2000), 226.

4. A. T. Robertson, *Word Pictures in the New Testament*, 6 vols. (Nashville: Broadman, 1930), 2:77.

Chapter 13—Call of the Disciples and the Great Sermon by the Lake

1. William Hendriksen, *The Gospel of Luke* (Grand Rapids: Baker, 1981), 334–35.
2. Marvin R. Vincent, *Word Studies in the New Testament*, 4 vols. (Peabody, MA: Hendrickson, 1886), 1:314.
3. R. C. H. Lenski, *The Interpretation of St. Luke's Gospel* (Minneapolis: Augsburg, 1961), 362–63.
4. Hendriksen, *Luke*, 361.

Chapter 14—Continuation of Miracles and Healings

1. Merrill F. Unger, *Unger's Commentary on the Old Testament* (Chattanooga, TN: AMG Publishers, 2002), 2077.
2. W. Robert Nicoll, *The Expositor's Greek Testament*, 5 vols. (Grand Rapids: Eerdmans, 1988), 1:515.
3. Mal Couch, gen. ed., *An Introduction to Classical Evangelical Hermeneutics* (Grand Rapids: Kregel, 2000), 213.
4. Stanley Toussaint, *Behold the King* (Portland, OR: Multnomah, 1980), 175–76.
5. R. C. H. Lenski, *The Interpretation of St. Luke's Gospel* (Minneapolis: Augsburg, 1961), 457.
6. William Hendriksen, *The Gospel of Luke* (Grand Rapids: Baker, 1981), 489.
7. C. Marvin Pate, *Luke* (Chicago: Moody Press, 1995), 209.
8. Ibid., 215.
9. J. Willcock, *The Preacher's Complete Homiletic Commentary on the Gospel According to St. Luke,* 31 vols. (Grand Rapids: Baker, n.d.), 23:264.

Chapter 16—Sending Forth of the Seventy Disciples

1. Mal Couch, "The War Over Words" in *The End Times Controversy,* ed. Thomas Ice (Eugene, OR: Harvest House, 2003), 287–88.

Chapter 17—Questioning of the Lawyer

1. Albert Barnes, *Barnes' Notes,* 14 vols. (Grand Rapids: Baker, 1983), 9:71.

Chapter 18—Teaching on Prayer

1. A. T. Robertson, *Word Pictures in the New Testament*, 6 vols. (Nashville: Broadman, 1930), 2:159.
2. William Hendriksen, *The Gospel of Luke* (Grand Rapids: Baker 1981), 612–13.

Chapter 20—Great Teaching Ministry of the Son of Man

1. J. Willcock, *The Preacher's Complete Homiletic Commentary on the Gospel According to St. Luke,* 31 vols. (Grand Rapids: Baker, n.d.), 23:342.
2. Ibid., 23:345.
3. A. T. Robertson, *Word Pictures in the New Testament*, 6 vols. (Nashville: Broadman, 1930), 2:205.
4. C. Marvin Pate, *Luke* (Chicago: Moody Press, 1995), 307.
5. R. C. H. Lenski, *The Interpretation of St. Luke's Gospel* (Minneapolis: Augsburg, 1961), 843.
6. Ibid.
7. Ibid., 844
8. William Whiston, trans., *The Works of Josephus,* "Antiquities" (Peabody: Hendrickson, 1987), 4:8; 23.
9. William Hendriksen, *The Gospel of Luke* (Grand Rapids: Baker, 1981), 794.

10. Pate, *Luke*, 325.

11. Willcock, *Preacher's Complete Homiletic Commentary*, 23:474.

12. Lenski, *Luke*, 880.

13. Korst Balz and Gerhard Schneider, *Exegetical Dictionary of the New Testament*, 3 vols. (Grand Rapids: Eerdmans, 1990), 3:35.

14. Lenski, *Luke*, 913.

15. Ibid., 920.

16. Ibid., 921.

17. Willcock, *Preacher's Complete Homiletic Commentary*, 23:499.

18. Lenski, *Luke*, 959.

Chapter 21—Authority of the Son of Man Revealed

1. Pate, *Luke*, 362.

2. Harold Hoehner, *Chronological Aspects of the Life of Christ* (Grand Rapids: Zondervan, 1977), 91–92.

Chapter 22—Final Discourse about Coming Judgment

1. Albert Barnes, *Barnes' Notes*, 14 vols. (Grand Rapids: Baker, 1983), 9:142.

2. R. C. H. Lenski, *The Interpretation of St. Luke's Gospel* (Minneapolis: Augsburg, 1961), 142.

3. Ibid.

Chapter 23—Final Hours with the Disciples

1. Merrill F. Unger, *Unger's Commentary on the Old Testament* (Chattanooga, TN: AMG Publishers, 2002), 116.

2. Ibid., 1575.

3. I. Howard Marshall, *The Gospel of Luke* (Grand Rapids: Eerdmans, 1995), 825.

Chapter 24—Arrest and Trials of the Son of Man

1. William Hendriksen, *The Gospel of Luke* (Grand Rapids: Baker, 1981), 988.

2. Ibid., 1008.

3. Albert Barnes, *Barnes' Notes*, 14 vols. (Grand Rapids: Baker, 1983), 9:154.

4. Hendriksen, *Luke*, 1017.

Chapter 26—Triumph over Death by the Son of Man

1. R. C. H. Lenski, *The Interpretation of St. Luke's Gospel* (Minneapolis: Augsburg, 1961), 1175–76.

Chapter 27—Appearances to the Disciples and the Ascension of the Son of Man

1. Frederick Godet, *A Commentary on the Gospel of St. Luke* (New York: I. K. Funk, 1881), 507.

2. C. Marvin Pate, *Luke* (Chicago: Moody Press, 1995), 474.

3. John F. Walvoord and Roy Zuck, gen. eds., *The Bible Knowledge Commentary*, New Testament (Wheaton, IL: Victor Books, 1978), 264.

4. Albert Barnes, *Barnes' Notes*, 14 vols. (Grand Rapids: Baker, 1983), 9:164.

5. Ibid., 167.

6. R. C. H. Lenski, *The Interpretation of St. Luke's Gospel* (Minneapolis: Augsburg, 1961), 1212.

7. John F. Walvoord, *The Millennial Kingdom* (Findlay, OH: Dunham, 1959), 230.

8. Ibid., 231.

9. Mal Couch, *An Introduction to Classical Evangelical Hermeneutics* (Grand Rapids: Kregel, 2000), 225.

About the Author

Mal Couch is founder and former president of Tyndale Theological Seminary and Biblical Institute in Fort Worth, Texas. He previously taught at Philadelphia College of the Bible, Moody Bible Institute, and Dallas Theological Seminary. His other publications include *The Hope of Christ's Return: A Premillennial Commentary on 1 and 2 Thessalonians, A Bible Handbook to Revelation,* and *Dictionary of Premillennial Theology.*

About the Other General Editor

Edward Hindson is professor of religion, dean of the Institute of Biblical Studies, and assistant to the chancellor at Liberty University in Lynchburg, Virginia. He has authored more than twenty books, served as coeditor of several Bible projects, and was one of the translators for the New King James Version of the Bible. Dr. Hindson has served as a visiting lecturer at Oxford University and Harvard Divinity School as well as numerous evangelical seminaries. He has taught more than fifty thousand students in the past twenty-five years.